JAN - 6 2003

ACROPOLIS RESTORATION

THE CCAM INTERVENTIONS

ACROPOLIS RESTORATION

THE CCAM INTERVENTIONS

EDITED BY RICHARD ECONOMAKIS

ACADEMY EDITIONS • LONDON

ACKNOWLEDGEMENTS

This book would not have been possible without the continuing support and encouragement of members of the Committee for the Conservation of the Acropolis Monuments. The initial conception for the publication was provided by Dr Andreas Papadakis. We would like to thank all the contributors to the book, especially Dr Charalambos Bouras for his advice and support; Dr Manolis Korres for his patience and hospitality; Dr Tasos Tanoulas for his tireless assistance; Dr Cornelia Hadziaslani, for her invaluable contributions and suggestions; Dr Fani Mallouchou-Tufano for her wholehearted involvement and insights; Dr Papanikolaou for his indefatigability and support; Dr Peter Calligas, Director of the Center for the Acropolis Studies; Dr Zambas; Dr Kouphopoulos; Dr Demetri Porphyrios for his recommendations; Dr Trianti for her assistance with permits; finally, Dr Margit Bendtsen for permission to use material from the publication *Sketches and Measurings – Danish Architects in Greece 1818-1862*, Copenhagen 1993.

The greatest appreciation and thanks go to Mario Bettella for his inspired and untiring work in designing the book; Natasha Robertson for her editorial work, enthusiasm and long working hours; Petra Roth for her patience and dedication in design and layouts; Lucy Coventry for her work in editing and proofing the texts. All original Greek texts were translated into the English by Richard Economakis. Translations from the German were provided by Pamela Johnston; further translations from the Greek were provided by Vivian Constantinopoulos. The essay 'Restoration and Value', pp204-207, remains copyright © Demetri Porphyrios. The text by Marcus Binney, p203, consists of selected excerpts from an article by the author in *The Times*, London, November 11th 1992.   RE

Photographic credits

Unless otherwise stated, all photographs are by Mario Bettella.

Additional photographic credits: S Gakis (photo courtesy of Mr George Economakis): p70 (above); German Archaeological Institute, Area Director K Nohlen, Istanbul: p201; G Kanellos (model): p180; M Kapon (artistic synthesis): pp96-97; Studio Kontos: p10; S Mavrommatis: pp125 (centre), 180; G Moutevelis: pp96-97; N Toganides: p131 (above); C Zambas: pp125 (above), 129 (above); All photographs for the article 'Education Programme on the Athenian Acropolis' belong to the archives of the Education Department of the Acropolis Ephorate; Special thanks to Fani Constantinou for permission to reproduce images belonging to the Photographic Archive of the Benaki Museum; Thanks go to Dr Otto Spoerri for assistance on the Acropolis and the Philopappos Hill.

Academy Group Ltd wishes to thank the Committee for the Conservation of the Acropolis Monuments for its kind permission to photograph the Acropolis Monuments.

Cover: The Caryatid Porch from the south; *Pages 2 & 3*: View of the Acropolis from Philopappos Hill; *Page 4*: The Acropolis seen from the Pnyx

Editorial Offices:
42 Leinster Gardens, London W2 3AN

Published in Great Britain in 1994 by
ACADEMY EDITIONS
an imprint of Academy Group Ltd
a member of VCH PUBLISHING GROUP

Distributed to the trade in the USA by
ST MARTIN'S PRESS 175 Fifth Avenue, New York, NY 10010

ISBN: 1 85490 344 6

Printed and bound in Singapore

CONTENTS

ACROPOLIS RESTORATION – AN EDITORIAL   8

RESTORATION WORK ON THE ACROPOLIS (1975-94) – CCAM   12

THE ARCHITECTURE OF THE ATHENIAN ACROPOLIS – TERMINOLOGY   16

THE CONSTRUCTION OF ANCIENT GREEK TEMPLES   *Manolis Korres*   20

THE SCULPTURAL ADORNMENT OF THE PARTHENON   *Manolis Korres*   28

THE HISTORY OF THE ACROPOLIS MONUMENTS   *Manolis Korres*   34

THE PROPYLAEA AND THE WESTERN ACCESS OF THE ACROPOLIS   *Tasos Tanoulas*   52

THE HISTORY OF INTERVENTIONS ON THE ACROPOLIS   *Fani Mallouchou-Tufano*   68

INTERNATIONAL CHARTER FOR THE CONSERVATION AND RESTORATION OF MONUMENTS AND SITES   86

THE INTERNATIONAL CHARTER OF VENICE AND THE RESTORATION OF CLASSICAL BUILDINGS   *Charalambos Bouras*   88

EDUCATIONAL PROGRAMMES ON THE ATHENIAN ACROPOLIS   *Cornelia Hadziaslani*   92

CURRENT PROBLEMS OF RESTORATION ON THE ACROPOLIS   *Charalambos Bouras*   100

STRUCTURAL INTERVENTIONS ON THE ACROPOLIS MONUMENTS   *Costas Zambas*   106

THE RESTORATION OF THE PARTHENON   *Manolis Korres*   110

THE RESTORATION OF THE ERECHTHEION   *Alexander Papanikolaou*   136

THE RESTORATION OF THE PROPYLAEA   *Tasos Tanoulas*   150

THE TEMPLE OF ATHENA NIKE   168

RECENT DISCOVERIES ON THE ACROPOLIS   *Manolis Korres*   174

NEW DISCOVERIES AT THE PROPYLAEA   *Tasos Tanoulas*   180

THE INTERNATIONAL DEBATE   184

CCAM QUESTIONNAIRE   212

RESTORATION AND VALUE   *Demetri Porphyrios*   206

RESTORING SYMBOLISM   *David Watkin*   210

ANASTYLOSIS AND HISTORICAL INTEGRITY   *Oswyn Murray*   212

A BUILDING SITE ONCE AGAIN   *Lothar Haselberger*   214

ARCHITECTURE AND POLITICS IN THE CLASSICAL CITY-STATE   *Helen Tatla*   218

THE VOICE OF TEIRESIAS   *Richard Economakis*   220

ACROPOLIS RESTORATION
AN EDITORIAL

For almost two and a half thousand years the Acropolis in Athens has stood as an embodiment of the highest achievements in western architecture and art. Still today, after its long passage through time, the ancient sanctuary looks out in undiminished grandeur over the broad plain of Attica, echoing a distant, heroic age that seems almost to have merged into the realm of myth. Here the works of the sculptor Phidias and the architects Iktinos, Callicrates and Mnesikles continue to capture the imagination of thousands of visitors who daily ascend the legendary Rock, reminding them of the flowering of Athens under the guidance of its statesman, Pericles, and the coming of age of a culture which permanently marked, indeed forms, the basis of our civilisation. Yet, for all its apparent agelessness, a darker reality hangs over the Acropolis – for until recently it has been quietly but steadily yielding its claim to immortality. Over the centuries the complex of exquisite marble temples and sacred structures has witnessed countless acts of vandalism, including wars, conversions, natural disasters, and more recently the ravages of mass tourism and atmospheric pollution. The last two factors have combined with the delayed but devastating effects of a series of flawed restorations that were effected between the end of the last century and the Second World War to threaten the very basis of the buildings' material and structural well-being.

Following an alarming exposé of the deteriorating state of the monuments that was prepared by scientists working for UNESCO in 1971, the Greek Ministry of Culture directed the Acropolis Ephorate to take urgent protective measures for the buildings. The magnitude of the problems eventually required the formation of a special task force, the Committee for the Conservation of the Acropolis Monuments (CCAM), which was invested with the necessary authority to carry out interventions by the Ministry in 1975. Since its creation the CCAM has exhaustively studied the ancient monuments and the problems that afflict them, charting the state of every architectural member, fallen fragment, and crack on the buildings and proceeding with restorative programmes in what is nothing less than a race against time to save the structures.

Any visitor to the Acropolis can see for himself the disastrous effects of acid rain and the increasing amounts of pollutant fuel emissions on the once-perfect surfaces of the marble buildings: delicate mouldings unrecognisable under coats of black soot, layers of marble flaking off or bursting, smooth surfaces crumbling like sugar at the touch of a hand. At the same time the oxidation of the exposed and uncoated iron cramps that were ignorantly or unwisely incorporated by older restorers have resulted in numerous new fractures, ruptured members and grotesquely discoloured stone surfaces. Before the CCAM was called in it was downright dangerous to move about the Acropolis.

From the start there was no question about having to go beyond mere conservation; drastic measures had to be taken urgently to add strength to the buildings, support collapsing members, repair earlier, ill-fated attempts to join broken elements. At the same time the unprecedented gathering of scattered fragments from around the Acropolis plateau led to the identification of a vast number of pieces that belong to the four main standing monuments. As these, too, were in dire

OPPOSITE: The Propylaea as seen from the Caryatid Porch

need of preservation it was decided that the best way to proceed was by repositioning as many of them as possible on the buildings. This afforded the fragments a greater degree of protection from the elements and made them more accessible than if they had been confined to a special storage area or shelter. Furthermore it offered the additional advantage of rendering the ruinous structures more architecturally intelligible to the visitor. Another important decision taken by the CCAM was the gradual replacement of the existing sculptures with accurate copies and their positioning in special museum displays to ensure their protection from atmospheric pollution.

The work that has been produced by the Committee and the manner by which it is decided has been positively received, indeed praised as exemplary by the international community. Certain objections have been raised, which are summarised in the 'Debate' section of this publication, that revolve mostly around the question of how far we are entitled to take restoration, even in the face of a drastic deterioration of the existing structures. As the team of restorers itself points out, an entire spectrum of possible actions presents itself with every restorative intervention. What has emerged with the new work on the Acropolis is an appreciation, paradoxical though it may sound, of the relative legitimacy of each facet of this spectrum, and, consequently, the importance of critical discussion in connection with any one proposal.

Since its inception the CCAM has had to operate within a complex world of scholarly debate. Like any interventions, its activities are bound to have critics; yet the Committee has not attempted to impose any one viewpoint over another. Almost every aspect of the work was decided after lengthy deliberation and democratic procedure. Especially as regards the care and discipline with which restorations are proceeding, there is everything to commend the new efforts. All work is being carried out in accordance with the principle of reversibility first stipulated by the CCAM. The main conservationist concerns are being dealt with as thoroughly as is possible: surfaces are being preserved patiently and painstakingly; the old rusted iron cramps are being removed systematically and replaced in uncorrodible titanium; structurally unsound sections of the buildings are being stabilised and strengthened; soot is being removed with the latest techniques available.

The chief protagonists of the restorations argue that the reincorporation of fallen material achieves two things at once; on the one hand it provides protection for the fragments, and on the other it invests the buildings with a new didactic value as it makes them more intelligible. If the contrast between old and new marble is as objectionable as some say it is, the CCAM need only apply a patina to the new surfaces. Better yet, it may merely exercise the Classical Greek ideal of patience, waiting, as Homer Thompson has urged us to do by recalling the restoration of the Stoa of Attalos in the Athenian Agora in the late fifties, for a few decades for the new marble to approximate the pleasant cream tones of the ancient material.

The efforts to protect the Acropolis Monuments constitute a duty that is as evident and old as the monuments themselves; for the ancient temples are products of the first marriage of the political concepts of freedom and collective responsibility which together form the Hellenic diptych of demokratia, which remains the western world's most cherished civic credo. As the spirit of democracy has haunted every subsequent generation, so have the creations of Phidias, Iktinos, Callicrates and Mnesikles. It is our task today to carry the enthusiasm of both ancient builders and modern restorers to the political arena, matching the interventions with the resolve and foresight that are necessary to reverse, once and for all, the real sources of deterioration that threaten the Periclean monuments.

Richard Economakis

OPPOSITE: Aerial view of the Acropolis from the southwest, with the theatre of Herod Atticus in the foreground and Mount Lykabettos in the distance

RESTORATION WORK
ON THE ACROPOLIS (1975-94)
CCAM

Since 1975 conservation and restoration work has been carried out on the various monuments of the Acropolis under the supervision of specially appointed experts – the Committee for the Conservation of the Acropolis Monuments – in cooperation with the Acropolis Ephorate of the Ministry of Culture. The work is financed jointly by the Greek state and the European Community and aims at dealing with the main problems affecting the monuments. These problems include cracking and fracturing of the marble on account of the oxidation of iron rods and fittings used in earlier attempts at restoration of the monuments, changes in the marble surface on account of the effects of atmospheric pollution and other biological and natural factors, the precarious structural condition of the monuments on account of their ruined state, and wear and tear to the Acropolis Rock itself (which constitutes a monument in its own right, as the bearer of the evidence of a long history) by the millions of visitors that tread its surface.

During the course of restoration work each of the monuments is carefully dismantled and the pieces are then treated individually on the ground. The oxidised metal elements are removed and replaced by others composed of titanium, the cracked pieces are stuck together, again with titanium reinforcing and a special cement compound. Wherever necessary, chiefly for structural reasons, certain blocks may be supplemented with new marble. When reassembling the monuments every effort is made to restore their original structure, rectifying the incorrect positioning of some pieces by previous restorers, and reinserting into the structure a large number of the pieces (whose exact position in the original structure has been securely identified) that until now had lain scattered over the Acropolis Rock. Throughout this process the surface of the marble undergoes treatment: the damaged stone, in the case of cracking and flaking, is sprayed and soaked, sealed and impregnated with inorganic materials whose properties and long-term behaviour are known. Moreover, in order to avoid irreversible damage, the architectural sculptures and reliefs have been moved to the museum and replaced on the monument with faithful copies made of a special cement whose colour and texture matches those of the surrounding monument.

An important feature of the Acropolis restoration project is the detailed documentation of all the phases of the work and the extensive use of the most well-tested and up-to-date technological aid. The latest engineering equipment has been brought in for the raising and removal of the various architectural blocks and for the construction of the various supplementary pieces. The project has also involved a pioneering use of titanium, the use of computers for the identification and repositioning of the pieces and for the handling of all the documentation, and, finally, the use of the latest methods and instruments for the analysis of the structural soundness of the monuments and their resistance to earthquakes. All the work is carried out according to the principles of the Charter of Venice, with further criteria such as the provision, as far as possible, of *reversibility* for whatever interventions are effected on the monuments, and above all the respect for the

OPPOSITE: Masons at work in the Parthenon cella

original state of the monuments – principles derived from the specific characteristics of Greek Classical architecture. The chief purpose of the restoration work is the conservation of the monuments of the Acropolis – the most recognisable and universal symbols of the Classical spirit – as works of art and as witnesses to the past.

Until now the CCAM has completed restoration work on the Erechtheion (1979-87), strengthened the slopes of the Acropolis Rock (1979-91), finished the first of twelve projected restoration programmes on the Parthenon (this one concerning the east side of the building), and installed removable walkways and paths for visitors through the ancient site. Operations continue on the Parthenon, involving the Pronaos, the cella walls and the Opisthonaos of the building, and were initiated systematically at the Propylaea in 1990. Here work has concentrated on the central building, and shall extend in the near future to the northwest wing of the monument, the Pinakotheke. A new restorative intervention (the third in a series) is scheduled at the temple of Athena Nike, pending the final approval of the specially commissioned survey of the structure, which has been completed. The process of recording, identifying, and allocating the fragments of architectural members, sculptures, inscriptions and other dedicatory offerings continues on the Acropolis, as does the creation of an extensive computer data bank with the material from the interventions (including photographs, drawings, and diaries). Finally special educational programmes have been instituted which bring young people to the Acropolis in order to sensitise them – especially if they are students in Greek schools – regarding matters of respect and care for ancient monuments.

The Committee for the Conservation of the Acropolis Monuments is made up of specialists and scientists of repute, Classical archaeologists, architects, architectural historians, conservators, structural engineers, and chemical engineers. The directors of the Acropolis Ephorate and the Departments of Antiquities and Restoration of the Greek Ministry of Culture participate 'ex officio' in the Committee. Presidents of the Committee have included the well-known and internationally respected archaeologists John Meliades, Nicholas Platon and George Mylonas. The composition of the Committee today is as follows:

President: Charalambos Bouras, Architect, Professor at the National Polytechnic. *Members*: Socrates Angelides, Structural Engineer, Professor at the National Polytechnic; Angelos Delivorrias, Archaeologist, Director of the Benaki Museum; George Despinis, Archaeologist, Professor at the University of Thessaloníki; Jordan Dimacopoulos, Architect, Head of the Department of Restoration of the Greek Ministry of Culture; George Dontas, Archaeologist, Honorary General Ephor of Antiquities of the Greek Ministry of Culture; Peter Calligas, Ephor of Antiquities, Director of the Acropolis Ephorate of the Greek Ministry of Culture; George Lavvas, Architect, Professor at the University of Athens; Basil Lambrinoudakis, Archaeologist, Professor at the University of Athens; Theodore Skoulikides, Chemical Engineer, Professor at the National Polytechnic; John Tzedakis, Ephor of Antiquities, Head of the Department of Prehistoric and Classical Antiquities of the Greek Ministry of Culture. *Secretary*: Helen Phocas-Logothetis, Archaeologist for the Greek Ministry of Culture.

The scientists and scholars in charge of the works that are being carried out under the supervision of the Committee and the Acropolis Ephorate are the following: *Restoration of the Erechtheion*: Alexander Papanikolaou, Architect; Costas Zambas, Civil Engineer. *Restoration of the Parthenon*: Manolis Korres, Architect; Costas Zambas, Civil Engineer; Associate Architects in charge of specific programmes: Peter Kouphopoulos, Nikos Toganides. *Restoration of the Propylaea*: Tasos Tanoulas, Architect; Maria Ioannidou, Civil Engineer. *Restora-*

tion of the Temple of Athena Nike: Demosthenes Giraud, Architect. *Consolidation of the rock slopes of the Acropolis*: Dionysios Monokrousos, Civil Engineer. *Conservation of the surfaces of the Acropolis monuments*: Supervisors Professor Theodore Skoulikides and Evi Papaconstantinou, Chemical Engineer; *Conservators responsible per monuments*: Amerimne Galanou, Yianna Dogani (Parthenon), Annita Moraïtou (Propylaea), Katie Babanika (Temple of Athena Nike). *Production of casts of architectural sculptures*: Alexander Mantis, Supervisor of Antiquities for the Acropolis Ephorate. *Cataloguing and placing of scattered fragments*: Christina Vlassopoulou, Supervisor of Antiquities for the Acropolis Ephorate; Archaeologist in charge: Constantine Kissas. *Creation of computer data base and information bank*: Fani Mallouchou-Tufano, Archaeologist. *Educational Programmes*: Cornelia Hadziaslani, Architect-Archaeologist.

Until the twenty-first century, which is now so near to us, the Acropolis shall give the impression of a large work site filled with scaffolds, machinery and technical personnel. It is an impression which parallels that which the ancient site must have given to the visitor in the age of Pericles, when this unique building programme was originally under way. To many it is a bothersome picture, but without doubt it is an unavoidable and creative one which shall ensure the preservation for the subsequent generations of an unequalled monumental complex, an indispensable part of not only the Greek cultural heritage but that of the world.

Fani Mallouchou-Tufano

The temple of Athena Nike seen through the scaffolding that covers the north wing of the Propylaea

THE ARCHITECTURE
OF THE ATHENIAN ACROPOLIS
CONCEPTS AND TERMINOLOGY

The Acropolis in Athens is a singularly well organised and preserved example of the ancient Greek *temenos* or walled sanctuary: as in most other Hellenic cities this site was located on an accessible, elevated landmass that was easily defensible. From here the temples, which were in effect the *oikiai* or homes of the patron gods and goddesses, could overlook and protect the populace. In times of war the city's defenders would seek the protection of the temenos walls as a last refuge.

As elsewhere, the Athenian Acropolis (Greek *acron* + *polis* = upper city) consisted of freestanding temples, religious structures, and large votive offerings (*choragic* monuments). The temples generally faced east but were usually conceived as *peripteral* structures, or freestanding buildings that were wrapped by colonnades (*peri* + *pteron* = surrounded by wings). Their two shorter sides were distinguished by pediments which represented the gabled ends of the earlier wooden structures from which monumental stone temples derived. The *tympana* or drums (vertical stone surfaces) that filled the pediments contained sculptural compositions representing mythological or historical scenes relating to the enshrined divinity. Temples normally consisted of *ptera* or colonnaded side wings (when temples were not *peripteral* they were either *prostyle*, featuring a single colonnaded porch on one pedimented side, or *amphiprostyle*, in which case they had colonnaded porches on the two pedimented sides), a cella or *naos*, which contained the monumental statue of the deity, a porch or *pronaos* from which the *naos* was entered (consisting either of columns framed between two *antae* or end pilasters or, as in the case of the Parthenon, a *prostyle* colonnade), an *adyton* or inner chamber that faced west, and an *opisthodomos* or *opisthonaos* from which the *adyton* was reached. As a rule the pedimented sides of temples contained an even number of columns (usually four, six, or eight) to ensure that the centre was marked by a void and thereby indicated entry; temples were therefore normally *tetrastyle*, *hexastyle*, or *octastyle*. The two longer sides almost always consisted of an odd number of columns, thereby presenting an occupied centre and notionally denying entry. Usually the total number of columns on the long sides of temples was twice the number on the short sides plus one.

Doric temples consisted of a *krepis* or stepped platform (normally comprising three steps), a column with twenty concave flutes separated by sharp *arrises* or edges, no base, a simple capital made up of a rounded *echinus* and a rectangular *abacus*, an architrave, a frieze consisting of *triglyphs* (representing the original wooden beam ends) and *metopes* or interstitial spaces, and a cornice surmounted by ornamental *acroteria*. Often the metopes contained relief sculptures with narrative mythological themes.

Ionic temples were different in that the columns had a base comprising an upper and a lower *torus* (Greek *speira*) and a central *scotia* (Greek *trochilos*), twenty-four flutes separated by flat *fillets* instead of arrises, and a capital consisting of four spiral *volutes* (Greek *helikes*). Furthermore the Ionic order either entirely omitted the frieze (as was often the case with temples in Asia Minor), or used it as an ornamental feature by wrapping it with relief sculpture. In general the Ionic order is taller and

OPPOSITE: The northeast corner of the temple of Athena Nike viewed through the central building of the Propylaea

FROM ABOVE: The entasis or vertical curvature of the Parthenon columns; a typical joint on the Parthenon, perfect to more than one thousandth of a millimetre. The fact that a joint is visible at all is due to the penetration, over the centuries, of microorganisms by a few millimetres along the exposed intersection of the blocks

more slender than the Doric; it is often more decorative, too, and makes freer use of sculptural elements, as in the case of the Caryatid Porch on the Erechtheion.

Perhaps because the Athenians were related to the Ionian Greeks who colonised Asia Minor (they were surrounded by often hostile Dorian city-states) or because they wished to take advantage of the full range of expressive possibilities contained in the two Classical Greek orders, they chose to use both architectural vocabularies on the Acropolis. Even the Parthenon, that most celebrated of Doric temples, contains numerous typically Ionic features, as are the columns of the adyton and the famous frieze by Phidias that surrounds the cella walls.

The four standing monuments on the Acropolis are unmatched in their combined structural clarity, aesthetic balance and architectural refinement. These qualities are manifested most clearly in the two main temples of the ancient temenos: though the Parthenon is in most respects a canonical octastyle peripteral Doric temple (and not an unusually large one at that), the carefully calculated proportional adjustments in its ordering system, its formal resolutions, and the subtleties in its construction together make it unique. The Erechtheion was already unusual for its age in its nature as an additive structure which utilised localised architectural 'events' to make contextual gestures on an urban level; what gives it its enduring qualities, however, is the combination of its formal complexity, the harmony of its diverse constituent elements, and the suppleness of its architectural and sculptural components.

Every architecture student has to some degree been familiarised with the Periclean refinements, but it is only upon visiting the Acropolis that one comes to fully appreciate their complexity, geometric exactitude, and sublime effect on the beholder, even at a great distance. Consider, for example, the *entasis* in the columns of the monuments; the characteristic curvature, that is, in the vertical profile of each support: this is nothing less than a perfect arc inscribed between the equally divided coordinates of the overall height of the column and the difference in width between the base and neck diameters. The peristyle columns incline inwards along projected axes that meet almost a mile above the Parthenon cornice; the flat surfaces of each column drum are adjusted against the horizontal plane by so much as is necessary to be perpendicular to the inclined columnar axes. As Manolis Korres has pointed out, stone joints are typically exact to *one thousandth of a millimetre*, an almost incredible figure even for today's high standards of accuracy.

The Erechtheion walls incline inward by 11.5mm between the *orthostate*, or top step of the krepis, and the level of the entablature. Like the Parthenon, this temple has a subtle horizontal curvature that carries from the base right up to the architrave and cornice, meaning that there are virtually no perfectly straight horizontal lines in any of the building's elevations. The Periclean monuments are in fact conceived on an Olympian scale as segments of gigantic geomorphic domes.

The reasons for these refinements were both to imbue the structures with the live musculature of load-bearing *agalmata* or votive sculptures and to correct the optical distortions ('sagging' of horizontal and 'bending' of vertical lines) that result in large post-and-lintel constructions. The optical refinements have been exquisitely married by the architects of the Parthenon to the disciplined plan of a peripteral Doric temple. This is most obvious in the way that the four corner columns are thickened to minimise the visual gap created by viewing these supports at an angle against the bright Attic sky. Furthermore these columns are placed closer to their immediately adjacent ones in order to resolve the notorious Doric paradox created by the need to omit the visually void metope fragments that would follow the end triglyphs in their 'normal' positions directly above their respective vertical supports. Unlike their later Hellenistic and Roman counterparts, Classical Greek architects did not approach the problem in a merely elevational way but chose to enhance the sculptural character of Doric temples by visually strengthening their corners. That they did so consciously is attested by earlier buildings like the temple of Athena at Paestum which, though 'logically' treated at the corners, were later deemed unsatisfactory when perceived with an eye for overall formal solidity. By the time of Callicrates and Iktinos the Doric order was understood to be essentially an architectural convention – a pictographic abbreviation that retained all the distinguishing features of post-and-lintel construction. As such, it was used primarily as a formal device. No earlier prototypical wooden temple would have needed to express beam ends (triglyphs) on the shorter gabled sides; to maintain a purely elevational rationale at the corners of the temples at the expense of their sculptural integrity would be contrary to the universality of Classical Greek thinking.

In many ways the Acropolis buildings are exercises in the marriage of type and contingency. The Erechtheion and Propylaea are the most obvious examples of this: the architect of the Erechtheion Mnesikles had to adapt an amphiprostyle Ionic temple to a complex topography which required him to reposition the west porch on the north side of the building. The resulting awkward plan was balanced by placing the smaller Caryatid Porch opposite the north porch. Mnesikles recognised that the south porch could not merely duplicate its counterpart on the other side of the building and chose to make reference to the immediate site contingencies here. The Caryatid Porch is therefore conceived on a scale that relates to the upper level of the Panathenaic Way or processional road that cuts through the Acropolis to the north of the Parthenon. As a result the Erechtheion is of a scale and formal complexity that sets it off against the Parthenon as a node or focal point rather than another directional east-west stoa or colonnade. Similarly the Propylaea were conceived on a monumental scale as a symmetrical building which had projecting colonnaded wings that wrapped the two sides of the ramped stairway leading up the western slope of the Acropolis. Here again Mnesikles was required to abandon his original scheme as it would have encroached on the sanctuary of Athena Nike, site of the slightly later Ionic temple of the same name. Consequently the south wing is both shallower and shorter than the north wing which houses the Pinakotheke. The south colonnade is in fact a screen which has as a primary function the establishment of a visual symmetry as one ascends to the temenos entrance.

Contrary to what many have made it out to be, the disalignment and apparently haphazard disposition of the monuments is part of a system of subtle inflections designed not to enforce axialities or link the buildings to some intellectualised nexus of relationships but to prompt the visitor to move along predetermined paths while appreciating the sculptural qualities of each building. The monuments stand alone and on their own terms, but are inseparable in their use of a common language of forms. They are conceived as a monumental quartet, or *tetras*, of civic and religious symbols conveyed through highly representational, idealised art forms.

Only a few of the architectural subtleties and innovations have here been described in connection with the Acropolis monuments. At the same time there is an entirely different set of refinements that relates to the symbolic content of each temple, and yet another set in connection with the artwork. Yet in spite of these elaborations the buildings are characterised by an unrivalled formal simplicity; they are among the purest expressions of the logic of load-bearing tectonics – monumental transformations of a universal vernacular vocabulary of forms. It is the timeless pertinence of this vocabulary that ennobles the Periclean monuments, and their unselfconscious pursuit of beauty that endears them to us.

Richard Economakis

FROM ABOVE: The horizontal curvature of the Parthenon, looking along its northern colonnade; the junction between a Parthenon column and the orthostate. The tonal differences in the latter show clearly where a narrow band was worked into the lower surface of the drum in order to prevent chipping of the edges in case of seismic activity

THE CONSTRUCTION
OF ANCIENT GREEK TEMPLES

Manolis Korres

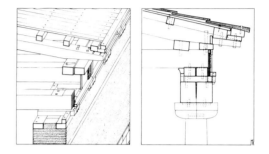

During the Geometric period, before the appearance of the canonical architectural orders, the walls of temples were mostly built with small, unworked stones and mud bricks; walls, in fact, made up the largest and most affordable part of the building mass. The most important part of the structure consisted of wood, which required superior structural technology and greater expense: skeletal structures and half-timber frames, columns and entablatures, doors and roofs. A repertoire of painted and applied themes, whether carved into the wood or as a series of local metal embossed details revealed the type, significance and ethnic and cultural identity of those buildings, and foreshadowed the appearance of the orders. In the Late Geometric period economic and social advances were accompanied by a continual development of vase making and terracotta modelling, but also by a continually increasing need for ornamented architecture, resulting in the increase in the size of temples, the replacement of perishable roofing materials with terracotta tiles and the covering of cornices, entablatures and other details with prefabricated terracotta vestments which protected and adorned the buildings. The industrial standardisation and the high level of precision of the rectangular roof tiles (measuring between four and six square feet) and other details dictated an impressive increase in the geometric regularity of temples and the development of metric canons in order to expedite this. The renewed appreciation of the ancient value of columns and entablatures as symbols or emblems for civic and, more importantly, religious buildings, resulted in the sudden concentration of attention and sculptural effort in an unprecedented architectural development of what was until then basic structural know-how. The change was not gradually progressive but precipitous. In a very short time the slender columns and light entablatures were replaced by the heaviest columns and entablatures many times thicker. At the same time the various architectural and decorative forms were fixed according to two basic systems, the Doric and Ionic. The replacement of older wooden constructional and decorative forms with equivalent ones in stone was not a simple, gradual development but a new eclectic creation, inspired only in part by the older wooden forms (which accounts for the problems inherent in modern attempts to reconstruct the wooden archetypes). For a while the terracotta vestments continued to be used on top of the new stone entablatures, but soon the sculptural refinement in stone of all details prevailed, something which had as a consequence the use of high-quality limestone for the erection of Doric temples and marble for the Ionic temples (in mainland Greece the Athenians were the first to use marble for Doric buildings).

That rapid development of architectural and building science would never have been possible without the existence of highly evolved metallurgical techniques. The easy quarrying and incredibly refined stone-dressing of Greek architecture was made possible thanks to the high level of metallurgical skills. From the development of woodworking tools new tools were created which were suitable for limestone, from which other ones were developed that could cut into marble. The quality of marble tools, as can be discerned in the working of the Parthenon, remains until now

FROM ABOVE: Reconstruction of the wooden origins of the Doric order; the Archaic hexastyle peripteral temple of Athena (the famed 'Hecatompedon'); OPPOSITE: View of the northwest corner of the Parthenon

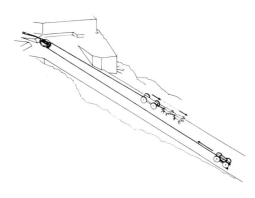

FROM ABOVE: Detail of an unfinished column drum from the Pre-Parthenon in which the successive stages of surface finishing are evident; diagram showing the method of raising heavy stone members onto the Acropolis Rock during the Classical period

unsurpassed. The contribution of the metallurgical industry is usually not stressed as much as it ought to be, as the history of art is concerned more directly with ideas and their originators rather than technology.

The systematic study of ancient Greek buildings reveals to us that the stone columns and architraves were conceived by their creators as monolithic forms. With the rapid increase, however, in the size of temples, columns and architraves began to be constructed out of numerous smaller stone sections. This was not only due to the difficulty in transporting colossal stones from quarries but also because the geological nature of most quarries did not permit the continual supply of consistent stone blocks of such large proportions. If the stone layers did not provide ready natural joints at favourable distances, the quarrying of limestone and, even more, marble was more economical if the stone masses had one dimension (the one vertical to the stone layers) not greater than sixty centimetres, so that narrow channels might suffice on either side for the extraction of a stone block, rather than the much wider and therefore more wasteful Archaic quarrying crevasses. Out of this came the *bilithic, trilithic* and *tetralithic,* along the width, construction of architraves or lintels, and the *polylithic,* along the height, construction of columns. Stones which had a smaller dimension that was much greater than sixty centimetres were usually the product of a careful selection in the stone quarry veins, where on the one side there was a ready natural joint and on the other it was possible to progressively extract smaller stones from narrower layers. On rare occasions regular mining trenches were opened which were wide enough to fit workmen. In the quarries the stone blocks were given a form just short of final. This was done to lighten the blocks as much as possible and to allow a closer inspection of the material for impurities. Finally, it was important to test-load at the quarries certain long and narrow blocks destined as beams by using loads many times heavier than those intended in order to be certain about the bending strength and safety of these units. The method used by the ancients to test the strength of marble can be said to be far more practical and safe than any modern structural computation systems. Stones were transported on sledges on downhill roads and carts drawn by many pairs of oxen or mules where the terrain was flat. The ascent to the Acropolis was accomplished by hauling the stones up two successive ramps from the area where later the Theatre of Herod Atticus was erected, to the Propylaea. When a cart reached the beginning of the ramp, strong ropes looped through a single gigantic pulley which was fixed at the top of the ramp fixed the cart to another one which had just delivered its load and was on its way back to the foot of the slope. The animals dragged the empty cart downward and thus pulled the loaded vehicle upward. (This method, which is described for the first time by Hero of Alexandria, continues to be used today with the help, of course, of mechanical pulling systems, as in the case of elevators and cable cars.) The positioning of the stones was accomplished with the help of cranes or strong scaffolds equipped with hoisting machines. In every case there were also light, strictly typical work scaffolds with floors that were able to move upward by one, two, or three Greek feet at a time. When a stone consisted of a complete architectural form, as in the case of a column capital, an architrave or a postament, it was possible to be positioned in a perfectly ready state. If, however, it was part of a continuous form consisting of many stones, it had to be positioned with only a finished resting surface (as with column drums) or only a finished resting surface and finished side contact surface (as in the case of a wall block). The upper surface of every column drum could only be worked after it was positioned and the upper surface of the blocks of a wall could only be prepared after all the stones of the respective course with its metal connecting ties were already in their place. This

method of operation ensured the safety of the stones prior to the final positioning and during the process of construction. It also provided a necessary external, unworked border for the final smoothing of the walls and coordinated completion of the building surfaces with geometric precision. Furthermore, it ensured the swifter execution of a work with an economy of space surrounding it.

The contact of the stone surfaces was direct, without the use of mortar, and made as perfectly as possible. Vertical joints were made perimetrically by joining surfaces which were finely smoothed along a thin border closest to the outside surfaces of the adjoining blocks (*anathyrosis*) while horizontal joints were, at least in the better buildings of the Classical period, made by the joining of perfectly flat stone surfaces, and not stones that were only levelled perimetrically, as is erroneously described in certain publications. Joints where there is no void even on the order of *one thousandth of a millimetre* have been achieved not with the method which was formerly held to be true of a rotational action (which would only be applicable with small column drums supplied with a central axis), but with a system of surface slabs, circular for columns and rectangular for the other stones. The surface plates were level and had an applied light red layer of paint (*miltologesis*) and came many times into contact with the resting surfaces of stones, on which they left impressions of colour which showed the precise positions where another light rubbing needed to be effected.

In order to bypass some unavoidable imperfections in the plate slabs themselves, but also for purely functional reasons, these instruments consisted of two complementary pieces capable of detecting the slightest inaccuracies (no larger than a thirtieth of a millimetre over a length and breadth of two metres). With one slab of the set the builders tested and adjusted always a single side of a joint, while with the other plate they tested and adjusted the opposite side. Thus through continual adjustments on both sides the complementary precision of the two surface plates was transferred with the sort of accuracy which today is equalled only through high-quality industrial equipment.

Structural or mechanical bonding was based chiefly on the way stones were interlocked and the considerable factor of frictional hold between stones. The wooden cylindrical *empolia* in the centre of columns served only as centring guides during the positioning of the drums and capitals. The linking of stones by means of metal ties and *gomphi* or dowels was intended to imbue the structure with an additional strength, mainly in anticipation of seismic activity. The fixing of the distances between clamps in accordance to set rules ensured the upholding of safety limitations in case of inner weaknesses in the stones. The rupture point of a clamp was always significantly smaller than the rupture point of the marble in the area around the tie (the various ancient cracks that can be observed today were effected only through the oxidation and expansion of certain clamps).

The final fine chiselling of the temple's visible surfaces began after the completion, from top to bottom, of the fluting of columns and the general vertical smoothing, or *kataxesis*, of the walls, and ended with the removal of the last superfluous layer of unworked stone (*apergon*) from the floors and the krepis. During this process the scaffold levels were gradually lowered, each time by one or two feet, serving at the same time for the application of painted and incised ornamentation. Work on sculpture progressed as with the architecture: the metopes and pedimental groups, which were made up of monolithic figures in the round, were prepared in the workshops prior to positioning. The Parthenon cella frieze (*zophoros*), a continuous relief sculpture consisting of numerous stones, was carved directly onto the building. Painted details (like those on the marble coffers) were

Scale model of a crane used on the Parthenon during Classical times

23

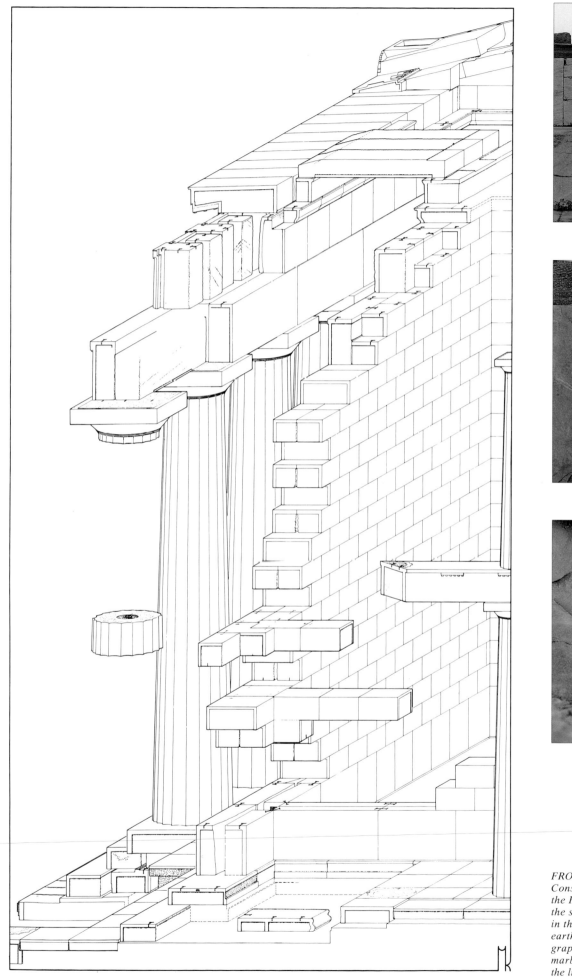

FROM OPPOSITE PAGE, L TO R:
Constructional axonometric analysis of part of
the Parthenon; constructional restoration of
the south wall of the Parthenon; a typical joint
in the Parthenon stylobate seen after recent
earthquake damage – the sequence of photo-
graphs shows how in the newly-revealed
marble cut it is almost impossible to discern
the line of the joint, so perfectly is it constructed

also sometimes prepared prior to positioning. The general painting of the triglyphs, architraves, columns and walls was effected immediately before the dismantling of the scaffolds. The colours hid the natural stains and veining of the stones (including marble elements, which, if left visible, would destroy the perfect visual continuity of columns, walls, etc) masked the blinding whiteness of Pentelic and other freshly-cut marble members, and rendered the architectural surfaces in colours and hues which had been established over the course of many generations.

The insistence of the ancients in moderating the whiteness and other aesthetic problems arising from the use of newly cut marble was such that they dressed these elements appropriately if these would either never be painted (as with socles) or remain white only for the duration of the construction work.

This dressing consisted of a very fine, homogeneous chiselling with fine pointed instruments of the surfaces so that the shine was dulled and the stone's veining and other imperfections were masked. This light stippling had nothing to do with the ordinary working of surfaces which preceded the final smoothing of a surface. In truth it was a purely decorative stippling on surfaces which were previously smoothed and shined. Because of the perfection in the surfaces the edges along the length of the joints were already perfectly sharp and consequently an unstippled zone along their length needed to be allowed in order to avoid damaging the edges. Regular zones of this type (taeniae) remain along the outward perimeter of every building block, including the outline of slightly projecting *aperga*.

The *taeniae*, *aperga*, *angones* and *scotiae* or *trochili* along the length of the joints are elements which in their simplest form had a purely functional purpose, and in their most developed were only partly functional, acting primarily as ornaments (hence 'decorative aperga'). The decorative aperga of a column or a wall also served an aesthetic purpose, as did, for example, colour schemes on smooth finished surfaces, but in a very different way. Decorative aperga emphasised the tectonic character of the building, underlining its nature as a composition of structural elements, while final removal of *aperga*, smoothing and colour schemes masked the blocks and stressed the plastic nature of the building which was meant to be seen at the same time as comprised of integral 'monolithic' plastic forms. Decorative aperga are usually the mark of a temporary building phase (as with the Parthenon prior to its completion or the never-completed Propylaea) but are also found in finished products, for example the Parthenon base, or the temple of Nike, where certain false joints were etched together with their respective taeniae, etc. In the first instance the removal of the aperga during the final stages of construction and the painting of the large surfaces constituted a radical metamorphosis of the building in which it abandoned its tectonic character and gained its projected plastic nature. Nevertheless the tectonic character was not lost, but simply rendered invisible, reappearing slowly with the passage of the centuries which faded the paints, moved the column drums and building blocks through seismic action and wore down the surfaces along the length of the joints and natural veining of the stones, resulting in the emphasis of each and every single stone. Of course today the natural ageing of the marble elements has accidentally given them shades and tones akin to those which they had when they were painted. The critics of the value of polychromy prefer the natural appearance of marble only because they have in mind its present state and because they have not imagined, or, better yet, witnessed the blinding whiteness of large newly-cut and smoothed surfaces of good Pentelic marble. The brilliance of a recently-smoothed Parthenon without its polychromy and painted tones made itself apparent when, despite the overcast weather, a thin layer of snow covered the surfaces of the northern side for a few hours after a recent blizzard.

The north side of the Parthenon covered in snow; OPPOSITE: Didactic restitution of the krepis, base, and orthostate of the south wall of the Pre-Parthenon

THE SCULPTURAL ADORNMENT
OF THE PARTHENON

Manolis Korres

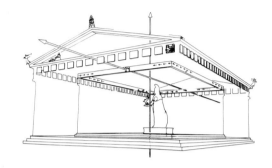

The term adornment (*diakosmos* or *kosmos* in Greek) as it is used today does not successfully render the ancient meaning of the word, especially as regards the subject of sculpture. Sculptural adornment denoted the highest human creation, equal even to the art of constructing temples, as it served the very same goals as sacred architecture: the fulfilment of religious duties, the expression of cultural values, as well as the intimation of political ideas. Naturally, however, its immediate and most tangible function was that of representation and the provision of narrative icons.

The adornment of Doric temples with sculpture was a rather typical phenomenon. However the case of the Parthenon is exceptional for a number of reasons. Its sculptures not only stand out because of their well known quality of design and execution, but even more so because of their quantity, being far more numerous that the average Greek temple. In most temples only a few of the metopes carried sculptures (at the Acropolis Hecatompedon and the temples of Selinous only the metopes of the east facades or cella facades were sculpted; at the temple of Zeus in Olympia only twelve out of eighty metopes were sculpted; and at the temple of Hephaistos in Athens only eighteen out of sixty-eight metopes were sculpted), in other temples all the metopes were unadorned – at the late Archaic temple on the Acropolis, at Paestum (Poseidonia), at Agrigento (Akragas), etc – and only rarely were these fully decorated with sculptures (as at the Treasury of the Athenians at Delphi, which featured thirty sculptured metopes). At the Parthenon the number of metopes was unusually large (ninety-two) and, even more unusually, *all* were sculpted.

The continuous (ie Ionic) frieze is found in only a few Doric temples and in any case only at the front or rear porch (as at the temple of Hephaistos or the temple of Poseidon at Sounion – the temple of Assos is yet another exception). At the Parthenon the frieze had a total length of a hundred and sixty metres and carried around on all four sides of the cella.

It is noteworthy that the thematic hierarchy of the Parthenon sculptures was organised vertically from the earthly subject of the frieze, the mythical content of the metopes, and the heavenly representations of the pediments; there was also a lengthwise thematic hierarchy: on the west and south sides the metopes do *not* contain deities, on the north side a few gods appear while on the east side *all* the metopes carry representations of the gods. The famous frieze contains deities only on the eastern side. The west pediment contains mostly heroes and only two gods, the east chiefly the Olympian gods including Zeus and no heroes (an equivalent hierarchy of themes can be seen in the frescoes and mosaics of churches: Christ *Pantokrator* 'Almighty' in the dome, the Virgin *Theometor* ('Mother of God') in the apse, secondary saints in secondary positions in the building, etc). The compositions followed rules which among other things served to bring out the best in every architectural frame. The square shape of the metope requires independent, self-contained themes, the lengthy frieze favours the development of continuous or progressive subjects, and the triangular pediment imposes special restrictions

Diagram showing the general arrangement of the Parthenon sculptures and the hierarchical thematic disposition on the longitudinal and vertical axes; OPPOSITE: Photomontage of the west side of the Parthenon with a scale model reconstruction of the west pedimental sculptures from the Acropolis museum

particularities in a unified scheme, but only the result of consecutive changes in the initial perfectly symmetrical plan of the temple.

The alterations were dictated by consecutive decisions to enlarge and expand the sculptural programme. It seems that instead of the frieze, simple unadorned metopes had been projected above the cella walls. Before the positioning of the stylobate of the east portico a decision was made to incorporate relief sculptures in the cella metopes, or to replace these entirely with an Ionic frieze. After the positioning of the first column drums of the east portico it was decided that an Ionic frieze should be added to the interior of the Pronaos. Then the already positioned drums were removed and their diameter was reduced. For the same purpose the east wall was built more to the west than had originally been planned. In general the erection of all the sides of the building was simultaneous, but nevertheless steadily behind the progress of the eastern side. At the moment when it was decided to add the lower frieze, the east side was ready up to the pediment with all the metopes in their positions, while in the other sides the architraves were in their places, but not the triglyphs or the metopes. These continual revisions to the programme could not possibly have been due to imperfections in the original studies and plans of the building. They must rather be due to the evolution and eventual prevalence of an opinion which had serious ethical and political dimensions. The metopes already provided allegorical allusions to the victories over the Persians (Trojan war, battle with Amazons), but said nothing about those who more recently had sacrificed even more, which was perhaps more proper. The Panathenaic frieze allowed the possibility to honour the state and to project the Athenian political system at a point in time when the need for an ethical justification towards allies and enemies appeared to be at its highest. Thus the building was not only a temple and monument to the Persian wars, but also a monument to the state.

The student of the Parthenon will feel that this temple is also in some way a monument to coexistence: regional deities and Olympian gods, citizens of two different political systems, Doric and Ionic forms and details (interior columns, Ionic and Lesbian cymas, anthemia, meanders, etc), Doric forms with Ionic proportions (Doric columns and especially the cella architraves). It is also a monument to the idea of *struggle*. In most metopes the theme is that of a struggle or contest, as in the west pediment. But that which is continually projected is not the victory of one faction, whether Gods, Lapiths or Greeks, nor, of course, defeat of another, whether Giants, Centaurs or Trojans. It is difficult to tell by looking at the metope sculptures just who shall be victorious, and the enemies are not shown to lack any hope of victory. Thus, as the outcome is not projected, what is represented is the very notion of struggle (*agon*), the idea, in other words, of the conflict between opposed supernatural, natural, historical, social, and even (why not?) personal, ideological and psychological forces (Centaurs).

As a monument to the Athenian political system the Parthenon contains a host of messages and meanings, but also intimations regarding the values and objectives of the Athenian State. It is evident that this large work on the Acropolis may be interpreted in various ways, even ways beyond the obvious which it may be possible to confirm as the subtle objectives of its creators.

Modifications in the proportional dispositions of the north peristyle colonnade of the Parthenon that were intended to allow a fuller development of the sculptural subject matter in the metopes. FROM ABOVE: General view of the northeast corner of the Parthenon; the second column from the left, showing a curious disalignment in the orthostate joints, which is now known to have been added at the start of the temple's construction to accommodate Phidias' revised metope sculptures; the third column from the left, showing an accurate joint alignment in the orthostate; OPPOSITE: The northeast corner of the Parthenon

THE HISTORY
OF THE ACROPOLIS MONUMENTS

Manolis Korres

The natural rock formation known as the Acropolis in Athens forms the nucleus of a five-thousand-year-old urban phenomenon. Its history is intimately linked to its nature as an elevated landmass that dominates the surrounding territory. The ancient Greek word *acropolis* itself denotes a defensible plateau at the centre or border of a city. As almost all Greek settlements were laid out around an acropolis (some cities, like Megara, even possessed two), it is clear that the presence of an appropriate natural fort was for Greek settlers one of the essential prerequisites for the selection of a site on which to build. Other important factors were the proximity of productive agricultural or pastoral territory sufficient for the maintenance and economic development of a sizeable population, and the existence of adequate land and sea connections for the expansion of commercial and other activities, especially if these could be economically and strategically controlled. The three most influencing parameters can therefore be summed up as security, economic sufficiency, and political control.

The Prehistoric Period

In the middle of the second millennium BC, the Attic basin, a variously flat and hilly expanse of some five hundred square kilometres which is hemmed in by mountains and the sea to the west, was an independent, self-sufficient productive region with a population of a few tens of thousands, concentrated in four or five larger settlements and numerous smaller ones. These settlements had spread across the natural subdivisions of the basin, and along major roads and highways which they came to control. The ethnic character of the inhabitants was the result of the absorption of pre-Hellenic Pelasgian elements by the stronger, more recently arrived Ionian Greeks. As elsewhere in Mycenaean Greece, society was organised along tribal lines, of which the more economically and militarily powerful ruled the land. The natural shape of the Attic basin favoured the eventual prevalence of one tribe over the entire region, allowing for the broader concentration of wealth, the development of a considerable military force and the transmission of political control through a system of hereditary monarchy. The necessary seat of this new state was a fortified plateau.

So it was that one thousand years before the erection of the Parthenon, and long before it was named 'acropolis', this natural rock formation (which subsequent generations recorded as having once been called Kranaa or Kekropia), was crowned by the walls of a fortified palace. At the time of its greatest development this building covered an area of some three thousand square metres, resembling, according to what we know, the palace at Mycenae: large rectangular courts and rooms clustered around columned halls, of which certain rubble foundations of massive proportions are still preserved.

On the eve of the great Dorian invasion in the thirteenth century BC, the upper part of the Acropolis rock was enclosed by a strong 'Cyclopean' circuit wall some 760 metres long and 4.5 metres wide (covering an area of 2.5 hectares), remains of

OPPOSITE: The Erechtheion seen at dusk with the Parthenon in the background

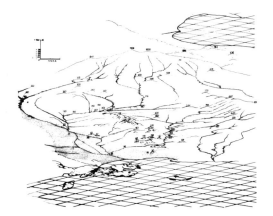

which exist on the south flank of the Propylaea and at great depth to the south of the Parthenon. Though it was headquarters and stronghold of a kingdom which held sway over the entire region, the Kekropian rock was not, as one might expect, even close to the geographical centre of the Attic basin. In fact, it is more than twenty kilometres distant from its natural northern border and only five kilometres from the coast. Whether the selection of this site was based on strategic criteria (as it allowed closer control of the coast and the borders of the neighbouring states of Salamis and Eleusis), or whether it came to be important by virtue of the fact that it was the home of the first clan which managed to prevail in the basin, is uncertain. The latter case appears, however, to have been more likely. According to Greek legend, Theseus laid the foundations of the future city-state by knitting numerous smaller settlements into a larger confederation (the Greek *synoekismos*), which would account for the plural *ai Athenai* ('the Athenas') – as opposed to 'Athena' – having established itself as the name of the city. That Kekropia was the base, in Mycenaean times, of the royal clan which instituted the confederation certainly suggests that this clan was the strongest and most influential in the area.

The advantages that came from the geographical situation of ancient Athens were largely economic. Athens directly controlled the lower half of the valley, which was the most fertile because of the earth deposits that were continually brought in and renewed by the Kifissós river. The most important Athenian agricultural industry was, of course, the olive. The olive oil that the city-state produced was precious not only as a food but as fuel for lamps, which for millennia remained the most common source of indoor lighting.

The importance of earth-renewing river water, life-giving rain water, drought-resisting dew, and nutritious, light-giving olive oil, found ample expression in the spiritual and artistic quests of the most ancient Athenians. The gods and mythological heroes, supernatural earth movers and genealogies that we associate with Athenian culture, all are creations of a religious, prescientific mode of thinking, in which true historical records merge with factual conjecture and symbolic representations of the forces of nature. The survival of an ethnically homogeneous Attic population, which had remained essentially unchanged after the absorption of the native Pelasgian element by the Ionian Greeks, justified the belief, held proudly by the Athenians, that they were direct descendants of the very first inhabitants of the region. Though identifying themselves as Ionians, a nation which, despite its long history in the Attic basin could lay no claim to being indigenous, the Athenians were zealous promoters and defenders of their aboriginal roots, however distant, remaining conscientious conservators of the most ancient Pelasgian traditions, now intimately linked to the Ionian. The product of this marriage of cultures was the marvellous mythical world of ancient Athens, which offered a wealth of subject matter for artists, including extensive iconographic programmes for the embellishment of Athenian temples.

As there are quite a few similarly defensible rock formations in the environs of the Acropolis, some of which have produced evidence of human presence since prehistoric times, the search for traces of the oldest settlements in the vicinity and the reasons for which the first builders chose the rock of the Acropolis as opposed to any of the other natural formations is of particular interest. A few Neolithic remains from the fourth millennium BC have come to light in the area of the Erechtheion, and even greater concentrations have been found on the southern foothills of the plateau. There are also traces of settlements from this period in the region of the Olympieion, where at a distance of some hundred and fifty metres from the river Ilissós a low, rocky escarpment is known to have existed, having since been levelled

The Attic basin in relief

and filled in. In the neolithic period, of course, antagonism between communities had yet to develop to such a degree as would require the large-scale concentration of power, and tall defensive plateaux were not necessary. The slopes of low hills were favoured in these times, especially if they were perforated by caves and natural shelters suitable for adaptation into sheepfolds and huts. We know, however, that the first priority in the selection of these primitive hill-forts was the existence in the immediate vicinity of spring or well-water nearby. Due to its unusual subterranean morphology, the Acropolis rock is the only natural formation in the region with significant water sources. Thus the area around its base was the preferred site of an unfortified neolithic community and, from the Mycenaean until the Archaic period, the rock itself served as the natural headquarters of successive military garrisons. Thucydides tells us that the most ancient name for the Acropolis was simply Polis (city) and that the oldest settlement stood in the region of the Olympieion (which is now occupied by the Temple of Oympian Zeus), site of the low, rocky escarpment mentioned earlier. The latter is confirmed not only by virtue of the large number of ancient shrines and sanctuaries unearthed there, but also by the numerous burials dating to the prehistoric and Geometric periods. It appears, then, that in its earliest stages of development, the city was bipolar; centred, in other words, simultaneously around the Acropolis and the Olympieion. With the growth of Athens, the term 'polis' was extended to the entire built area, and the larger of the two hills was given the distinguishing name acropolis (ie 'city on the hill').

The urban fabric of ancient Athens suggests that until the early Archaic period a simple walled enclosure wrapped the oldest part of town around the Acropolis, of which the largest dimensions were perhaps some seven hundred by five hundred metres. This primitive circuit wall was evidently rendered obsolete by the outward growth of the city, but not without having a direct influence on the town plan – an unbuilt zone some twelve metres wide which hugged this perimetric construction was later to develop into the famed Street of the Tripods, a broad boulevard which was left open on one side to allow room for the erection of large choragic monuments.

The uninterrupted development of the city upon and around the Acropolis ensured the passing down from generation to generation of the significance of the plateau as cradle and cultural epicentre of the city of Athens, as well as its great flourishing from the Archaic till the third century AD; from thence on to the nineteenth century its unaltered characteristics and, above all, the advantages offered by its well-waters ensured its continuing use as a fort capable of successfully withstanding the most persistent sieges. 1833 saw the beginning of a new period in which the Acropolis is no longer keep or religious centre. Rather, it has assumed the role of monumental historical complex, visited by millions, the object of archaeological research, scientific studies, restoration programmes, debates centring around the question of aesthetics, and, for a few decades, the inspiration for a series of planning decisions affecting a vastly enlarged area of the city.

Thus, for the various different reasons discussed, the Acropolis rock remains the nucleus of one of the world's most ancient urban phenomena.

The Archaic Period
The available documentation for the oldest religious structures on the Acropolis (dating to the eighth and seventh centuries BC) is unfortunately scanty, having been obliterated by the vigorous building activities of the many successive periods. Their existence is, however, confirmed by the surviving written records and a few existing stone bases for wooden columns, but chiefly from the rich remains of a great variety

Model of the Acropolis Rock during the Neolithic period

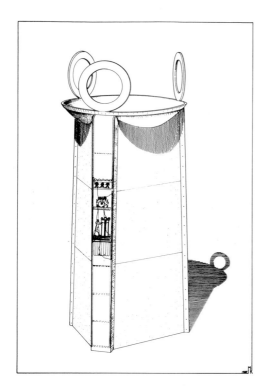

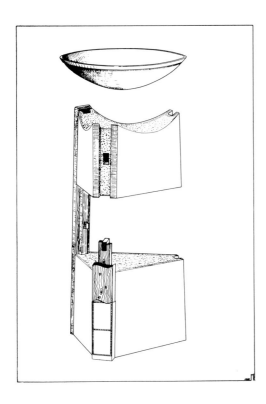

Drawing of a votive tripod from the early Archaic period. The full restoration was made on the basis of surviving fragments that are shown below

of terracotta roof details, most of which can be assigned to the end of this period. The great variety of these sculptured architectural features testifies to the existence not only of numerous secondary or ancillary buildings in this period, but of more than one large temple. These temples, which are now known to have had stone bases and half-timbered brick walls enhanced by rich wooden, terracotta, and metal decorative elements, must have stood directly above the foundations of the ruined Mycenaean palace in the location now occupied by the Erechtheion, the area just south of the Erechtheion, and the north flank of the Parthenon. One can only assume that these temples were the direct predecessors in both location and ritual function of the later, well known Archaic and Classical buildings. In the immediate vicinity of these temples large votive offerings, chiefly tripods, are known to have once stood, of which remains dating to the seventh century BC have survived, and which bear witness to the wealth of the donors and artistic merit of the craftsmen that they employed.

At the beginning of the sixth century BC the growing rivalry between social classes led to civil unrest, but this was defused by the laws instituted by Solon which released hard-pressed citizens from their debt and permitted a series of face-saving legal compromises to be arranged. In all likelihood the first large stone temple of Athena (known today by the generic Greek term Hecatompedos or 'Hundred-Footer') was built during this period. Its dedication is dated conjecturally to the year 566-5 BC, during which time that most ancient event, instituted by the hero-king Theseus and known as the Great Panathenaic Festival, was radically reorganised. After the discovery in 1847 of architectural and, in 1888, sculptural fragments from this Archaic temple, a number of reconstructions of the building and its pediments were put forward (Wiegand, Heberday, Buscher, Schrader, Schuchhardt, Dinsmoor, Plommer and Beyer), without, however, there having ever been general agreement about the original location of some of these fragments, or, for that matter, about the precise location of the building. Nevertheless all the more recent observations concur in that this limestone temple was a hexastyle peripteral structure, situated roughly where the Parthenon was later to stand.

The pedimental sculptures contained symbolic representations of bulls being devoured by lions, gigantic heraldic serpents, the reception of Herakles on Olympus, a sacred procession, the benign three-bodied daemon with symbols of well-being in his hands, and the battle between Herakles and the giant Triton. The sole marble members of the temple were the upper part of the sculptured eaves, the metopes, some embellished with sculpture – a four-horse chariot in full frontal view, the Gorgon, lions – some with simple painted or etched motifs, and the acroteria, which took the form of anthemia at the pediment apexes and sphinxes at the corners. Hymettian marble was used throughout, which was the sculptural material *par excellence* during the reign of Peisistratos. The most famed statues from this period from the Kerameikos cemetery or the Acropolis, like the shapely 'good shepherd' (or calf bearer) which is now on display at the Acropolis Museum, were carved out of this material.

In 527 BC Peisistratos was succeeded by his sons. An enormous Doric temple at the Olympieion measuring 110 metres long was included in their building programme, as was a second peripteral temple of Athena on the Acropolis, intended to replace an older temple ('Archaios Naos' or 'Ancient Temple') from the Geometric period. The foundations of this new temple are still visible on the south side of the Erechtheion, as are numerous architectural members and pedimental sculptures. These sculptures, together with the pedimental tympana, the cornices and the decorative edges of the roof and eaves, are carved out of Parian marble, a material which by this time had replaced the Hymetteian in the sculptor's workshop.

Hymetteian marble was also used in this new temple, but only for the plain metopes and as a roofing material. The subject matter for the east pediment was the battle between gods and giants with Athena and Zeus acting as protagonists. The west pediment contained a large composition of bulls and lions.

The two peripteral limestone temples were the most central and largest, but by no means the only structures on the Acropolis. Sculptural ensembles like the 'olive tree pediment', the 'Hydra pediment' or the 'red pediment' and countless architectural members testify to the existence of a few other limestone Archaic buildings, which were apparently all built in the Doric style and had columns only on the main facades. In the various specialised publications which feature these buildings they are listed under indicative headings like 'building A', 'building B', 'building C', etc, which in reality indicate only the various groupings of related architectural members. The original location of these buildings is not known, but it is reasonable to assume that, inasmuch as these structures are the corresponding predecessors of later, well known buildings of the Classical period, they most probably occupied the same or immediately adjacent sites. This is further reinforced by the observation that, in general, when Greek temples were rebuilt they completely replaced older buildings. The same is true with the sacred roads and avenues, sanctuaries, and especially the boundary walls that separated the different sacred sites. The central road axis of the Acropolis commenced from the western gate of the Mycenaean circuit wall, which occupied the same place as the imposing central doorway of the Propylaea, and after a curved, mostly uphill run ended at the southeast part of the wall, on the south side of which must have been located the gate where the original smoothly graded ascent of the southern ramp once lay. Another smaller road also commenced from the western gate and with a more northern course ended close to the Erechtheion. On either side of the two roads the ground surface levels were divided into bordering temeni or sanctuaries all of which had their own surrounding walls with an entrance or gateway. The irregular shape of the entire complex did not allow, naturally, for the creation of regularised, rectilinear sites, but at the same time precluded sinuous or curved boundaries The use of simple straight-line divisions or, in the worst case, polygonal lines for boundary walls and the incorporation of at least one right angle in every accidental four-sided or five-sided site was one of the main characteristics of ancient Greek urban design. This guiding principle was followed by the subdivision of the Acropolis by means of roads and dividing walls. The gradually rotating orientation of the various sites from the central sanctuary of Athena to the shrine of Pandion to the southeast was the result of their tangental arrangement (achieved by means of parallel and angular alignments) in relation to the curved, polygonal central road, which in turn was the outcome of sectional alignments along an earlier curved path which was probably already in existence when the Mycenaean palace was being built. The forms that were already developed during the Archaic period were firmly connected to a specific use and stolidly resisted every later attempt to transform or alter them, even when this obstructed the completion of the most important state plans, as in the case of the Classical Propylaea. Their transformation was possible only if it benefited those same sanctuaries without harming neighbouring ones, as was done, for instance, during the great widening of the Acropolis to the south after the Persian wars.

The uses of the temeni, or enclosed sanctuaries, were almost exclusively religious. The two most centrally located and largest sites on either side of the central road were dedicated to Athena for the different aspects or manifestations of her persona: as peaceful Polias or protectress of the city to the north, and in her ancient guise as warrior goddess and fighting Pallas or Parthenos to the south (where

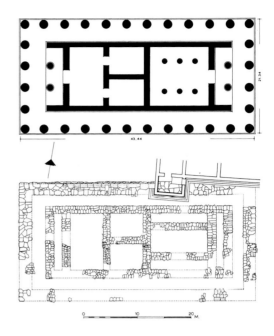

The hexastyle peripteral temple of Athena Polias, known as the 'Ancient Temple'

she also assumed the complementary role of Ergane). The other, smaller but well known sanctuaries at the southwestern tip of the Acropolis plateau were dedicated to yet other manifestations of Athena (Nike, Hygeia). A few large temeni were dedicated to other Olympian gods: Zeus at the highest point of the plateau (northeast of the Parthenon), Artemis Epipyrgeia (Of the Towers) near the temple of Athena Nike, and Artemis Brauroneia to the right after the Propylaea (her worship in this guise had been introduced by Peisistratos, who traced his ancestry to the town of Brauron). Many temeni were dedicated to the mythical hero-kings, guarantors and protectors of the indigenous ancestry of the Athenians, and to mythical figures related to them: Erechtheus, Kekrops, Boutos, Pandion, Pandrosos, Aglauros, the Arrephoroi and Erichthonios on the north and east sides of the Acropolis. In the northwest corner of the citadel a large water reservoir was built, as were a few buildings which served purely functional purposes. Finally there are parts of the Acropolis the uses of which remain completely unknown.

It should be clear now that the overall urban and architectural synthesis of the Acropolis was not the result of a single architectural concept or the application of any given aesthetic criteria, but mostly the outcome of an additive, continual process in which numerous ancient deeds and decisions continued to be binding, yet helped, in the long run, to guide and contain subsequent building activity. The orientation of axes were determined by general planning principles related to the subdivisions of the available space and certain specific principles regarding the orientation of temples toward the rising sun during the holy day assigned to the particular deity (with all the inaccuracies of the ancient calendar). What usually remained for architects to do was the synthetic act of incorporating new building designs into the existing, highly particular built context with all the older uses and particular conditions, and of course the study of aesthetic and constructional details in connection with the complexities of execution. The offhand interpretation or critique of an ancient Greek building from the sole point of view of architectural composition and in ignorance of the real conditions related to its creation, and the attribution to this creation of fanciful or unworthy characteristics by modern theorists is an act which wrongs the ancients. The true valour of their work is not contingent on the modern emphasis on isolated artistic genius and idiosyncrasy, but rather on the maturing of older types and the as yet unsurpassed, continual refinement of aesthetic and sculptural form.

These qualities may also be attributed to the buildings on the Archaic Acropolis, where the absence of any concern for general composition is as evident as the unprecedented care for the integrity of every form. On an urban scale the Acropolis complex was rich and diverse. Amongst the smaller structures two large, geometrically crystalline temples appeared to sprout without any transition from an irregular ground surface covered with natural clefts and angular projections, surrounded by a completely uneven and semi-ruinous wall of massive 'Cyclopian' masonry. Even the design of the temples, though part of a unified conception, at times presented an obvious, intentional lack of coordination in its parts. Exaggerated column capitals, massive architraves, overly-pronounced cornices on the lowest parts of the pediments, larger-than-life figures in the centre of pedimental compositions and much smaller ones in the corners, etc. Yet the forms in themselves are superb. The capitals as complete sculptural elements are exquisite, the cornices and the various parts of the sculptural groups are characterised by a supreme compositional unity.

The dynamic aesthetic qualities of the religious buildings was complemented by the countless marble and bronze votive offerings. Most splendid were the life-size equestrian statues and the *korai* (maidens), most of which were the creations of celebrated sculptors like the famous Antenor. An important monument, to judge from its proportions, was a tall Ionic column, certainly the largest in mainland Greece, the capital of which was 2.5 metres wide. From the various indications it would appear that this column stood on the grave of Kekrops.

In 510 BC the tyranny was ended after an organised mobilisation of certain aristocrats and knights. One of these was Kleisthenes, who in the end chose to collaborate with the *deme*, or free state. This collaboration led to the first arrangement and consolidation of democracy in 508. Two years later an important dedication was made on the Acropolis: a bronze four-horse chariot just outside the western gate of the still-preserved Mycenaean walls, following a victory against the Thebans and Chalcidaeans, who, egged-on by Sparta, had attempted a military confrontation with the newly-formed democratic state. In the meantime the construction of the gigantic Olympieion was halted as it meant continuing a programme that had been initiated by the defunct tyranny; perhaps in order to compensate for the discontinued work the first plans were made for the erection of the Parthenon, which would replace the peripteral Peisistrateian temple. This new temple would be made of limestone with columns roughly the size of those of the Olympieion, yet would have a canonic hexastyle plan like the building it was replacing, and not octastyle like the Olympieion.

The construction of this building would demand the transposition and lifting of thousands of stones weighing between two and fifteen tonnes from the quarries in Piraeus, which were already prepared for the now-abandoned Olympieion. Of this work, only a portion of which was ever realised and survives in the stereobate of the Parthenon, opinions vary. Some consider the remains to be the only executed part of a Pre-Parthenon from the end of the sixth and beginning of the fifth century BC that measured thirty-one by seventy-seven metres (Doerpfeld) and others an integral part, a podium, from the completed Pre-Parthenon from the second decade of the fifth century BC (Dinsmoor). The first theory would appear today to be the most likely. At any rate the difference in chronology between the two purported structures is so small, only a decade, as not to seriously conflict with the dating of the structure by Dinsmoor on the basis of related artefacts.

The Classical Period

The famous battle of Marathon (490 BC) was without doubt the greatest milestone in the history of the Athenian state and its cultural evolution. Great, costly public dedications were set up in Athens, Delphi, and elsewhere, that honoured and gave thanks to the gods, exalted the victors (and artists) and promoted the arts. The most splendid of all public projects was the first marble Parthenon, thanks to which the first systematic use of Pentelic marble was initiated. Until then Doric temples had always been built of limestone and only special details like the eaves and certain elements of the entablatures had occasionally been rendered in marble. In some older Athenian temples the gradual replacement of the upper parts of temples with marble details had been completed (the Archaic Parthenon, the temple of Athena Polias), or had even had their elevations, bit by costly bit, rebuilt in marble (as in the temple of Delphi through donations of the Athenian Alcmaeonids); but the construction of the new Parthenon from the ground up entirely in marble can only be compared with the temples in Ionia. An Ionic characteristic of the new Doric Parthenon was not only the material of its construction, but the monumentally proportioned cymation that was added at the base of the walls. The new building programme also included a propylon unique in its magnitude that was placed at the location of the ancient Mycenaean gate. The new marble hexastyle Parthenon, like

FROM ABOVE: Column drums and part of the entablature of the temple of Athena Polias in the north circuit wall of the Acropolis, placed there as a visual reminder of the Persian Wars

its predecessor, was founded on the same gigantic limestone base, but did not completely cover it (there is a difference of nine metres in length and five metres in width between this platform and the Parthenon footprint, which constitutes one of the most important indications that plans had been made for an earlier, ultimately unrealised, gigantic limestone temple). From various indications it may be concluded that the construction of the new temple did not entirely obliterate the older building. One part of the nave of the limestone building may well have survived briefly in the centre of the new peripteral structure, the construction of which progressed chiefly along the colonnade and the extremities of the nave. Column drums, architraves, etc, from the partial dismantling of the limestone temple, were used contemporaneously or subsequently on the lowest portion of the new south wall, and the related metopes were applied as a monumental dressing for the Mycenaean walls just outside the west gate prior to the commencement of works on the Propylon in 490 BC. The construction of the first marble Parthenon had progressed up to the height of the second or third column drum course when it was halted, most probably because of the institution of a military alert following the enthronement of the new Persian monarch Xerxes in 485 BC. Themistocles, the enlightened leader of the Athenians, had sagely focused all state efforts on the fortification of the port of Piraeus and the creation of a military fleet. This fleet eventually crushed the Persian forces at the battle of Salamis (480 BC), but the enemy had by then wreaked havoc on the Acropolis. The temple of Athena Polias, the east part of the Archaic Parthenon, the smaller ancillary buildings and almost all the dedications were torn down or consumed in the fire set by the Persian army. The burning of the wooden scaffolding of the unfinished temple and the monumental Propylon caused thermal fissures that left most of the marble elements irreparably damaged. In the following year the Persian army suffered a major defeat at Plataea and was thrown out of Greece. It seems that after the battle the victors swore (according to fourth century BC testimonies) not to rebuild those temples that were destroyed in the war for thirty years. This postponement of temple-building activity was instituted both for practical and symbolic reasons. Priority was wisely given to defensive works and economic restructuring. At the same time the pointed preservation of these buildings in a state of ruin was calculated to contribute to the heightening of national consciousness. This marriage of a spirit of material economy and symbolic projection characterises many postwar works in Classical Athens. The fallen architraves, triglyphs, cornices, etc, of the temple of Athena Polias and the semi-destroyed building blocks and column drums of the Archaic Parthenon were not thrown out as useless material but were creatively reused in 479 BC for the erection of a new north wall to the Acropolis; particular care in construction was afforded to those positions along the wall which would be most visible from the Agora, which was in effect the political centre of the city. Unusually, the cella, or at least a part of the cella, of the temple of Athena Polias was repaired and maintained for worship.

With the passage of time the scene of the Greco-Persian war was transferred continually eastward, largely due to the efforts and foresight of Kimon. His signal victory at the battle of Eurymedon (467 BC) ensured among other things the construction of the gigantic south wall by which the Acropolis achieved, more or less, its present extent and appearance.

About thirty years after the battle of Plataea, Athenian power was at its zenith. The signing of treaties with the Persians and the rival city-state of Sparta allowed the Athenians to turn unmolested to the creation of the most splendid public buildings and monuments, for which they had already secured adequate economic funds and,

ABOVE: Model views of the Classical Acropolis; OPPOSITE, FROM ABOVE: Perspective view and plan of the Classical Acropolis: 1 Propylaea, 2 Temple of Athena Nike, 3 Parthenon, 4 Erechtheion, 5 Bronze Athena, 6 Chalkotheke, 7 Artemis Brauronia; 8 Altar of Athena; 9 Arrhephoreion

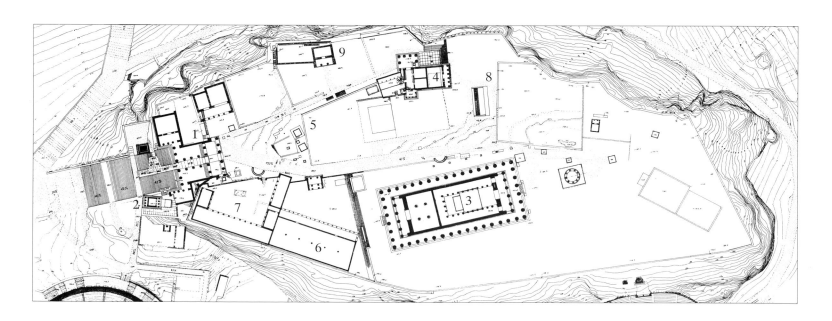

most importantly, unrivalled spiritual resources. On the Acropolis the result of this unprecedented combination was the Parthenon and, next in splendour, the Erechtheion, the Propylaea, and a great number of smaller buildings and votive offerings, many of which were veritable masterpieces of art and architecture.

The projection and realisation of any public work on the Acropolis and the rest of the city involved the submission of an appropriate proposal on behalf of any single citizen to the City Council and the approval of the Council following a discussion. Public works required the approval of cost estimates and methods of funding. The chief sources of funding were the temple treasuries, the treasuries of other large public institutions, the spoils of war, and certain percentages, usually amounting to 166 per cent, from the yearly tributes of the allied city-states to the treasury of the Delian League, which had been transferred in 454 BC from the sacred island of Delos to Athens.

From the records of the City Council decisions a synoptic text regarding the particular object of the resolution was composed and displayed publicly in certain well frequented places on the Acropolis or the Agora, or both, concurrently. These texts spelled out the general extent of the projects, the dates and time of their execution, the costs, the architects, and the special committees that were made responsible for the supervision of works and the keeping to the specific agreements and terms. The handling of funds was the task of special administrators whose term was yearly and ended with a fiscal accounting.

This accounting listed the sums received by a particular committee and their provenance, together with the sums carried over from the previous year's committee, the amounts it had expended for the provision of the various supplies and materials, services and wages, and the amounts the committee had moved from one treasury to another. The publication of these accounts was ensured by carving them onto marble plaques. Epigraphic records of this sort have survived in fragments which have provided us with interesting details regarding the yearly progress of the construction of the Parthenon and the Propylaea, and much more analytically the last phase of the construction of the Erechtheion.

During the four decades since the start of the construction of the first Archaic marble Parthenon new ideas and new techniques had been introduced to the arts and cultural manifestations, and the initial plan for the temple had been greatly surpassed.

The new plan needed to reflect the new, vastly improved ideas and abilities of the state. However it had to be realised by using the largest possible number of marble blocks from the Pre-Parthenon. This condition, which was a supreme example of Athenian restraint and foresight, aimed not only at cutting costs, but also at generating an ethical restoration, inasmuch as it reversed, to a large degree, what was until then considered to be a *fait accompli* of the war, namely the rendering useless of the previous temple during its construction. Now, once again, the discarded material that had for decades been considered useless would find a good practical function. The humbling effects of the Persian incursion were thus followed by a redemption of original value. For the architects, however, the difficulties were only mounting. These were eventually overcome by means and methods that were especially conceived for this building. Many previously unquestioned Classical canons were violated. The result, however, was above all criticism that was based on older general principles, and very soon every nuance and modification effected on the architecture of the Parthenon became part of a new, more valid and accepted system of principles. Construction commenced in 447 BC and was completed in 438 BC, which was a year in which the Great Panathenaic Festival took place. The

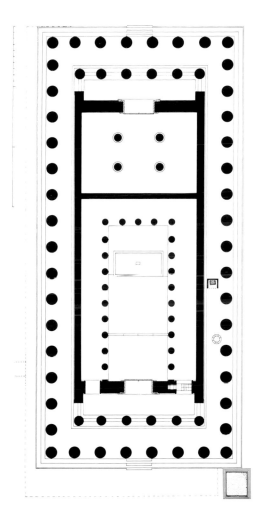

The newly revised plan of the Parthenon;
OPPOSITE: Perspective reconstruction of the Parthenon Pronaos

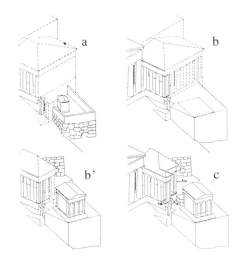

FROM ABOVE: The recently discovered shrine in the north peristyle colonnade of the Parthenon; revisions to the plan of the southwest chamber of the Propylaea

pedimental sculptures were all in place by 431 BC. The classical Parthenon was the religious antecedent of the older limestone temples on the site; at the same time, however, it was a new public votive offering which began as a monument to the victory at the battle of Marathon and was completed, after scores of new victories, as a monument to Athenian power.

Immediately after the completion of the Parthenon, work on the Erechtheion and Propylaea was started, as were the construction of certain upper parts of the south Acropolis wall and the levelling of related surface areas. A common problem faced by the building committees and the architects was the following: as the sacred structures and monuments of older periods were smaller and sometimes very close to each other, the replacement of the more important ones with new, significantly larger buildings would be possible only at the expense of open space or by totally obliterating neighbouring monuments. The latter were often so splendid as to preclude their destruction or relocation. To this problem solutions had to be given according to the particular situation. A small temple, the existence of which was ascertained recently, existed on the site of the Parthenon and had been preserved intact until then thanks to the contained, one-sided expansion of the Pre-Parthenon to the south which required the costly construction of the gigantic foundation platform. The new increase in the width of the Parthenon could not be contained to the south. It was extended to the north, without, however, eliminating the small temple. By carefully arranging the plan and orientation of the Parthenon the small shrine remained in place between the peristyle colonnade and the cella wall, by means of a rectangular opening that had been purposefully incorporated into the peristyle floor. In the exact same place a new shrine was soon constructed together with its related altar.

Similar phenomena are known from earlier excavations at the Erechtheion and the Propylaea. The asymmetrical form of these two buildings is due primarily to the form and shape of earlier buildings, monumental or purely functional, which it was not permissible to remove. It is evident that the plan of the Erechtheion was designed to be asymmetrical and irregular from the beginning because of the great importance of the older sanctuaries and buildings that had to be preserved around and even inside the new structure. On the other hand, the original plan of the Propylaea was symmetrical. The obstacles that were presented by the neighbouring sanctuaries, particularly on the side of the Temple of Artemis Brauroneia, must have initially impressed the architect Mnesikles and the collaborating committee as being negotiable. It seems, however, that in the end they were not, as plans for the great northeast hall were scrapped at a very early stage of the works, and the final form of the southwest wing was revised three times. Designs for a large southeast stoa were considered feasible until the end; its construction would require only a moderate intervention on the so-called North Building, and yet were never realised, perhaps because of the fact that it was an intervention or because of the start of the Peloponnesian war and the general interruption of the works. This interruption, it should be pointed out, was final. The last stage of construction, which required the smoothing of the wall surfaces and the floors of the completed parts of the building, was never carried out. On the contrary, the construction and completion of a large part of the Erechtheion actually took place during the height of the Peloponnesian war. The fluting of the columns of the east side of the temple was finished in 409 BC and a short time later the building was complete. The Erechtheion combined under one roof the various functions which preexisted on the site and at the same time replaced the neighbouring limestone temple of Athena Polias, which after the Persian destruction and the re-incorporation of material from its walls into the new north circuit wall, remained in use as a simple, repaired cella that temporarily housed the various site functions pending the completion of the new marble temples. Nevertheless, even after the completion of the new temples, the west part of this cella, known commonly as the Opisthodomos, was preserved for decades, or even centuries, despite the fact that it stood at a very short distance from the Caryatids. This Opisthodomos, which contained in separate rooms the treasury of Athena and of the other gods, was damaged once more by an accidental fire or arson around the end of the fifth century BC or in the third decade of the fourth. Other treasuries and places intended for the safekeeping of valuables was the Chalkotheke, the large colonnaded building along the length of the south circuit wall (of which only a few foundations stones have survived), the west chamber of the Parthenon, and of course its spacious eastern side. The treasury committee was responsible for the keeping of these valuables, a part of which were also the movable and therefore potentially replaceable elements of the shrines and temples, like the gold cloak of the chryselephantine statue of Athena Parthenos (which weighed around 1.5 tonnes), or the valuable door-coverings of the Parthenon. Every treasurer was entrusted with one of the many keys of the treasury door. The committee annually counted and weighed the precious metal objects and composed records which were published as marble-carved treasury inscriptions.

Among the large monuments were countless smaller ones, many votive offerings, some public and some private. The most splendid and precious were made of bronze. The centrally-placed gigantic bronze statue of Athena Promachos, which was an early work by Phidias, was a dedication to the victory at the battle of Marathon, though it was realised three decades after the event. Another important public monument was a large bronze ship of which only two of the inscribed supporting stones survive. Other monuments included larger-than-life-size bronze Trojan horse at the restructured Brauroneion with its new limestone Doric buildings, the 'Lemnian' Athena by Phidias, the numerous statues in front of the Parthenon columns, the bronze generals Konon and Timotheos that were placed on a semicircular marble exedra to the north of the Parthenon and a later, similar structure inside the Propylaea on which stood Kifessodotos and another general. Large gold-covered shields were dedicated to Athena by Alexander following the battle of the Granikos (334 BC), which were fixed to the architraves of the Parthenon.

The political and economic decay of the city after the fourth century BC is embedded in the history of the Acropolis monuments. In 304 BC the western chamber of the Parthenon was used as a place of residence for general Demetrios Poliorketes and in 295 Lachares, the bankrupt leader of the Athenians, denuded the statue of the Parthenos in order to melt down the gold. At the end of the third century BC king Attalos I of Pergamon dedicated a long monument along the length of the south retaining wall commemorating the Gaulish wars. Numerous scattered stones from this structure survive, most probably from the base. At the beginning of the second century BC Antiochos IV, known as Epiphanes, dedicated a gigantic shield on the Acropolis which was decorated with a Gorgoneion, or head of Medusa, which was hung on the south wall. During the same period Eumenes of Pergamon and a little later his brother Attalos II donated to the city of Athens the famous stoas which came to be known by their respective names, and were subsequently honoured by the Athenians with large monuments consisting of a massive pillar and a bronze four-horse chariot placed at the peak. At least two such monuments were erected on the Acropolis, one exactly at the northeast corner of the Parthenon and the surviving one to the right of the Propylaea (left of the building as one ascends the Acropolis). In

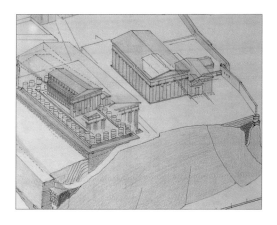

FROM ABOVE: Perspective view of the Erechtheion from the southwest; successive phases of the temples of Athena, axonometric representation with colour-coded outlines. Green: temple of Athena Polias, Geometric period (the so-called 'Ancient Temple', seventh century BC). Pink: limestone Archaic temples in the location of the later Parthenon, the 'Hecatompedon' temple (c570 BC), while the new temple of Athena Polias (525 BC) keeps its name 'Ancient Temple'. Yellow: the unfinished Pre-Parthenon. Blue: Classical period Parthenon, Erechtheion, Propylaea

The interior of the Parthenon after the fire of AD 267

AD 31 the Athenians altered the inscriptions on these monuments and re-dedicated them to the emperors Augustus and Agrippa, respectively. Under Augustus the interior of the Erechtheion suffered serious damages from a fire and during its repair underwent a few essential changes, of which the most serious from a stylistic point of view was the placement of windows in the spaces between the engaged columns of the west elevation (the windows have passed into the repertoire of late classicism because they were erroneously recorded as having been part of the original building by Stuart and Inwood). Around that time a nine-columned circular temple of Roma and Augustus was constructed in front of the Parthenon, a classicising structure which copied the stylistic elements of the Erechtheion. The architect of this building was perhaps the same one who intervened on the Erechtheion. The greatest part of this circular temple survives today.

Under the emperor Nero a three-line golden inscription was placed between the shields along the length of the architrave of the east side of the Parthenon in his honour, and in the next century a statue of Hadrian was placed alongside the chryselephantine Athena of Phidias. In the Propylaea marble door surrounds were positioned in place of the original wooden ones which had burned in a fire.

The Roman Period until 1687

The third century BC was the worst for the Athenian monuments. In 267 the Heruli, originating in the north of Europe, overran Greece causing serious destruction. Virtually all the public buildings were set on fire. The heavy damage caused by the intense thermal activity is visible on the original walls of the stoa of Attalos, the interior of the Parthenon, the Erechtheion and the Theatre of Herod Atticus, and on the surviving stones of numerous other monuments. If the barbarians alone were responsible for the destructions, the inability of the Athenians to restitute the damage was due to something much worse, namely the economic and demographic withering of the city, which had already begun in the age of the Antonines. The maintenance until then of the shining monuments balanced, somewhat, the unhappy reality of the situation. After the destruction, however, the state of the city better reflected the material strength of Athenian society. The ruined monuments were not repaired but systematically destroyed, aided by the reappropriation of building material for the cheapest possible strengthening of the old defensive walls and the fortification of the central part of the city. The part that was walled between the stoa of Attalos, the Library of Hadrian, and the Pantheon, up to the Theatre of Herod Atticus, the stoa of Eumenes and the Theatre of Dionysos, was a twelfth of the immediately preceding area and a half of the area during the earliest Archaic period!

In the next century the Parthenon, which for many decades had remained unroofed and whose cella colonnade was seriously damaged, was repaired with marble blocks that were removed from the bases of various classical monuments and material from the dismantling of a stoa, which had a total length of around two hundred metres, which had not been destroyed by the Heruli. The new roof covered only the cella, was steeper than the ancient one and used cheap terracotta roof tiles. The peristyle has remained unroofed ever since. At the end of the fourth century AD and the beginning of the fifth extensive demolitions of temples and other ancient buildings were carried out on the Acropolis. The Brauroneion, the Arrephorion, the northeast building and many more were pulled down around that period. Stones from those buildings were used for the construction of a Nymphaeum, of which one part survives attached to the remaining wall of the stoa of Eumenes, next the Theatre of Herod Atticus, on the same line with a surviving wall of the third century AD.

Under the reign of Justinian the Parthenon and Erechtheion were transformed into Christian churches, with relatively small interventions and the addition of a semicircular apse on the east side, between the columns. The transformation of the Parthenon contributed to its eventual survival as a building, but at the same time was an excuse for new, planned destructions: the defacing of the metopes along the length of the east, north and west side of the building and the disappearance of the greatest part of the east pedimental sculpture.

From inscriptions on the columns of the Parthenon we may deduce that prior to the year AD 841 the diocese of Athens was elevated to an archdiocese and before the year 981 to a metropolitan seat (some two-hundred and thirty Christian inscriptions are documented from the Parthenon and scores of others from the Propylaea and the Theseion, which cover ten centuries).

During the office of metropolitan Nikolaos Aghiotheodorites (1166-75), the east wall of the Parthenon was rebuilt and the apse was significantly enlarged, assuming a semi-hexagonal form. Immediately afterwards, under metropolitan Michael Choniates (1175-1204), the church was extensively decorated with frescoes.

In 1204 Athens fell to the Franks, and with a Papal volition of November 27th, 1206 the new archbishop, Berard, assumed leadership over the churches throughout the Athenian province. The Parthenon was now the metropolitan cathedral of the Duchy of Athens. Around that time a lofty tower was built in the northwest corner of the Parthenon cella, which was constructed of marble chiefly from the partial demolition of the monument of Philopappos and partly from the Propylaea and other monuments. A tower was also built at the south wing of the Propylaea and later an octagonal tower at the northeast corner of the Acropolis. In the same period a new, circuit wall was added to the west side of the plateau and the east and south, which followed the all but vanished outline of the Theatre of Dionysos.

After the bloody battle of Kopaïs (1311), the Duchy fell to the chiefs of the Catalan Company, who established their own guard and government on the Acropolis. In 1388 the Acropolis was occupied by the Florentine Neri Acciauoli. The Propylaea were subsequently transformed into his palatial residence, with the addition of floors immediately above the central building and the Pinakotheke, and the addition of new fortifications and towers along the perimeter of the complex.

In 1394 Neri was buried in the Parthenon. According to his will the entire town would become property of the Latin church of the Theotokos, (*Santa Maria di Atene*, as the Parthenon was then called) and the Venetians would oversee the carrying out of the will. Under the supervision of the Venetians in 1401 the strong but worn walls of the Acropolis were repaired.

The Acropolis was reclaimed in 1403 by Antonio Acciauoli, son of Neri. The palace (Propylaea) was extended with new additions. From Neri's will and the writings of the Italian visitor Nicolo da Martoni we have valuable information about the Parthenon. For the smaller buildings, like, for example, the church at the Erechtheion, the information is scanty. Another church, San Bartolomeo, was built to the east of the Pinakotheke. In 1451 the Venetian aristocrat Chiara Zorzi, widow of Neri II, was married in the Parthenon to her compatriot Bartolomeo Contarini.

In 1456 the Turkish army wrested the city of Athens from the Venetians and in 1458 the Acropolis fell in its turn. The last Duke of Athens departed. Only the last archbishop Nicolo Protimo stayed behind, but he, too, for a very short while. In 1460 the Parthenon was transformed into a Turkish mosque and a minaret was added to the upper part of the Frankish tower.

During the next two centuries the Acropolis, castle of Athens, was a place virtually forgotten by Europe. Only after the middle of the seventeenth century

FROM ABOVE: The twelveth-century apse of the Christian Parthenon; model of the Acropolis during the period when it served as a fort for the Florentine Acciauoli dynasty

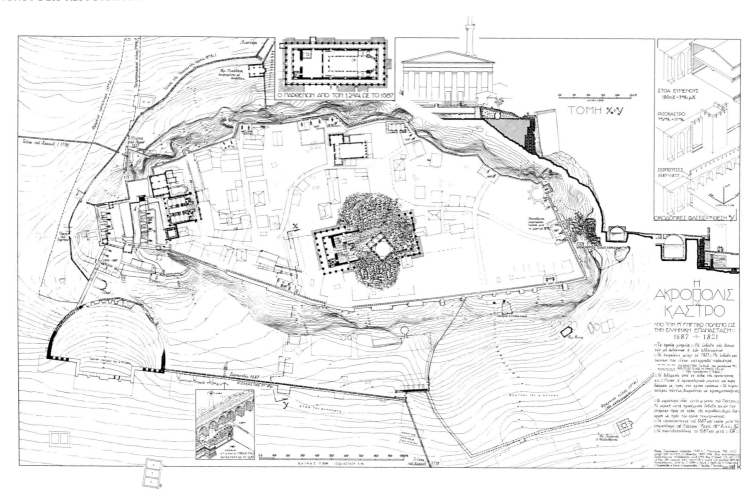

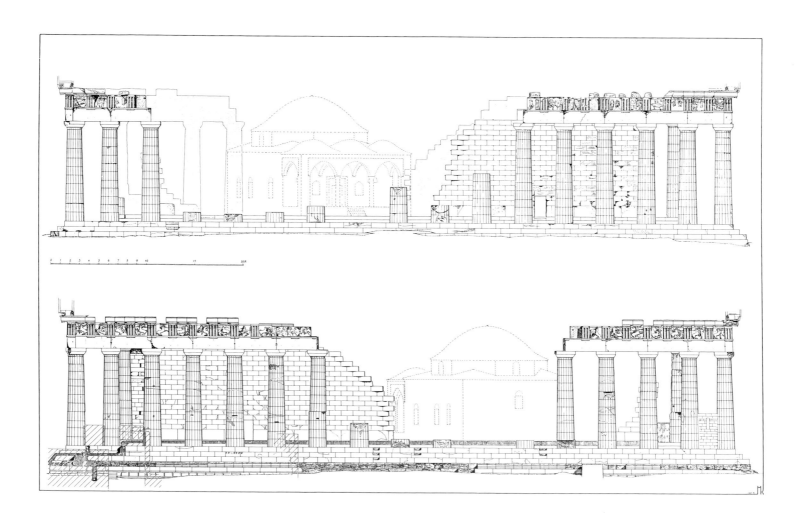

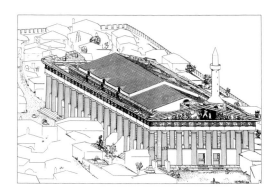

would there be new testimonies from visitors to the site: J Giraud, E Celebi, JP Babin, J Spon, G Wheler, F Vernon, G de la Guilletieres, Olier, Marchese de Nointele, G Magni, B Randolph. In September 1687 the Venetian general Morosini besieged the Acropolis. The Turks had previously reinforced their defences with new walls on the south side of the plateau and a new battlement at the Propylaea, for the construction of which they had dismantled the temple of Nike, which had until then stood in excellent condition. Behind this battlement stood, still intact, the facade of the Propylaea, while behind it a large part of the building lay in ruins following an older gunpowder explosion (c1640). It appears that this catastrophe had not sufficiently instructed the Turks, who once again used the Propylaea and the Parthenon as gunpowder arsenals. On September 22nd, 1687 the southeast corner of the Propylaea exploded from the ignition of the stored gunpowder and, four days later, the Parthenon from a far greater concentration of explosives. The roof, the later interior columns, the lateral walls, the ancient Pronaos and large parts of the peristyle colonnade were victims of this combination of Turkish and European carelessness. The latter already knew that they could not field sufficient military muscle to hold on to the territories they were only temporarily capturing. After a few months the Venetians withdrew, leaving the Acropolis once again to the Turks, thereby demonstrating that the Parthenon was sacrificed for the mere purpose of displaying momentary strength, and not for some serious programme of national and religious prevalence of the West in Greece.

Before their departure the Venetians attempted to remove a few sculptures from the west pediment but were clumsy and rushed in their efforts, causing once-famed masterpieces of art to fall and be shattered. Nevertheless various technical difficulties did not permit them to carry through with a ready plan of exploding the walls and sides of the Acropolis rock, by which they hoped to render the castle useless to their enemies.

FROM ABOVE: The Parthenon just before the explosion of 1687; the explosion that destroyed the Parthenon on September 26th, 1687 (drawing by Manolis Korres); OPPOSITE, FROM ABOVE: Plan of the Acropolis in 1687; the Parthenon in 1800, long elevation

THE PROPYLAEA
AND THE WESTERN ACCESS
OF THE ACROPOLIS

Tasos Tanoulas

The Propylaea of the Athenian Acropolis, one of the most original and sophisticated architectural creations of Classical antiquity, occupied the top of the western slope of the Acropolis, which is the only negotiable access to the summit of the rock. Its purpose was to mark in a monumental manner the end of the access and the entrance to the holy precinct. The complex was planned by the architect Mnesikles as a part of the Periclean project which turned the Acropolis into the symbol *par excellence* of Classical culture; the Parthenon, the Erechtheion and the temple of Athena Nike being the other main elements of the same project. The construction of the Propylaea started just after the completion of the Parthenon in 437 BC and ended in 432 BC. During this process, Mnesikles appears to have changed some elements of the plan, and finally to have curtailed it substantially by not building the two large wings to the north and east of the central building, and by not fully developing the southern wing. The walls, floors and *krepis* surfaces of the Propylaea, having never received the final treatment, are very instructive about the building techniques and processes applied by the Athenians of the fifth century BC in order to achieve perfection in marble. Despite their ultimately unfinished state, the Mnesiklean Propylaea are so well crafted as to have earned the admiration of the architects' contemporaries and of the generations to come.

Mnesikles' inventive mind provided ready solutions to the structural and artistic problems emerging from the new building type he created: the two main Classical orders, Doric and Ionic, being visible together for the first time on the exterior of the same building, the juxtaposition of two scales of the Doric order, the differentiation of levels, and the use of grey marble to achieve subtle perceptual effects, were all combined to translate both the function of the building and the constraints of its situation on the sloping rock into architectural terms of great beauty.

Today the monuments of the Acropolis might be thought of as *palimpsests* retaining, in their fabric or on their surfaces, the traces of successive historic interventions. In order to interpret these traces one has to examine them together with the testimonies provided both by travellers who visited Athens in the period from the late Middle Ages until the nineteenth century, and by nineteenth-century archaeological research. These testimonies consist of texts and illustrations which must be mutually compared and cross-referenced, a procedure that allows the identification of later structural phases of the Propylaea and the western access to the Acropolis.

The earliest interventions on the Mnesiklean building are most probably the marble pieces added in special cuttings of the superstructure in the northern wing. They are very likely repairs made after an earthquake that struck in 426 BC. Another early intervention is a marble floor in the central passageway, which must be attributed to the late fifth century BC. Furthermore, one has to mention the statues, stelae, and other votive offerings, traces of which still survive on the classical fabric of the monument. It is worth recording five cuttings surviving on the north side of the south colonnade of the central passageway and on the southern doorjamb of the

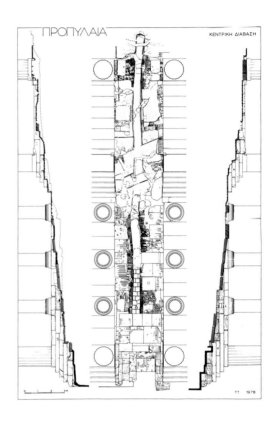

The central passageway of the Propylaea, actual state. Plan and face of the vertical sides; OPPOSITE: View of the Propylaea from the southwest, with the temple of Athena Nike to the left

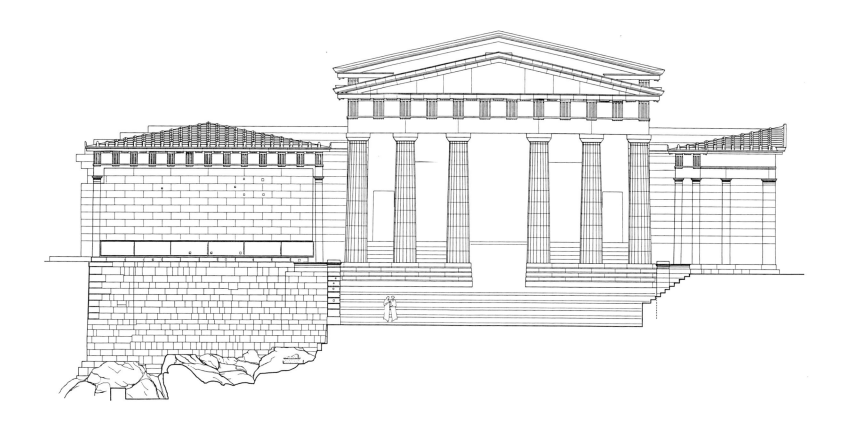

The Propylaea in the fifth century BC. FROM ABOVE: West elevation; section on the central axis of the central building, looking north

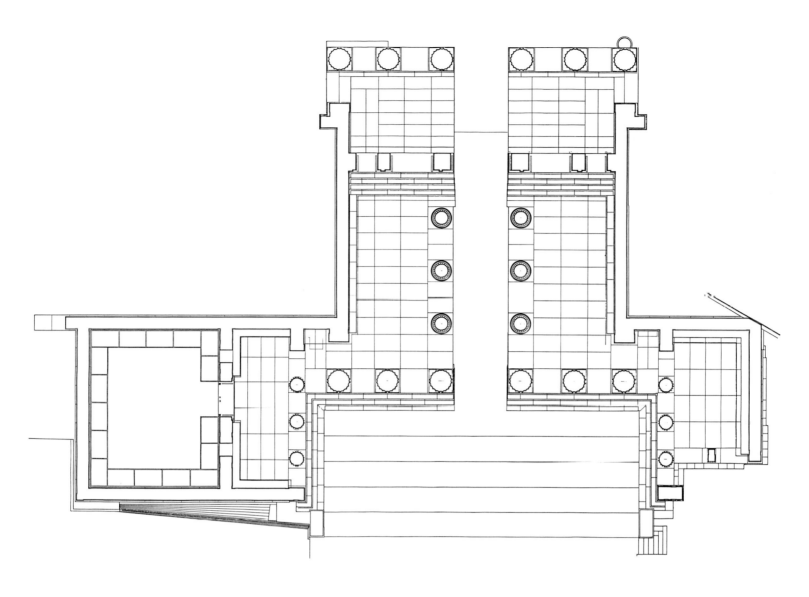

The Propylaea in the fifth century BC. FROM ABOVE: plan; section in the Pinakotheke, looking south

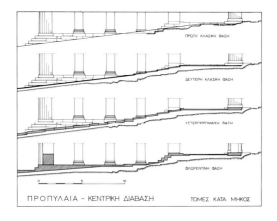

FROM ABOVE: The western access to the Acropolis in the fifth century BC (model belonging to the American School of Classical Studies in Athens); fifth century AD repairs on the upper parts of the triglyphs of the northern wall of the Propylaea; cross sections of the successive structural phases traced in the central passageway (from above: first Classical phase, with pressed earth in the natural cavities of the rock, second Classical phase, with pavement and a central drain channel, Post-Herulian phase with pavement of second-hand marble slabs and central drain channel, Florentine phase, fifteenth century AD, unifying the floor in the western hall, the two upper stairs of the krepis of the western facade); cuttings on the northern side of the southern interior colonnade and on the southern jamb of the central door

central door; these cutting are aligned roughly with the slope of the central passageway, and were used for the suspension of ornamental or functional objects. Different cuttings are visible on the southern wall of the central building, and one of them still retains the iron clamp used for the suspension of such objects. On the eastern wall of the southern wing ten cuttings occur, similar to the ones on the central building wall; they might have been used for the suspension of offerings related to the sanctuary of Athena Nike or the other small sanctuaries in the area. Clearly, then, interventions at the Propylaea had already commenced during Classical times with the adornment of the complex for ceremonial purposes.

In 174 BC, near the southwest corner of the north wing, a tall pedestal was erected carrying the statue of Eumenes II, king of Pergamon; this is now known as the Pedestal of Agrippa whose statue replaced the previous one in the first century BC. In the first century AD a marble flight of steps replaced the ramp that formed part of the original Classical complex. Traces in the superstructure of the northern wing, some slabs from the central building's ceilings and, also, the marble portals of the entrance doors of the central building indicate a Roman intervention, most probably of the second century AD.

History records that the Heruli devastated Athens and, probably, the Acropolis in AD 267; this event is conventionally considered to be the beginning of the Middle Ages in Greece. A short time after the departure of the Heruli, the Athenians encircled their city and the southern slope of the Acropolis with the so called Post-Herulian wall.

The Acropolis itself was fortified as well: a Post-Herulian gate, known today as the Beulé gate, cut through the Roman flight of steps to the west of the Propylaea. To the west of the Nike tower a second gate was built, protected by a tower standing, respectively, on its western side. At the same time the famed Klepsydra spring was covered with a vaulted structure that was protected by the Post-Herulian wall and connected to the Mnesiklean terrace by means of a covered staircase with a vaulted roof. The purpose of this arrangement was to secure the Klepsydra water source for the defenders of the Acropolis in case of siege.

There is evidence that the lateral wings of the Propylaea had been deprived of their roofs and wooden ceilings sometime in late antiquity, possibly in 267. Evidence to corroborate this are the gutters that were cut in the floor of the lateral wings at a very early period, and a recently discovered marble tile from the Pinakotheke built into the Justinianic cistern behind the Propylaea, dated to the sixth century AD.

Athens remained the stronghold of pagan culture down to the sixth century AD. This accounts for the fact that no Classical monument in Athens was converted into a Christian church before the end of the sixth century. On the Acropolis the Parthenon and the Erechtheion were eventually turned into churches, but not before the second half of the sixth century. A small church that was built in the southern wing of the Propylaea dates, in all likelihood, from the same period. This church appears to have been a one-aisled basilica, with a wooden roof sloping to the north and west.

Cuttings from this period surviving on the colonnade of the northern wing of the Propylaea indicate a sloping wooden roof, which covered a terrace isolated from the outside by means of a wall or fence; this terrace occupied the angle between the northern half of the central building and the northern wing. The roofed area of the terrace communicated with a room behind the two westernmost spaces – both being free of walls – of the colonnade. The rest of the portico of the north wing must have been left unroofed, but the Pinakotheke itself appears to have received a new roof.

To this period must be attributed the cistern in the area of the northeastern wing

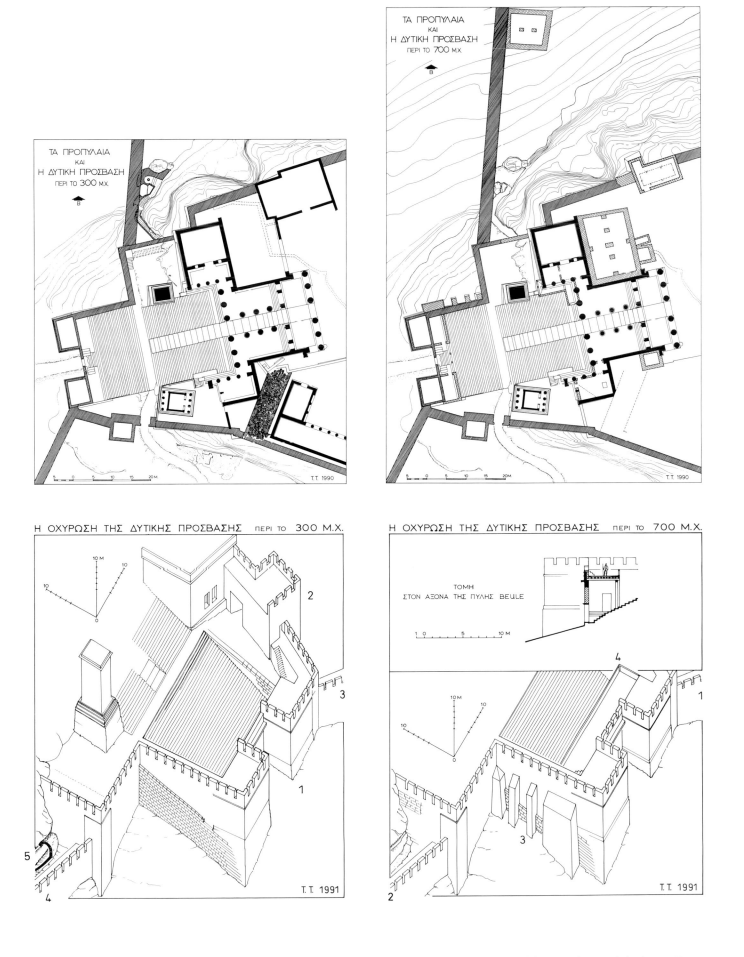

FROM ABOVE, L TO R: Plan of the Propylaea and the Acropolis western access about 300 AD; plan of the Propylaea and the Acropolis western access about 700 AD; the fortifications of the Acropolis western access about 300 AD. Isometric view from the northwest; the fortifications of the Acropolis western access about 700 AD. Isometric view from the northwest

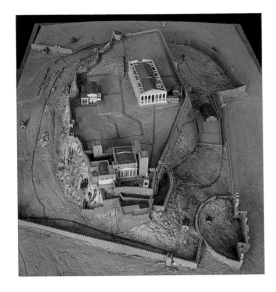

FROM ABOVE: *Model of the Acropolis in the second half of the fifteenth century, view from the northwest (the intercolumniations of the northern portico of the Erechtheion are occupied by walls with pointed arched openings); detail of the same with the Propylaea and the western access, view from the southwest*

built with marble blocks. In this complex there is a big hall with thirteen large columns. Above these columns there are beams thirty feet long, and above them there are marble slabs. A great and admirable work to see'. The second description is by another Italian, one of the most curious and famous personalities of the quattrocento, Ciriaco Pizzicoli from Ancona, considered by many as the first modern antiquarian. During his second stay in Athens in 1444, he paid a visit to the Duke of Athens in his palace, which was in the Propylaea. He says: 'When I decided to visit prince Nerio Acciauoli, a Florentine, who at that time was prince of Athens, I was informed that he lived on the Acropolis, at the summit of the town. We saw the admirable portico of four marble columns of finest craftsmanship, upon which rest ten marble beams. Then we came to the main hall where we saw three pairs of oversized columns, three feet in diameter, which supported marble coffered slabs, and twenty-four smooth marble beams, put three on each line. They seem to be about twenty-four feet long and three feet wide. The exquisite marble walls of this hall are made of smoothed blocks of equal size. This hall is accessible through only one oversized and magnificent entrance'. The comparison of these two early descriptions prove that the changes discussed above took place sometime between the respective visits of these travellers to Athens and, more specifically, under the rule of Antonio Acciauoli, who was a half-Greek by birth. This Acciauoli reigned for a relatively long period – 1403 to 1435 – and left behind him the reputation of a great builder.

Pizzicoli's description of the Propylaea makes it clear that he entered the building from the eastern portico, the four central columns of which were practically free of masonry; only the lower parts of the intercolumniations were occupied by low walls pierced by doors. The northern and southern columns alone were concealed in the masonry of modern buildings. Inside the lateral walls of the portico there were two rooms, roofed with timber floors which formed galleries, accessible from the vestibule by means of staircases; above the vestibule and the galleries the entering visitor could see the whole classical roof. The beam sockets for the floors of these galleries can still be seen on the walls of the monument. The eastern portico served as a vestibule to the western hall of the central building, which was used as a reception hall, retaining all the splendour of the marble walls, Ionic columns and coffered ceilings.

A gate wall formed a court that faced the eastern front of the palace. In order to protect this gate the wall to the north formed a triangular bastion-like projection; a similar projection was added on the outside of the massive Frankish military building further to the north, in order to protect the door between this building and the northern Acropolis wall. An oblong building bearing a south-sloping roof was attached on the southern wall of the western hall of the central building, in order to protect the last entrance to the Acropolis that was built by Antonio Acciauoli to the south of the Propylaea complex.

The intercolumniations of the ancient building's western front were finally entirely closed with walls, which only fully covered the inner side of the columns. This explains the fact that Pizzicoli did not perceive the Doric columns from inside the western hall of the central building, which was used as a reception hall. The western side of the recess between the central building and the northern wing was closed with a wall, in order to provide a solid defensible front to the palace on this side. The Middle Byzantine terrace in front of the central building was extended down to the ancient krepis of the southern wing, and the gap between the two upper stairs at the middle of the krepis of the central building was filled in. Inside the western hall, the ramp of the central passageway was covered by a horizontal floor, and the gap at the middle of the stairs along the door wall was also filled in, because the central passageway was not used any more to access the Acropolis plateau. A second floor was added at the top of the central building, using the coffered ceiling as a floor. The roof of this second storey was wooden and surrounded by crenellations, part of which survived until the end of the seventeenth century The southern wing of the Propylaea was now occupied by a tower twenty-six metres high, which later became known as the Frankish Tower. This tower did not communicate with any part of the residential area in the Propylaea, and had only one entrance on its western side.

The last entrance to the Acropolis plateau (to the south of the Propylaea's southern wing) was accessible by means of an extension of the Frankish ramp. For the sake of this extension, the western part of the southern wing was dismantled and built into the tower; for the same purpose, the structures that were built in the area of the Athena Nike sanctuary during the middle Byzantine and Frankish periods were demolished.

The Turks captured the Acropolis in 1458. The new conquerors initially respected the monuments, which at that time were almost intact, and Sultan Mohamed II came to Athens himself to visit them. The model shows the Acropolis in the second half of the fifteenth century. The general picture is the one under the last years of the Florentine government: the Propylaea have assumed the form of the Florentine palace, the Parthenon that of a church with a bell tower, and the Erechtheion has the form it had attained as the residence of the Latin bishop of Athens. But the massive western bastion which enveloped the Beulé gate must be attributed to an attempt by the Turks to fortify the Acropolis in order to accommodate modern artillery techniques. A comparison with the fortification techniques employed in the well known examples in the East proves that most probably this adaptation of the western access to the Acropolis had not taken place before the last decades of the fifteenth century.

The Turkish occupation put a barrier between East and West and the mutual intercourse between the two regions of Christendom ceased. Athens was further isolated as it was not on the usual routes of traders or pilgrims to the Holy Land, which went through Crete, Rhodes and Cyprus. But in the seventeenth century Athens began to be rediscovered by Western Europeans and as a result there is a good deal of first-hand contemporary information about the city and the Acropolis. Jacob Spon and Georges Wheler visited the Acropolis in 1676. According to them the upper floor of the ducal residence in the Propylaea served as residence to the *disdar*, the Turkish governor of the Acropolis. But unfortunately, sometime before, the Turks had converted the magnificent Ionic hall to a gunpowder magazine. For the communication of this magazine with the raised ground level to the south of the central building, a door was cut in the middle of the marble wall's height. In October 1640 lightning had caused the explosion of the gunpowder which, in Wheler's own words, 'blew part of the roof, whereon the Haga's house stood, together with him and his whole family up into the air. The walls of the building held fast, being of marble, and very thick. Yet they were so cracked in some places, that one may still thrust one's hand through them. But the part of the building towards the front, which looketh westwards, received no harm, either walls or roof'. In addition to the above information, Spon's detailed description of the construction of the ceiling of the western hall makes it clear that this part of the building, together with the Ionic columns which supported it, survived the explosion. On drawings dated between 1671 and 1687, the pediment can still be seen surmounted by a high crenellated wall, which is the western front of the upper floor added by the Acciauoli.

Eleven years after Spon's and Wheler's visit to Athens the Turks, expecting the

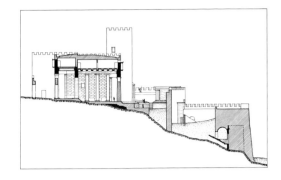

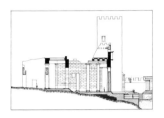

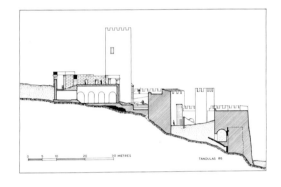

FROM ABOVE: Central section of the Propylaea and the Acropolis western access, before the explosion in the central building in 1640, looking south; central section of the Propylaea looking south, after the explosion in the central building in 1640; central section of the Propylaea and the Acropolis western access after the construction of the third cannon battery in the Propylaea

FROM ABOVE: View of the entrance to the Acropolis with the restored temple of Athena Nike as depicted by Th du Moncel, 1843 (Du Moncel, Vues Pittoresques des Monuments d'Athènes, Paris 1845, fig 1); plan of the Acropolis showing the excavations up to 1847, drawing by C Penrose (C Penrose, An Investigation of the Principles of Athenian Architecture, 2nd ed, London 1888, fig II); general view of the Acropolis from the southwest, ca 1860. On the south side of the hill the discarded earth from the excavations is clearly visible (Benaki Museum Photographic Archive)

under the direct supervision of architect E Laurent was commenced immediately following the recovery of this material: the northern wall and the antae of the entrance were restored up to the height of the architrave, the south and west walls up to about the middle of their height. All the columns on the east elevation were restored, as were the three northern columns of the west elevation together with their architraves; the first from the north coffered ceiling slab over the Pronaos was repositioned as well. During the restoration of the temple its architectural members were used as ordinary building material: marble blocks were placed in random positions on the walls, often reversed, while various scattered pieces from other monuments were freely incorporated, particularly pieces belonging originally to the neighbouring Propylaea. For the filling-in of certain missing stones marble was used in the more architecturally significant parts of the building, like the stylobate, the antae and columns, while limestone was used to plug the gaps in the walls. In the new members the shapes and profiles were rendered in a very simplified, schematic way, revealing, in spite of the restorers' innocent intention to differentiate between old and new, the hastiness in the execution of the work and above all the well known absence, in those early days of the revived Greek state, of experienced or specialised stone masons and marble craftsmen. The rebuilding of the temple of Athena Nike was the first full reconstruction of a Classical monument in Greece and, in the literal sense of the term, Europe. It was realised in a climate of general euphoria and enthusiasm and corresponded in the best way to the visions of the new classicists. In their eyes the restored temple at the entrance of the Acropolis figured as an obvious symbol of the rebirth of the Greek nation as well as the ancient ideals of beauty.

The person of the Athenian archaeologist Kyriakos Pittakis, successor to Ludwig Ross in the Greek Archaeological Service, dominated the works on the Acropolis from July of 1836 until the end of the Othonian period. Raised under the shadow of the holy rock, the native Pittakis would devote his entire life with unique faith and passion to the revelation and elevation in the public consciousness of the Acropolis monuments, the recovery, collection, and protection of scattered antiquities, and the publication of ancient inscriptions. His first collaborators were Schaubert and Laurent, and the sculptor and caster E Imhoff and his helper J Andreoli, while from 1840 onwards he began to work closely with the other Greek archaeologist of that period, Alexander Rizos Rangavis, representative of the newly founded Greek Archaeological Society.

The work of Pittakis, which was characterised by continual, only briefly interrupted excavations, general clearing, removal of earth and dismantling of the more recent additions to the Acropolis, were not confined only to the large monuments but extended to their general surroundings: in 1836-38 he dismantled the remains of the medieval palace in the Propylaea, the Frankish domes in the Pinakotheke and the Turkish domes in the central part of the building and excavated the interior of the structure. From 1837 he extended the excavations to the Erechtheion and the area between the Erechtheion and the Parthenon. He subsequently excavated, in 1838-39, the east stoa of the Propylaea and cleared the area to the east up to the Parthenon. At the same time he cleared the area to the east of the Erechtheion and excavated the Parthenon Pronaos. Works of clearing and excavations were resumed in 1844-45, at which time the ruins of the Turkish gunpowder arsenal were removed from the north portico of the Erechtheion, and the area to the north of the Parthenon together with the ascent to the Propylaea were excavated. In 1848-49 the clearing operations of Pittakis were extended to the northeast of the Propylaea up to the Erechtheion, while in the period between 1856 and 1860 the last large scale excavations by the Athenian archaeologist were carried out on the

Acropolis. Then, with the possibility of erecting a Museum on the Acropolis, the area opposite the northeast angle of the Parthenon was cleared and the open space between the Propylaea, the Parthenon and the Erechtheion was excavated. In the process of these works the large reservoir in front of the west side of the Parthenon – which had served until then as a kind of temporary 'museum' – was dismantled, and the ancient steps that were carved into the natural face of the rock leading to the Parthenon were thus uncovered. At the end of these works Pittakis considered that the excavations on the Acropolis had been completed, as the natural rock had been fully unearthed in the area between the three main monuments, a large number of later buildings on the hill had been removed, and an impressive number of finds had been discovered.

Indeed, a host of diverse material had been retrieved from these works on the Acropolis, including fallen architectural members, fragments from the sculptural decoration of the monuments, fragments from the numerous dedications which adorned the Rock during ancient times and other small statuary and ceramic pieces. New evidence regarding the original arrangement and the later phases of the monuments was thereby made public: at the Erechtheion the excavations reached as deep as the Christian floor of the building, revealing graves and the large reservoir in the west chamber, while around the exterior of the building the main body and fragments of the sixth Caryatid together with the head of the fourth were brought to light. In the area east of the Propylaea up to the western facade of the Parthenon thirty statue bases were found among the fragments of sculptural groups and inscriptions. More inscriptions and statuary were unearthed during the excavation of the Parthenon Pronaos, while a virtual hoard of inscriptions was brought to the surface at the western ascent to the Acropolis. Pittakis fought hard to protect this material from the ravenous intentions of the various collectors who visited the Acropolis: he created 'archaeological collections' inside the four large monuments and various later structures on the plateau, in the large reservoir to the west of the Parthenon, in a smaller reservoir known as 'tholos' (dome) and in a Turkish house east of the Erechtheion, and his tactics of incorporating fragments in the south circuit wall of the Acropolis or hanging them like picture frames on the interior of the Pinakotheke in order to protect them became legendary.

Meanwhile Pittakis, who considered that 'it is a sacred work to concern oneself with the discovery of the monuments of the ancient Greeks and to repair and reconstruct these' carried on with their restoration by repositioning on the buildings the members which were brought to light by the continual removal of the surface strata. He began with the Erechtheion, where in the period between 1837 and 1840 he re-erected a large part of the long north and south walls of the building, the northwest anta to a height of seven courses, and filled in and secured the western columns of the north porch and the engaged columns of the western wall, of which he fully restored the southernmost. Finally at the south porch (the famous Caryatid Porch of the building) he repositioned the fourth Kore (Caryatid), which had collapsed during the second siege of the Acropolis (1827-33). This Caryatid was completed by Imhoff, who repositioned the head that had been recovered in the recent excavations. The well known researcher of the Parthenon Alexis Paccard, who was one of the first winners of the Prix de Rome prize to visit Greece, worked on the restoration of the Caryatid Porch between the years 1846 and 1847. He repositioned the sixth Kore, which had been restored by Andreoli, and placed a clay cast, gift of the British Museum, in the place of the third Caryatid which had been carried off by Lord Elgin. Paccard also completed in marble the architraves, orthostates and the cornice of the portico's podium. From 1841 Pittakis expanded

FROM ABOVE: The archaeological collection of Pittakis at the Propylaea, as depicted by L Winstrup, 1850 (the Royal Academy Library, Architectural Drawings, LAW 032); view of the Caryatid Porch from the southeast after its restoration by Paccard (photograph by Robertson, ca 1855, from the Benaki Museum Photographic Archives)

73

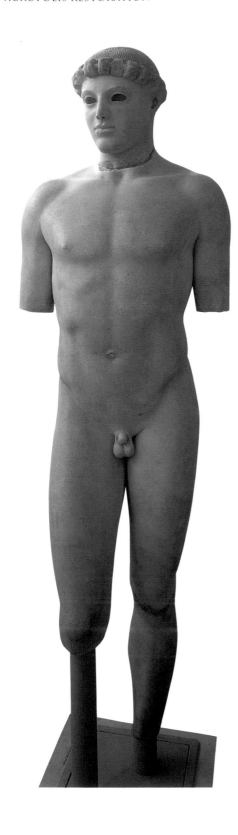

*The 'Kritias Boy', from just before 480 BC
(Acropolis Museum)*

his restoration activities to the Parthenon: with the help of Rangavis he restored a number of columns on the north facade, the ninth and eleventh (from the east) complete with capitals, the sixth and seventh to about two thirds of their height, while three drums were replaced on the eighth column of the south facade. The two collaborators rebuilt a significant part of the long cella walls, repositioning no less than 158 fallen marble blocks. In 1843-44 they completed the restoration of the temple of Athena Nike, where they raised the remaining parts of the incomplete south and west walls, almost all the architraves, the coffered ceilings of the two porches, and the southwest column, and in 1846-47 they fitted the building with clay casts of the three stones from its sculptured frieze that remain in the British Museum. The last interventions by Pittakis on the Acropolis were the restoration in 1850 of the staircase leading up to the Propylaea, with the repositioning of thirty-five ancient steps in accordance with the plans of the French architect Prosper Desbuisson and the repair, in 1854, of the external west side of the Pinakotheke's podium, which was in very poor condition.

Empiricism, improvisation and purism reached their zenith during the interventions of the Pittakis era. The extent of interventions was more than often accidental: Pittakis himself declared to visitors on the Acropolis and in his announcements to the members of the Greek Archaeological Society that he wished to continue his restorations, at least at the Erechtheion and the Parthenon, as far as the surviving amount of fallen ancient building material permitted him. But the final extent of the works depended on the available economic means and working staff. Equally haphazard were the decisions to conserve or obliterate surviving material from post-classical phases in the various parts of the monuments, which depended entirely on whether or not operations had extended this or that far. A similar approach was extended to the handling of ancient building material during its reincorporation into the structures: no serious attempt was made to determine the original position of the scattered material on the walls, the initial orientation of fallen stones, or even their provenance. A new aspect of these restorations was the introduction of machine-made bricks in order to support ancient members, complete them if they were only partly preserved, fill in openings in various parts of the monuments, and restore the initial width of their walls, methods which accorded with the other realities relating to the execution of works, namely economic adversity and the absence of an experienced workforce. The completion of ancient members with bricks had an unforeseen advantage of protecting their surfaces from the tendency to chisel them flat in order to facilitate the positioning of stone infill pieces; large, long iron connecting beams in the shape of a shallow U were used to piece stone members together, which were secured externally without the use of lead. Contrarily, Paccard introduced new methods of restoration in his intervention on the Caryatid Porch like the chiselling of fractured surfaces on the ancient members in order to facilitate their completion with new marble pieces, or the embedding of new metal ties in the ancient stones, both of which had extremely detrimental effects on the original material. Lastly, the understandable desire to differentiate the newly restored sections of the buildings from the ancient material was achieved with the intrusive carving on the new surfaces of the dates of their execution.

During this period the first words of protest regarding the haphazard and imprecise manner by which work was being carried out on the Acropolis were heard, coming from the circles of the first European 'scientists' who were involved with research in Athens, who did not comprehend and were suspicious of the 'charmingly rustic' Pittakis, who was a product of pre-scientific, popular conceptions regarding the ancient monuments. To his list of critics was added, by his refusal to accept any personal responsibility for the works being carried out, his one-time colleague, the Constantinopolitan scholar, politician, diplomat and archaeologist Rangavis, transferring to the field of archaeology the infighting between autochthonous and non-Helladic (that is, not born within the boundaries of the newly-formed Hellenic kingdom) Greeks that was shaking the country in those days. At the same time the continually growing numbers of visitors to the Acropolis, who were in their majority British subjects, cultured representatives of a rising and well-to-do social class inspired by the prevailing conceptions of the aesthetic and psychological effect of the monuments, began to express doubts regarding the usefulness, extent, and aesthetic result of those restorative interventions, and especially the interventions on the Parthenon, which sought to bring out the artistic value of the Classical monument at the expense of the much preferred character of the building as the romantic ruin *par excellence*: the seeds of what came historically to be known as the 'Question of the Parthenon Restoration' had already been sown. But the lovers of the Picturesque need not be troubled: the restorations of the Othonian period certainly gave shape, weight and mass to the ancient buildings, mainly emphasising their purely archaeological nature and that of their immediate surroundings, but the haphazard and extemporised way by which restoration work was executed, the inconsistency and mottled effect of the reused and newly introduced materials far from detracted from the appearance of the ruins or weakened their picturesque effect. The radical changes had not been effected yet.

In the period of Panayiotis Eustratiades' ephorate (1863-84), as successor to Pittakis in the Archaeological service and the interventions on the Acropolis, the most significant operations were the erection of a Museum and the dismantling of the Frankish Tower at the Propylaea, which for centuries commanded the entrance to the holy rock. The construction of the Museum – an old dream of both Klenze and Pittakis – provided a reason for the carrying out of clearing operations in the region to the south and southeast of the Parthenon, where in 1865 an area of a thousand square metres was dug to a depth of some thirteen metres, revealing antiquities of great importance to the history of art like the 'Kritias Boy', the 'Calf-bearer' or the head of Athena from the pediment of the Gigantomachy, forerunners of all that would follow. The museum would be completed in 1874 to the plans of Panagis Kalkos: a simple, discreet building of purely functional character, which did not seek to present itself as competitive to the architecture of the monuments, and to which the various 'collections' on the Acropolis started to be transferred in stages. In those years foreign researchers would carry out additional 'excavations' at various places on the Acropolis, seeking evidence for their theses. This tradition had been started in 1852/53 by Ernest Beulé, who in digging around the western ascent to the Acropolis discovered the so-called defensive Late Roman Gate. Carl Botticher followed suit by exploring the Parthenon in 1862 and removing a large part of the remains of the apse dating from the Christian phase of the building, while at the same time excavating the Erechtheion interior until striking natural rock. In 1864 the architect Ernst Ziller, while searching for evidence regarding the question of the curvature of the Parthenon krepis, which preoccupied the scientific world at the time, effected two deep probing cuts on the south side of the monument, going as far as the natural rock and leaving us with one of the most valuable stratigraphical records of the period. Soon afterwards Marcel Lambert and H Blondel would conduct surface digs in 1877 and 1879 northwest and north of the Erechtheion, respectively. Nevertheless the most important excavations of the period were those of Richard Bohn in 1880 at the Beulé Gate and the western ascent to the Acropolis, the Propylaea and the tower of Nike, which led to the publication of the first

The 'Calf-bearer', c570 BC (Acropolis Museum)

FROM ABOVE: View of the Parthenon from the northwest by H C Stilling, 1853 (Kunstakademiet, Copenhagen); view of the restored temple of Athena Nike from the northeast. (Photograph by P Sebah, 1872-75. Archives of the CCAM); view of the Propylaea from the west. The Pittakis steps are visible (Photograph by Stillman, ca 1869, Benaki Museum Photographic Archives)

complete reconstruction drawings of the Mnesikleian building.

Under Eustratiades no large restorative interventions were carried out on the Acropolis monuments. Two, however, are worthy of note: in 1872 Kalkos, as was recently revealed, built a brick arch supported by a wall of stones and bricks in order to secure the lintel of the west door of the Parthenon, while at the same time the sculptor and caster Napoleone Martinelli, working at the time with the Archaeological Service, carried out conservation work on the west frieze of the building and completed in marble the architraves below the frieze. In 1878 the Archaeological Society repaired under the supervision of Lyssandros Kautantzoglou, the most important Greek Classical architect of this period, the two retaining walls north of the Podium of Agrippa and west of the Pinakotheke in the Propylaea, maintaining, as was proudly emphasised in the report on the works, 'precisely the ancient masonry line and techniques' with the incorporation of certain of the 'better preserved ancient limestone cornerstones . . . in order to ascertain the fact that in the repairs no deviation from the ancient line was effected nor use of alien material'. This is one of the earliest expressions of the pure classicising spirit that would prevail in the interventions on the Acropolis in the last quarter of the nineteenth century.

Prior to this operation the dismantling of the Frankish Tower at the Propylaea had been effected, from June 21st until September 20th, 1875, under the direct supervision of the energetic Martinelli. This intervention, the purist nature of which far surpassed Klenze's proposals, sparked an intense debate. In Greece the historical research of Spyridon Zambelios and especially Constantine Paparigopoulos had led, from the middle of the century, to the reappraisal of the nation's medieval history, which was now appreciated as an inseparable link in its cultural continuity. At the same time abroad, artists protested the radical reduction of the romantic landscape of the Acropolis and historians the eradication of representative evidence for the temporal supremacy during medieval times of the west in this easternmost reach of Europe. The dismantling of the Frankish Tower was effected by the Greek Archaeological Society, immovable ideological venue of a pure classicism throughout the nineteenth century, in the midst of external pressures and a national crisis of doubt – with the rekindling of the 'Eastern Question' – which encouraged the tendency of modern Greeks to seek shelter in the brilliant ancient Greek legacy which provided abundant fuel for national confidence and certainty. This tendency was maintained and inflamed by consecutive national crises up to the end of the century – the economic disaster of 1893, the defeat during the Greco-Turkish war of 1897 – settling finally on the unanimously desired restoration of the greatest national symbol, namely the monumental complex of the Athenian Acropolis. Panayiotis Kavvadias and Nikolaos Balanos undertook to satisfy this need through drastic but very effective means beginning in 1885.

This Panayiotis Kavvadias, a dominant figure in the Greek archaeological scene at the turn of the century who was General Ephor of Antiquities from 1885 and General Secretary of the Archaeological Society from 1895, commenced to excavate the Acropolis Rock on 11th November, 1885 with a specific programme and system, which consisted of: a) the excavation of the entire Acropolis up to the natural rock surface; b) the execution of a detailed drawing survey of the rock and the surviving ruins and, where necessary, the photographing of these; following the digs, the resurfacing with earth of the rock face with the same carefully sieved earth and whatever scattered, amorphous, rubble stones might have been gathered, with the intent to restore, as much as possible, the ground level as it might have been in the fifth century BC; c) ensuring that certain important remains are left visible; d) the

FROM ABOVE: View of the interior of the Parthenon from the east in 1872-75. The brick arch over the west portal is visible, as are the interior brick facings of the cella walls from the Pittakis period. Numerous architectural members and sculptural pieces can be seen grouped inside the building, including parts of the Parthenon frieze (photograph by P Sebah 1872-75, archives of the CCAM); general view of the Acropolis rock from the east. The Frankish tower is still standing in the distance (photograph by P Sebah, 1872-75, archives of the Committee for the Conservation of the Acropolis Monuments); view of the Propylaea with the Frankish tower shortly before its demolition (photograph by P Sebah, 1872-75, archives of the CCAM)

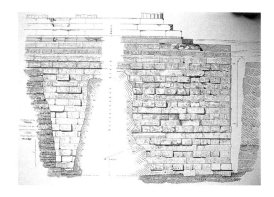

FROM ABOVE: The area south of the Parthenon recorded by E Ziller, 1864 (JA Bundgaard, The excavation of the Athenian Acropolis, 1882-90, Copenhagen 1974, vol II, fig 227); excavations by Kavvadias and Kawerau south of the Acropolis. The stereobate of the building is visible to its full height (photograph from the German Archaeological Institute of Athens, neg number Ak 112); OPPOSITE, FROM ABOVE: Archaic pedimental sculptures depicting Athena in the 'Battle of Giants' discovered by Kavvadias (Acropolis Museum); Archaic limestone 'Three-bodied Daemon' discovered by Kavvadias (Acropolis Museum)

clearing of the Acropolis of all the remaining later buildings; e) the gathering and ordering of significant scattered architectural members in piles, the search for members which might belong to the four large monuments and their positioning at their perimeter, together with the removal from these areas of any foreign (to the surviving monuments) elements. Kavvadias would carry out this programme without interruption and firmly until the year 1890.

The excavation began in the region to the northeast of the Propylaea and moved in an eastward direction. In 1886 it was extended to three areas: along the length of the North Circuit Wall which lies between the Propylaea and the Erechtheion, between the Erechtheion and the Parthenon (in the area of the Archaic Temple), as well as to the east of the Parthenon. In 1887 the entire area to the east of the Erechtheion was excavated. The dig would continue in the same year along the length of the East Circuit Wall up to the Belvedere and from there to the region between the new Museum and the Parthenon. This area, its extension to the south, the area between the Parthenon and the South Circuit Wall of the Acropolis, as well as the interior of the Museum, would undergo systematic excavations in 1888. The excavation reached its greatest depth of fourteen metres here, uncovering the twenty-two courses of the Parthenon *stereobate*. In 1889 a surface survey and clearing operations were carried out along the length of the South Circuit Wall, the area to the west of the Parthenon up to the Propylaea, the interior of the Parthenon (in the no-longer paved parts of the floor), and between the Parthenon and the remains of the ancient temple of Athena. The interior of the Pinakotheke was also excavated, as well as the area around the Tower (ie the base) of the temple of Athena Nike and the southwest wing of the Propylaea, while at the end of the year and in the beginning of 1890 the ongoing operations covered the north sector of the western ascent to the Acropolis from the Beulé Gate up to the Propylaea. In February 1890 the excavation had been completed. As Kavvadias wrote, 'on all of the Acropolis not the smallest amount of earth remained which was not removed and sifted until the natural rock surface was exposed; even where it was apparent that in earlier years excavations had taken place, the earth was nevertheless removed and searched'. During the course of the operations the last medieval and later constructions were removed from the Rock, including the vaults of the late Roman reservoir to the northeast of the Propylaea, the 'tholos' structure east of the Erechtheion, the remains of a significant medieval building to the south of the Parthenon, the later fortifications of the Beulé Gate, the 'Tholikon', the last remaining part of the 'Serpentzé' wall between the Beulé Gate and the Theatre of Herod Atticus, even the 'walls' built with the recovered fragments by Pittakis, while in 1887-88 a second Museum, nicknamed 'Mikro' ('Little' building) was constructed to the east of the first Museum according to the plans of the excavation architect George Kawerau.

According to our modern criteria the excavation was executed in an unscientific and unsystematic way, without a daily record of the works and, most importantly, without a stratigraphical study. The operation's photographic records are also scanty, limited to general views, while the measured drawings by Kawerau and, occasionally, by Wilhelm Dörpfeld are inconsistently rendered. Its results, however, were truly, to use Kavvadias' own expression, 'most significant, unexpected and awesome': remains from the most ancient phases of the life of the Acropolis came to light, including the Mycenaean circuit walls, the northeast entrance, traces of the Mycenaean palace and remains of houses, building 'B' under the Pinakotheke, the Archaic temple of Athena, the Arrephoros stair, the East Building, the Workshop to the south of the Parthenon, the Brauroneion, the Chalkotheke, and the temple of Rome and Augustus. In addition the famous Archaic Kore statues and a host of

limestone Archaic sculptures and architectural members were recovered, as were numerous inscriptions, pottery pieces and bronze artefacts and idols, which today grace the Acropolis Museum and the National Archaeological Museum. These finds gave an enormous boost to the scientific study of the history of the Acropolis Rock, the knowledge of its topography, the pre-classical buildings that graced it, together with the various inscriptions, pottery finds, and the evolution of sculpture in ancient Athens. The stated goals of Kavvadias had been achieved when in February of 1890 he announced with great pride in the journal *Archaiologikon Deltion*: 'Thus does Greece deliver the Acropolis back to the civilised world, cleansed of all barbaric additions, a noble monument to the Greek genius, a modest and unique treasury of superb works of ancient art which call indiscriminately all civilised nations to study, cooperate and compete in due civil spirit toward the promotion of the science of archaeology'.

A strong earthquake in Athens in 1894, which caused many fragments to fall from the architraves of the Parthenon Opisthodomos, led to the decision to proceed with a serious surgical intervention on the monument. Times, however, had begun to change: in the transitional phase of Greek archaeology from an amateur affectation with antiquities to a science, an intense concern was being nurtured regarding the manner of intervening on a monument, the global importance of which has begun to be appreciated in Greece as well. The relevant authorities turned to three researchers thoroughly familiar with the Parthenon, namely Francis Crammer Penrose, Joseph Durm, and Lucien Magne, who composed the first analyses of the problems of the monument and the manner by which to deal with them. The exchange of views and the discussions which were carried out culminated in certain basic decisions like the exclusion of a reconstruction of the monument and the execution of a simple intervention aimed at strengthening the damaged parts of the building, incorporating certain substitutions and completions of ancient members with new marble and a few limited new additions, depending on the specific situation. It was decided that work be done *'according to the ancient method'* through the use of metal ties, lead-filled or covered in cement, for the vertical and horizontal joining of the members. The general supervision of the works was charged to the three specialists, while the immediate supervision was entrusted to the 'Committee for the Conservation of the Parthenon', in which representatives of the administration, the academic world as well as architects of those foreign archaeological schools that were already operating in Greece took part. The legal engineer of Public Works Nikolaos Balanos was soon called to join the Committee; he immediately undertook the direction of the operations, gradually extending his activities, independently and unchecked, to the other monuments on the Acropolis for a full forty years until the Second World War.

Due to unfavourable outside circumstances, the interventions on the Parthenon began only in 1898. In this first phase they would last until 1902. They included consolidation work and the replacement of parts of capitals and architraves on the Opisthodomos colonnade and the western facade of the building, the replacement of the greater part of the backing blocks of the western frieze as well as numerous *thranoi*, the consolidation of the orthostate of the western pediment, together with the dismantling, conservation and repositioning of the members of the two corners of the pediment. Similar works of dismantling, strengthening and reassembling members also took place on the westernmost cornice of the north peristyle as well as on stone members at the two corners of the temple's east pediment.

In the years to follow Balanos oversaw the restoration of the Erechtheion (1902-09) and the Propylaea (1909-17); by this point he was working alone, free from the supervision of the two committees, and in collaboration with the General Ephorate of Antiquities and the Archaeological Society, which had undertaken the financing of the works. At the Erechtheion Balanos completed the restoration of the south wall to its full height and restored the western elevation more or less to the condition it was in after the interventions of the Roman period by repositioning the largest part of the entablature and the northernmost section of the pediment; in the eastern facade he pieced together the southeast column together with the surviving architraves and cornices and reassembled the frieze from fallen fragments. He also dismantled and reassembled the northwest pilaster of the monument and drastically intervened in its two famous porticoes which thus virtually changed appearance. In the north portico he repositioned all the architraves, the largest part of the frieze, the backing blocks, and the cornices. He completed and repaired with new marble the northwest column and the middle column of the western side and restored the ancient roof by repositioning the beams and coffers. Balanos also repositioned the pediment tympana. In the south portico (the celebrated Caryatid Porch) he replaced Paccard's restorations of the podium and the architraves, returned all the coffered slabs of the roof to their original positions, conserved and repaired the Caryatids and relieved them of the weight of the roof by transferring it by means of an iron beam which he built into the architraves to the corner pilasters of the portico, and through iron posts that he placed between the statues. At the Propylaea Balanos intervened in the east portico of the central building, where he completed and repaired the columns, repositioned the architraves and restored the northern section of the overlying frieze, the coffered ceiling, the pediment, as well as a part of the tiled roof at the northeastern corner. In the west hall he restored the northeastern portion of the coffered ceiling. In order to support the ceiling he raised the eastern column of the northern Ionic colonnade together with its superimposed architrave, as well as the last course of the main wall.

Balanos again intervened on the Parthenon during the period between 1923 and 1933, during which time he restored nine columns of the northern peristyle colonnade with their architraves, triglyphs, the backing blocks of the metopes and the cornices, two columns completely and three partly from the south colonnade, and certain members from the entablature. In the eastern facade of the building he completed and reinforced certain members of the horizontal cornice; similar work was carried out on the raking cornices of the east pediment, to which he added a new tympanum orthostate, and placed cement casts of four pedimental sculptures in their place, which were sent courtesy of the British Museum. Balanos proceeded with very limited work on the first from south column of the Pronaos colonnade and on the southeast pilaster of the cella. Finally, he removed the brick dressings of the Pittakis era from the long north and south walls of the cella as well and the brick arch of 1872 from the door of the Opisthodomos of the building. There he replaced the ancient lintel with reinforced concrete, while strengthening by means of a metal beam its ruinous backing block.

The last intervention by Balanos on the Acropolis was the new restoration of the temple of Athena Nike during the eve of the Second World War. Elderly and ill from 1935 to 1939, at which point he was forced to abandon the work, he proceeded to dismantle the building as it had been restored at the beginning of the nineteenth century because it was in danger of collapsing due to a sudden settlement of its krepidoma; he also dismantled the tower below the monument, the interior of which he excavated together with archaeologist G Welter, uncovering the remains of a tower from the Mycenaean fortifications of the Acropolis as well as remains from the pre-Classical cult of Athena. Balanos subsequently rearranged the interior of the

FROM ABOVE: The Erechtheion in 1902, at the beginning of the Balanos interventions (archives of the CCAM); the east facade of the Propylaea during the interventions of Balanos (archives of the CCAM)

tower to make it accessible to visitors, restored its exterior walls, and proceeded with the definitive restoration of the temple up to the level of the orthostates and a trial restoration up to the level of the architraves. The restoration of the temple was completed in 1940 by Anastasios Orlandos with the repositioning of the building's entablature, the columns and the pilasters or antae of its entrance. During the intervention the limestone infill of previous restorations was replaced with marble, and accurate copies of the capital and column base of the missing anta were inserted; during the positioning of the members numerous mistakes from the earlier interventions were made good.

Balanos acted in a period in which a new set of concerns had arisen in Europe in the field of monument restoration, thanks to the theories of Camillo Boito, Luca Beltrami and Alois Riegl, which called for a scientific and critical approach to the problems of restoration. These concerns appear to have been ignored by Balanos, who was a civil engineer with a French education, having graduated from the École des Ponts et Chaussées in Paris. He himself consciously continued the work of nineteenth-century classicist architects and archaeologists. The primary goal of his interventions remained the upgrading of the artistic and environmental values of the monumental buildings, while his methods continued to be in large degree empirical and improvised. Wishing to '. . . give a more complete impression of the monuments as if these had suffered smaller damages . . .' and elevate them '. . . through the restoration of a part of their magnificence . . .', Balanos exceeded the limit of simple strengthening interventions which had been stipulated by the first committees formed to oversee the works, and proceeded with more comprehensive restorations of parts of the monuments with the relocation of scattered fragments, without, however, carefully studying and documenting his work, which often saw material being positioned haphazardly. Equally haphazard was the ultimate limit of intervention, which now depended on the number of ancient members which were recognised and identified, a process which remained incomplete and fragmentary as Balanos lacked specialised archaeological knowledge and ignored the method of recognition and interpretation of marble traces which had begun to be applied by his contemporary architects and archaeologists. Balanos gave special attention to the aesthetic upgrading of the monuments, using Pentelic marble for the completion and replacement of ancient parts, the sole exception being the intervention on the two colonnades and the lintel of the western door of the Parthenon, where in order to achieve a better, in his view, chromatic consistency between the new pieces and the ancient members he chose to use reinforced concrete. By continuing to use, like his predecessors, the scattered ancient members as common building material, he often completed, always for the same reasons of aesthetics but also for reasons of economy, the architectural members of the monuments with fragments of ancient stones; he even created new pieces out of these stones, particularly coffers and capitals to replace missing parts, by assembling ancient fragments of various provenances from which he did not even hesitate to violently cut the broken surfaces in order to create flat contact surfaces. In order to differentiate the new additions and infill from the ancient members Balanos many times treated the final surface-work differently or positioned inscriptions with the date of the interventions. Where Balanos displayed an unforgivable carelessness, particularly if one takes into account his speciality, is in the technological domain: during the application of the 'ancient technique' in the assembling of members he used common metal ties of random size and composition, cast poorly or not at all in lead or covered with cement plaster, all of which was effected without taking into consideration the ancient samples and without the least previous study and research into the appropriate sizes of metal elements or the composition of ties. At the same time he built large metal elements, which consisted of rods, plates and iron beams, into the ancient members for structural reasons and in order to support more extensive portions of the monuments, destroying large masses of ancient material during the actual act of incorporation.

The period's growing sensitivity to matters regarding the conservation of antiquities was reflected mostly in the argumentation which erupted each time before interventions on the Parthenon were announced: in 1904 the Parisian art review 'Le Musée' published the *Protestation des écrivains et des artistes contre la restauration du Parthénon*, which was presented and discussed at the first International Archaeological Congress in Athens in 1905, together with the subject of the protection of the West Frieze of the building, which had already arisen. The *Question of the Restoration of the Parthenon* was rekindled in 1921-22 with the publication of the intention of Balanos to proceed with the restoration of the north peristyle colonnade of the monument: the issue divided the archaeological and architectural worlds in Greece and abroad, with professionals and academics expressing opinions which ranged from the rejection of the proposal on the basis of aesthetic and historical criteria, to its acceptance with few or many comments and cautions regarding the manner and the precision of carrying out the intervention, its extent, and the material which was proposed to be used in the new additions. At any rate in its own day the work of Balanos won the general agreement and praise of his contemporaries, particularly the scientists who were working on the Acropolis at the time. Balanos himself won fame and glory both in Greece and abroad, his interventions establishing internationally the term *anastylosis*; the critique which was expounded for the first time at the conference of the International Office of Museums in Athens in 1931 regarding the techniques and the materials that Balanos had decided to use during the erection of parts of the monuments came far too late.

There is no doubt that the restorative interventions of Balanos succeeded in their immediate aesthetic goals, as they gave the ruined Acropolis monuments a part of their lost grandeur. But the inability of Balanos to understand the individual value and tectonic functions of the ancient architectural members in the classical Greek system of load-bearing construction together with their use during the interventions as common building material led to the loss of the authentic structure of the monuments and their essential degradation. Finally, the uncritical use of modern technology would very soon have fatal consequences on the buildings.

The interventions of Kavvadias and Balanos radically changed the Acropolis landscape, definitively eradicating the accidental picturesqueness of the Rock by restituting the ground surface to a level considered equivalent to that of classical times and the buildings to grand, yet 'artificial', ruins, bearers to a large degree of the initial designs and forms. The resulting impression of the Acropolis is familiar today to the entire world; it is an impression which is taken in and transmitted by the multitudes of visitors who have converged at this site *en masse* since the end of the Second World War. During this later period the appearance of the monuments has not changed much, though they are directly caught up, together with the rest of the country's antiquities, with the problems stemming from the development of mass tourism in Greece, the subsequent demand for an 'embellishment' of the site, the projection and elevation of the monuments as touristic centres of attraction and the increase in formal clarity and didactic content of the buildings as objects of cultural significance to the wider masses. After Balanos the protection of the monuments fell into the hands of the Restoration Service of the Ministry of Culture, headed by Anastasios Orlandos, the instrumental and pioneering Greek architectural scholar

and energetic restorer of monuments, in collaboration with the respective Greek archaeological ephorate.

Orlandos essentially intervened on the Acropolis only at the Propylaea, where from 1947 to 1957 he restored the southwest wing with the removal of the last remains of the Frankish Tower, reconstituted the southwest column, the western anta and the middle pillar; he also repositioned the overlying architrave with the help of an iron rod that was incorporated in the unit. In 1955 he proceeded with works of consolidation in the foundations of the west wall of the Pinakotheke, while in 1956/57 he transformed the western approach to the Acropolis by building a ramp in accordance with recent architectural research.

Orlandos was especially interested in the Parthenon, which he had already begun to study systematically during the war; his research would result, much later, in the publication of the *Architecture of the Parthenon* (*Architectonike tou Parthenonos*), which was the first general survey of the monument in the Greek language. During the forties and fifties the responsible authorities were intensely troubled about the issues of removing the medieval staircase from the western porch of the Parthenon and the roofing of the western wing in order to protect Phidias' frieze. The proposal to remove the staircase because it was a later addition without special value, and because it had, on the contrary, a destructive and intrusive effect on the sovereign aesthetic value of the Parthenon, was the position espoused by Orlandos, John Meliades (ephor of the Acropolis from 1941 to 1960, with a brief interruption, and the man responsible for the extension of the Acropolis Museum and the restitution of the displays in the Museum from 1953 to 1964), and other archaeologists. The proposal collided with more recent conceptions regarding the need to respect the historical value of the monument and its representative remains, which by now had appeared in the Greek archaeological world, and the scheme was abandoned. A similar fate awaited Orlandos' proposal to roof the western wing of the Parthenon, which was repeatedly discussed, decided, and begun to be executed with the carving between 1954 and 1958, in new marble, of various roof members (beams and coffers), which were fated to remain on the ground. The only work which was carried out by the crews of the Restoration Service at the beginning of the sixties was the completion in marble of the gaps in the Parthenon floor, meant to block the access of rain water to the foundations, the closing with marble of the later openings in the side walls of the nave and the completion, with Piraean porous limestone, of certain places on the stereobate of the monument. At the same time in 1960 specialised sculptors would complete in marble certain gaps in the stones of the western frieze, as well as the neighbouring members in the slabs that lie between the beams and the taenia of the architrave.

Yet the postwar era is sealed by the danger of a collapse of the monumental buildings, which began to appear very early with the cracking and breaking of the marble pieces, due to the oxidation and subsequent expansion of the ironwork incorporated into these by Balanos. Already from 1943 John Meliades determined '. . . that the damages to the monuments and the Parthenon in particular are due firstly to the criminal way in which the marble elements were joined by unprotected iron ties and . . . secondly . . . to the effects of atmospheric pollution and the growth of lichen'. These problems are, to this day, continually worsening: the collapse of sizeable fragments from the monuments are more and more frequent, and, in addition, acid rain washes away unique details from the sculptural ornamentation of the monuments. To these are added the footsteps of millions of visitors to the Acropolis every year, which wear out precious traces from the floors of the buildings and the Rock itself – invaluable witnesses of its many centuries of life.

These problems are being addressed as best as possible by the Acropolis Ephorate, which was exclusively responsible after 1960 for the protection of the monuments, through a series of conservation works like consolidations and the joining of fragments and chippings, replacements, where possible, of iron ties with copper ones, and the draining of building floors, particularly those of the Parthenon and Erechtheion. It is, however, obvious that these measures are not sufficient. From the middle of the sixties the Greek and international press and popular opinion were sensitised to the problems of the Acropolis monuments. In 1968 and 1969 UNESCO experts expressed the urgency of the situation in site visits and stressed the need for a more comprehensive handling of the problems. All this led the Greek state to found, in 1975, a multidisciplinary scientific committee consisting of specialists, archaeologists, architects, civil engineers and chemical engineers. The 'Committee for the Conservation of the Acropolis Monuments' finally undertook, under new conditions and a new spirit, to press on with the battle to save the monumental building complex of the Acropolis, which, despite all, remains 'evergreen and unaging', as Plutarch once said, a timeless expression of one of the greatest periods of creation in the history of humanity.

INTERNATIONAL CHARTER FOR THE CONSERVATION AND RESTORATION OF MONUMENTS AND SITES

International Council of Monuments and Sites (ICOMOS)

Imbued with a message from the past, the historic monuments of generations of people remain to the present day as living witnesses of their age-old traditions. People are becoming more and more conscious of the unity of human values and regard ancient monuments as a common heritage. The common responsibility to safeguard them for future generations is recognised. It is our duty to hand them on in the full richness of their authenticity. It is essential that the principles guiding the preservation and restoration of ancient buildings should be agreed and be laid down on an international basis, with each country being responsible for applying the plan within the framework of its own culture and traditions.

The Second International Congress of Architects and Technicians of Historic Monuments, which met in Venice from May 25th to 31st 1964, approved the following text:

DEFINITIONS

Article 1   *The concept of an historic monument embraces not only the single architectural work but also the urban or rural setting in which is found the evidence of a particular civilisation, a significant development, or an historic event. This applies not only to great works of art but also to more modest works of the past which have acquired cultural significance with the passing of time.*

Article 2   *The conservation and restoration of monuments must have recourse to all the sciences and techniques which can contribute to the study and safeguarding of the architectural heritage.*

Article 3   *The intention in conserving and restoring monuments is to safeguard them no less as works of art than as historical evidence.*

CONSERVATION

Article 4   *It is essential to the conservation of monuments that they be maintained on a permanent basis.*

Article 5   *The conservation of monuments is always facilitated by making use of them for some socially useful purpose. Such use is therefore desirable but it must not change the layout or decoration of the building. It is within these limits only that modifications demanded by a change of function should be envisaged and may be permitted.*

Article 6   *The conservation of a monument implies preserving a setting which is not out of scale. Wherever the traditional setting exists, it must be kept. No new construction, demolition or modification which would alter the relations of mass and colour must be allowed.*

Article 7   *A monument is inseparable from the history to which it bears witness and from the setting in which it occurs. The moving of all or part of a monument cannot be allowed except where the safeguarding of that monument demands it or where it is justified by national or international interests of paramount importance.*

Article 8   *Items of sculpture, painting or decoration which form an integral part of a monument may only be removed from it if this is the sole means of ensuring their preservation.*

RESTORATION

Article 9   *The process of restoration is a highly specialised operation. Its aim is to preserve and reveal the aesthetic and historic value of the monument and is based on respect for original material and authentic documents. It must stop at the point where conjecture begins, and in this case moreover any extra work which is indispensable must be distinct from the architectural composition and must bear a contemporary stamp. The* *restoration in any case must be preceded and followed by an archaeological and historical study of the monument.*

Article 10   *Where traditional techniques prove inadequate, the consolidation of a monument can be achieved by the use of any modern technique for conservation and construction, the efficacy of which has been shown by scientific data and proved by experience.*

Article 11   *The valid contributions of all periods to the building of a monument must be respected, since unity of style is not the aim of a restoration. When a building includes the superimposed work of different periods, the revealing of the underlying state can only be justified in exceptional circumstances and when what is removed is of little interest and the material which is brought to light is of great historical, archaeological or aesthetic value, and its state of preservation good enough to justify the action. Evaluation of the importance of the elements involved and the decision as to what may be destroyed cannot rest solely on the individual in charge of the work.*

Article 12   *Replacements of missing parts must integrate harmoniously with the whole, but at the same time must be distinguishable from the original so that restoration does not falsify the artistic or historic evidence.*

Article 13   *Additions cannot be allowed except in so far as they do not detract from the interesting parts of the building, its traditional setting, the balance of its composition and its relation with its surroundings.*

HISTORIC SITES

Article 14   *The sites of monuments must be the object of special care in order to safeguard their integrity and ensure that they are cleared and presented in a seemly manner. The work of conservation and restoration carried out in such places should be inspired by the principles set forth in the foregoing articles.*

EXCAVATIONS

Article 15   *Excavations should be carried out in accordance with scientific standards and the recommendation defining international principles to be applied in the case of archaeological excavation adopted by UNESCO in 1956. Ruins must be maintained and measures necessary for the permanent conservation and protection of architectural features and of objects discovered must be taken. Furthermore, every means must be taken to facilitate the understanding of the monument and to reveal it without ever distorting its meaning.*

All reconstruction work should however be ruled out a priori. Only anastylosis, that is to say, the assembling of existing but dismembered parts can be permitted. The material used for integration should be recognisable and its use should be the least that will ensure the conservation of a monument and the reinstatement of its form.

PUBLICATION

Article 16   *In all works of preservation, restoration or excavation, there should always be precise documentation in the form of analytical and critical reports, illustrated with drawings and photographs. Every stage of the work of clearing, consolidation, rearrangement and integration, as well as technical and formal features identified during the course of the work, should be included. This record should be placed in the archives of a public institution and made available to research workers. It is recommended that the report should be published.*

This text consists of selected excerpts from the International Charter for the Conservation and Restoration of Monuments and Sites, known also as the 'Charter of Venice'. It does not include the original references to its relation to the Charter of Athens and the list of participants.

THE INTERNATIONAL CHARTER OF VENICE AND THE RESTORATION OF CLASSICAL BUILDINGS

Charalambos Bouras

In what way do monuments from Classical antiquity differ from other buildings that constitute the world's architectural heritage? An analytical response to this question would lead us to the formulation of a precise strategy for certain monuments of Greco-Roman civilisation, one that relates specifically to the international framework of principles for the protection and restitution of this inheritance known as the 'International Charter of Venice'.

From its inception in 1975 until today, the Committee for the Conservation of the Acropolis Monuments has never ceased to discuss in detail the related theoretical topics in its effort to bolster its work on objective and generally accepted issues. Thus it has tried to address the opening question while remaining faithful, as much as was deemed possible, to the stipulations of the Charter of Venice. It has thereby determined that Classical monuments, particularly those buildings that directly concern the Committee: a) have a very large historical and aesthetic value and relatively small functional value, b) are constituted primarily of architectural members, carved out of stone, that have an inherent structural and aesthetic integrity, c) have become widely known in their present ruinous state, simultaneously acquiring value as symbols in their more-or-less fixed twentieth-century form, and d) precisely because they are ruinous have lost their original protection against adverse weather conditions.

These particularities led the Committee for the Conservation of the Acropolis Monuments to promote five new articles which in a way complement the Charter of Venice and cover in a unified manner the requirements that they have created. But let us first examine the Charter itself and the ways in which the persons and parties responsible for the works on the Athenian Acropolis have upheld it.

The International Charter of Venice was drafted in May 1966 on the occasion of the second international conference of architects and building technicians involved in the restoration and maintenance of monuments, that was held in Venice. It consisted of a re-examination of a similar Charter of 1931 and summarised the experiences and lessons of almost twenty years of intense postwar restoration activity. For obvious reasons the creators of the Charter were almost entirely concerned with medieval and later buildings that were in use immediately before the war and not with the very special case of Classical monuments. The Charter text does not refer (except perhaps in article 3) to the objective values of which monuments are the bearers, and it is noteworthy that during the drafting of the text there were no contributions by representatives of countries of which the architectural heritage includes buildings analogous with those of Greece (like Turkey, Syria, Jordan or Lebanon). It should also be pointed out that not all countries that were directly concerned with and addressed by the Charter signed the document, Great Britain most notably.

Nevertheless the Charter of Venice has become widely accepted because of its concise, uncomplicated character. The various motions that have at times been put forward calling for its extension and updating (Colloque Paris 1976, Lausanne 1991)

were not put into effect and did not lead to revisions.

During the drafting and formulation of the programmes of the Committee for the Conservation of the Acropolis Monuments the provisions of the Charter of Venice have continued to be respected, despite their flaws. In the publication entitled 'Study for the Preservation of the Parthenon' by Manolis Korres and the author of this paper (Athens 1983), a detailed presentation was made of articles 2, 3, 5, 6, 8-12, 15, and 16 of the Charter. Their implementation in the case of Classical monuments was interpreted as follows:

1) The scientific diversity both of the members of the Committee and the personnel of the Technical Office of the Acropolis fully satisfies the requirements of article 2 of the Charter.

2) Article 3 is considered to be self-evident. The intention to upgrade the monuments by re-incorporating missing architectural members is meant to complete their form as much as possible, as it considers these to be works of art. The ongoing work and scientific research aim to secure the historical testimony provided by monuments.

3) As regards buildings that are no longer in use (as in the case of the temples and stoas of the Greeks), article 5 becomes meaningful only where monuments are considered to have value as exhibits, that is cultural artefacts analogous to the exhibits in a museum. This interpretation, together with the requirements of article 15 of the Charter, obviates the need to make every monument more appreciable and known in every way possible.

4) Article 6 does not greatly concern the Acropolis monuments, the immediate environment of which has been freed of obstructive contemporary buildings and all other forms of nuisance.

5) Endless discussions have been conducted regarding the requirements of article 8, given that the atmospheric pollution of Athens has caused significant surface damage to the sculptures that embellish the Acropolis monuments. All parties involved in the discussions now accept that the '. . . sole manner by which to secure the preservation' of the sculptures in danger is their transference to a controlled environment, in other words a museum.

6) The restorations effected on Classical monuments, particularly those on the Athenian Acropolis, are in fact few and in the majority of the cases imposed by unique circumstances. The extensive archaeological research that has been completed for the most important of those buildings guarantees absolute certainty about their original form and appearance. Thus the instructions of article 9 of the Charter are properly addressed.

7) According to article 10, all interventions that are implemented on Classical monuments make use of *traditional* techniques and materials with a proven resistance to the effects of time.

8) Important additions and extensions to Classical monuments and especially those of the Acropolis that have been effected from antiquity till this day (including those that remain from earlier interventions by archaeologists) are wholly respected (as stipulated by article 11).

9) The differentiation of the new stone parts from the original ancient material, as stipulated in article 12 of the Charter, may not be achieved without a negative aesthetic effect on the building or the part of the building that is being restored, because of the absolute harmony of the various architectural members. It is essential, therefore, that the differentiation be rendered subtly. The amount of new material that can be used in a restoration is not specified by the Charter, but efforts are being made to limit it as much as possible.

10) Article 15, which refers specifically to restoration, the re-incorporation, in other words, of architectural members that have been removed from their original position, is the most relevant to Classical monuments. It is noteworthy that the article does not preclude restoration with contemporary materials provided that it is done with the least amount necessary for the restitution of the ancient structure. This principle is upheld on the Acropolis and other ancient monuments in Greece, as, for example, at Epidaurus.

11) Finally, article 16 stipulates a systematic justification and creation of relevant archives that are accessible to researchers and publications. All this is unwaveringly upheld in the works of the Committee on the Acropolis.

Let us return to the points raised in the first paragraphs of this discussion and examine the five articles which, according to the views of the Committee, ought to complete the Charter by making specific reference to the special needs of Classical monuments.

a) Reversibility. The acceptance of the possibility of restituting a monument to the condition it was in prior to the intervention. Reversibility is ensured with Classical monuments on the one hand by the avoidance of direct intervention on the ancient architectural members and on the other by exhaustive justification (by means of measured drawings and photographs) prior to every modification. It should be noted that the full implementation of the principle of reversibility is possible only in Classical buildings of antiquity in which the distinct architectural parts are not connected by means of mortar and stucco.

b) Maintenance of the integrity of the different architectural elements and their basic structural functions.

c) Limiting interventions as much as possible to those parts of the monuments that have been affected by earlier restoration work.

d) Ensuring the self-protection of the ruin from the elements.

e) Limitation to a minimum of changes to the general appearance of the monument.

The Parthenon seen through the scaffolds that surround the north wing of the Propylaea

EDUCATIONAL PROGRAMMES ON THE ATHENIAN ACROPOLIS

Cornelia Hadziaslani

On September 26th 1987, exactly three hundred years after the destruction of the Parthenon by troops under the command of the Venetian general Morosini, the Acropolis Ephorate inaugurated a new museum, the Centre for the Acropolis Studies. It was housed in the old building in the Makriyiannis lot (adjacent to Makriyiannis Street on the south slope of the Acropolis), which was constructed in 1836 by Bavarian army engineer W Weiler to serve as a military hospital. The building is one of the oldest and most important examples of Neoclassicism in Greece. In 1930 the Athenian police were stationed here; when an adequate site was being sought in 1975 for the new Acropolis Museum, Prime Minister Constantine Karamanlis arranged for the removal of the civil force. In 1985 the building started being repaired in order to shelter copies of the Parthenon sculptures (known as the 'Elgin Marbles'). Two years later, under the former Director of the Acropolis Ephorate Dr Evi Touloupa (who was responsible for investing the Centre with its present character and functions), the building was officially opened by the Minister of Culture Melina Mercouri. Under the present Director Dr P Calligas the Centre is the seat of an expanding archaeological Ephorate bustling with activities that centre on archaeological and architectural studies.

In 1989 the international competition for the new Acropolis Museum was held at the centre. Some 438 entries were submitted to an international jury. In 1990, the prizewinning study confirmed the Makriyiannis lot as the eventual building site and the Centre for the Acropolis Studies was officially incorporated as part of the complex.

The Centre acts as the Educational Centre of the First Ephorate of Prehistoric and Classical Antiquities in Greece and is used as a preparative stepping stone for visitors of all ages to the Acropolis. It thus represents an area of communication with the wider public interested in archaeological, historical, architectural and artistic subjects related to the Acropolis. Furthermore, the Centre caters to the promotion of studies focusing on the Acropolis and its monuments.

The building consists of three floors and a basement, each of which is being used for specific functions and displays. I will briefly describe the exhibition areas. The ground floor is dedicated to the Parthenon sculptures; casts of the metopes, the frieze and the pediments, all of which were carefully studied and arranged by the archaeologist A Mantis, give the visitor a rare, comprehensive view of the sculptures that includes all those which are presently housed in museums around the world.

The two celebrated pedimental compositions of the Parthenon, each of which is twenty-five metres long and 3.2 metres tall and illustrate, respectively, the birth of Athena (east front) and the competition between Athena and Poseidon for the patronage of Athens (west front), are exhibited in the two main exhibition halls flanking the entrance, together with the fifteen surviving metopes from the south elevation of the temple. Reconstructions of other metopes are currently being prepared for exhibition. Copies of the surviving 110 metres (out of an original total of 160) of the Parthenon Frieze illustrating the Panathenaic Procession are affixed to

OPPOSITE, FROM ABOVE L TO R: Demonstration of ancient marble cutting techniques; touring the site; measuring a mutule with architect Tasos Tanoulas; learning to cut and finish a marble block; modelling demonstration by Greek sculptor Stelios Triantis at the Centre for the Acropolis Studies; learning how to cast in plaster

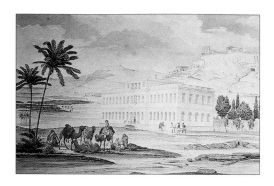

FROM ABOVE: The old Makriyiannis building, now the centre for the Acropolis Studies, seen from the south; watercolour of the building just after its construction

the walls of the entrance and the two adjacent corridors.

These casts have their own history. In 1846 the British government donated a series of copies of the famed 'Elgin Marbles' to the newly independent Greek state. Since the fifties the cast collection has continued to be enriched with new matrices and casts, most of which are now on display. These acquisitions are hugely important because they provide possibilities of comparative and highly detailed research. The matrices are especially valuable as they bear details that the originals may have lost today. The Centre also functions as a school for students of casting and conservation techniques. The Casts and Matrices Archive is housed in the basement to facilitate work.

The second floor of the Centre is taken up mostly by the exhibition 'Acropolis: Conservation, Restoration and Research'. Its purpose is to make known to the general public the work accomplished by the Committee for the Conservation of the Acropolis Monuments (CCAM) since 1975, which comprises both the preliminary studies for restoring the monuments and carrying out the programme and the application of new techniques and methods. Included in the exhibited material are numerous old photographs showing some of the works executed in the nineteenth and early twentieth century which gave the Acropolis its present form, now familiar to millions of people around the world.

A special presentation on the same floor focuses on the project for the consolidation of the Acropolis rock slopes; works in progress on the main ancient temples, that is the Erechtheion (which was the first restoration project to be completed by the Committee), the Parthenon, the Propylaea, and the temple of Athena Nike; ways and means of documenting both the studies and progress of operations, presented through a series of drawings and models; the project to document the architectural members scattered around the Acropolis, showing how they are inventoried, classified and reassigned to buildings; and finally the related physiochemical and static problems, which are the main causes of deterioration in the buildings. The ultimate aim of the exhibit is to project a comprehensive view of the recent research carried out on the archaeology, architecture, and history of the buildings, research that has yielded a veritable harvest of new data and enormously enriched our knowledge of these unique structures. The exhibition currently on show is already the third in a continuing series, as every two to three years it is updated with the latest material arising from the progress of the ongoing restoration works.

The Centre also houses a collection of superb models and drawings that were put together mostly by the architect Manolis Korres in order to better inform the visitor on the historical evolution of the Acropolis and the construction of ancient Greek temples. Five models representing the state of the Acropolis rock during successive historical periods (Neolithic, Archaic, Classical, and Medieval), a model of the city of Athens during the third century AD, models of the Erechtheion, the temple of Athena Nike and the theatre of Dionysos during the classical period, all constitute a very important part of the exhibition, as do several drawings of the Parthenon as a church, a mosque, and during and after the great explosion of 1687. The special exhibition 'From Pentelikon to the Parthenon' illustrates, through reconstruction drawings and models, the phases a piece of marble underwent from the moment it was chosen at the quarry to the moment of its final finishing on the surface of the temple itself. Models of ancient building devices and samples of tools and their distinctive traces, the various fastenings that were used, etc, complete this exhibit.

The exhibition 'Terracotta Tiles from the Athenian Acropolis', studied and put together by the archaeologist C Vlassopoulou, provides the visitor with general information on the construction of ancient roofs, both terracotta and marble, and a complete analysis of ancient terracotta tiles focusing on their composition and decoration, and the uses of polychromy in antiquity.

On this same floor there is an auditorium (seating 250 people), in which all the education services are initiated. Students are taken regularly to the Acropolis itself, but the Centre is always considered as the first step before any visit to the archaeological site. The philosophy of the Education Department and the programmes that have been developed are laid out below.

The Education Department of the Acropolis Ephorate was created in 1987 (the year of the inauguration of the Centre for the Acropolis Studies) by the First Ephorate of Prehistoric and Classical Antiquities (the Acropolis Ephorate) in collaboration with the Committee for the Conservation of the Acropolis Monuments, and is based on the belief that:

1 An intimate knowledge of the art and history of the Acropolis monuments and a familiarity with the essence of Classical architecture should be the prerogative of all people today and not that of a select circle of experts.

2 An understanding and appreciation of the Athenian Acropolis is part of the curriculum in the majority of schools worldwide and forms, of course, a substantial part of the history taught in schools throughout Greece; virtually every Greek school sends its students on a visit to the Acropolis. In fact, one to two thousand pupils visit the Acropolis every day in autumn and spring. The Ephorate is dedicated to the continual improvement of conditions for visiting groups of students.

3 The first step towards ensuring the respect and continuing conservation of a monument is through education; related curricula should begin at an even earlier age than what is currently required in schools.

These principles constitute the framework within which the Education Department is seeking to effect positive changes in educational practices today. The aim is to provide people of different ages and different levels of education with the opportunity to enhance their understanding of Classical civilisation. Lectures, film projections, and guided tours by Acropolis personnel are organised on a monthly basis Two 'Acropolis Laboratories' are presented every year: events are coordinated so as to interest all groups, be they scholars, adult education seminar participants, or school students. The active support of the 'Friends of the Acropolis' is a valuable contribution.

Due to the large number of people interested in the Acropolis, priority is given to school pupils and teachers, whatever their field. Education services are currently offered through special seminars for teachers and their pupils, 'open days' organised on the Acropolis (drawing around eight hundred pupils per day) or at the Centre (where one to five hundred pupils participate daily, depending on the subject), school visits (between thirty and forty pupils normally attending, ie around one class per visit), and the loan of pedagogic material. All these services, it should be mentioned, are provided free of charge.

I will briefly expand on each of the services provided by the Education Department, giving particular emphasis on the use of the Acropolis and the Centre for the initiation of the non-specialists (especially school pupils and their teachers) in Classical architecture and current attitudes towards restoration. The first task that the Ephorate set itself was to study how the area of the Acropolis could best be utilised so that the pupils' visit could be of the utmost benefit to them. The result was the programme 'A Day at the Acropolis'. The emphasis of this programme is on the architectural and archaeological analysis of the ancient buildings, construction methods, the analysis of the damage caused to the monuments over the two-and-a-half thousand years of their life, as well as today's conservation and restoration methodologies.

Casts and moulds at the Centre for the Acropolis Studies

FROM ABOVE: Didactic model of the artificial terraces on the Acropolis with removable buildings; samples of casts and moulds from the special educational kits provided by the Centre for the Acropolis Studies; the special kits that were prepared for visiting teachers and pupils

The archaeological site is organised so as to present visitors with a full perspective of the above subjects through visual, hearing, and touching experiences. Fifty trained volunteer university students are stationed around the site, each presenting a different part of the work. The presentations are coordinated to provide a full description of the temples and the ongoing or completed restoration works. Attending school pupils can thus learn about things not ordinarily covered in the available text books, guide books, and leaflets: about the ancient building accounts, the development of the construction of an ancient building, the cost of materials, and the transportation and labour that was involved in the erection of each edifice. Using replicas of the ancient tools they can work directly on marble and learn to distinguish the different tool traces on contemporary and ancient blocks. Often they are even encouraged to sculpturally reproduce architectural members in soap.

The construction of a wall by placing and joining the stones without the use of mortar is explained in detail and duplicated physically. The original connectors, clamps and rectangular dowels are shown and matched against their original cuttings by the pupils. The staff demonstrates the ancient procedure of pouring molten lead around the connectors to complete the bond, to absorb earthquake vibrations, and to preclude the possibility of rust arising from the metal components. They also illustrate the use of the *polos* (a wooden cylinder) and *empolion* (a truncated pyramid of wood) to align column drums vertically.

Ancient methods of transporting and hoisting marble blocks are reproduced by the technical staff with the help of sketches and models. Today's most common methods are also displayed as a means of comparison (the comparative juxtaposition of a model of a fifth-century BC crane against the modern crane designed specially for the Parthenon restoration tends to excite particular interest). The pupil has the opportunity to watch and in some cases to participate in moving marble blocks horizontally and vertically by hand or with the help of tools and machinery. Pupils are taught to distinguish traces of paint on the monuments and are shown coloured reconstructions; they are encouraged to colour a line drawing of a painted coffered ceiling panel or of cymatia with reference to the originals and to the polychromatic palette. They are also offered the opportunity to learn about ancient tiles, both of marble and clay, and are even encouraged to make their own.

The other major focus of this programme is a detailed analysis of the stages of the scholarly research, conservation and restoration work currently in motion. The estimated number of stone building fragments on the Acropolis is between fifty to seventy thousand; the principles, as well as the difficulties, of their classification in categories are carefully illustrated alongside samples from the archive index of the scattered architectural members. Pupils are taught to distinguish the Doric, Ionic and Corinthian orders in the thousands of fragments on the site, aided by a diagram and the staff.

The methods of photographic documentation of antiquities are illustrated in a special display at the Centre, as is documentation by scale drawing. Pupils can assist the architects, watch how detailed measurements are made, how they are translated into a sketch and finally into a scale architectural drawing. Precision instruments are made available for close scrutiny by the new initiates.

The major causes and types of stone decay are presented and discussed at length. Marble fragments selected to illustrate each type of damage are placed side by side and pupils have the opportunity to examine for themselves the wear on the stone surfaces. The types of deterioration normally displayed are those resulting from atmospheric pollution and acid rain, oxidation and expansion of iron clamps from older interventions, biodeterioration, fire, plant roots, bird droppings, wartime shelling and bombardment, vandalism, and from combinations of the above.

Special research studies aimed at counteracting these sorts of damages are meticulously illustrated: for example, diagrams showing the corrosion of the metopes, antiseismic studies, etc. Staff demonstrates cleaning and maintenance procedures, the equipment, and the chemicals involved. Attending pupils can gaze through a stereoscopic microscope and even work on specially chosen fragments.

The principles for the restoration of the Acropolis monuments are analysed with reference to the Charter of Venice and the principle of 'reversibility' first stipulated by the Committee for the Conservation of the Acropolis Monuments. The decision of the Committee to restore to their original positions the various fragments that were scattered around the site or incorrectly positioned in previous interventions (including architectural members now housed in museums around the world), is discussed *in situ*. Furthermore, staff explain why elements that are intended to replace lost parts of the monuments should be both distinguishable from the authentic parts in order to prevent false impressions and not too different in form or colour so as not to disturb the harmony of the monuments. The replacement of a ruinous block by an accurate copy in marble is enacted: first a mould is produced, which is subsequently copied in marble with the help of a pointing instrument or (automatically) by means of a pantograph. The joining of old and new pieces through reinforcements made of titanium is examined next.

'A Day at the Acropolis' takes place for three consecutive days every spring: some eight hundred to one thousand pupils participate in each of the open days, representing a total of eighty different schools (primary and secondary) from around Greece every year. The accompanying teachers that are selected are different every year, the programme being part of an expanding national curriculum. Fifty students from the Faculties of Archaeology and Architecture of the University of Athens present a total of twenty-five workshops. The students are trained by the Acropolis staff (who presented the first 'Day at the Acropolis' programme in 1986) during the course of five intensive four-hour seminars. All of the 'open day' programmes that are presented by students are organised on a voluntary basis, the students being specially appointed after a request made to their professors. Through their participation they acquire a more extensive knowledge of the Acropolis and inside experience on educational programmes and proceedings, all very valuable exposure for them as in the future many might staff the Archaeological Service and schools throughout the country.

The twenty-five workshops form the basis of most of the Centre's programmes. The majority of these have by now taken their final form as a Teacher's Pack or a Museum Kit, and can be loaned to teachers. Several guided trails on the history, architecture, sculpture and restoration of the monuments are also active. The goal is to train the teachers and to encourage them to bring their pupils to the Acropolis on their own, to prepare the young scholars in their charge and to enable them to run workshops with the help of the loan material without the presence of trained staff.

The programme 'A Day at the Centre for the Acropolis Studies' was instituted for the first time in 1989. All the exhibits at the Centre are used, and the full range of workshops is made available. Many well known Greek artists present these workshops, helping in their way to bridge the historical gap between ancient and contemporary culture. The Parthenon sculptures are analysed in detail, pediments are recreated by means of holography, and their composition represented through role-play. Needless to say, mythological storytelling crops up everywhere. The South Metopes of the Parthenon, illustrating the battle between Centaurs and Lapiths, are presented and acted out by the pupils. With the help of computers and image-processing through computer graphics, the pupils have the opportunity to put together fragments

FROM ABOVE: Educational material intended for instruction in the three Greek architecture orders; chiselling equipment available to students learning marble cutting techniques; didactic reconstruction of ancient Greek musical instruments that appear on the Parthenon frieze

Identifying themes in miniature casts of the Parthenon frieze

of broken metopes, to colour architectural members, and make a synthesis of architectural elements. The Parthenon Frieze is studied and put together by analysing and recreating its subject matter, namely the Panathenaic Procession.

Mythology and everyday life in Classical Athens are jointly discussed through the Frieze's exquisite relief figures. Cult statues and votive offerings are used to analyse, explain and recreate worship and customs, materials and techniques. A description of the 'Athena Parthenos', the colossal gold and ivory statue by Phidias, provides the opportunity to discuss the use of matrices and procedures. The process of creating a marble sculpture, the production of clay works of art, the transfer in plaster and transcription on marble, all takes place in front of the pediments during the special programmes. Pupils are welcome to ask for details, to participate and even to carve directly in stone. The process of producing a bronze sculpture with the lost wax method is presented with reference to the huge 'Athena Promachos' statue by Phidias which guarded the Acropolis. The 'Diipetes Xoanon', which was the Archaic wooden statue in the Erechtheion, is the hint to discuss and work with wood. Likewise, a terracotta acroterion which forms part of the Tiles Exhibition, is the hint to discuss and work in clay. As ancient Greek sculptures were normally painted, techniques and painting possibilities are made available to pupils.

The Centre for the Acropolis Studies is a cast museum, and on each day of the programme the laboratories and the Cast Archive are open to the public. Visitors are free to observe the stages of construction of the different types of moulds and casts, every guest being entitled to witness and take part in the pouring of an individual cast.

Additionally, the second floor houses a presentation of the system of modules, styles, forms, and decorative themes from ancient Greek architecture, the sensitive combinations of which produced the perfect classical aesthetic achievements which have so indelibly marked the development of western culture.

The open yard facing the Centre is being excavated to allow the future construction of the new Acropolis Museum. The archaeologists in charge routinely explain the different stages followed in an excavation in order to make a piece of earth and its contents contribute fully to the knowledge of our past.

In January 1991 the Minister of Culture accepted the Committee's proposal and decided to proceed with the most important intervention on the Parthenon, namely the removal of the Parthenon Frieze for its protection. Subsequently the Centre produced the programme entitled 'A Day with the Parthenon Frieze'. This programme is based on a new concept and inaugurated a new series of flexible programmes. It is addressed to around one hundred pupils per day who participate after a slide presentation in eight workshops which are divided into groups of pupils who are led around the museum every fifteen minutes. They first sculpt in marble and get a taste of the difficulties of this craft. Then they make a scaled cast of a Parthenon Frieze block, paint it, and locate it in the exhibition, thus piecing together the various thematic groups in the Panathenaic Procession. Subsequently the pupils are encouraged to make an archaeological and stylistic analysis of one frieze block. They search for different kinds of garments worn by the ancient participants, try to find and identify ancient musical instruments, and look for the different animals (horses, cattle and rams). Finally they are encouraged to identify the Gods of Olympus and act out their characters. This particular programme lasts three hours and requires the assistance of around ten university students. Depending on the availability of the students it can be easily repeated, as well as enlarged or reduced thematically. The success and flexibility of this programme resulted in the next ones:

'A Day with the History of the Acropolis' focuses on the collection of models and drawings at the Centre. The subjects are the Neolithic, Archaic, Classical and

Medieval periods; the 1687 explosion; the stripping of the Parthenon sculptures by Lord Elgin; the Balanos restorations; and the Committee for the Conservation of the Acropolis Monuments restoration works.

'A Day with the Acropolis Monuments': like the previous programme, it is also focused on the models in the Centre's collection. The subjects are the Acropolis Rock and the complex of temples (the Parthenon, Erechtheion, Propylaea and temple of Athena Nike), the Brauroneion sanctuary, the Chalkotheke and the Arrephorion, the votive offerings, and finally the ancient processions and sacrifices that took place around the various altars on the Acropolis.

'A Day Building the Acropolis': this programme centres on the collection of models and drawings in the special exhibition 'From Pentelikon to the Parthenon'. The subjects are: building inscriptions, the orders of Classical Hellenic architecture, columns and capitals, floors and walls, putting blocks together and fastening them, roofs, ceilings, tiles, sculpture, ornament and applied colours, techniques of stone carving, and, finally, sculpting in soap.

'A Day Building Your Own Temple': integrated with the above programme, the project encourages pupils to articulate the necessary phases that they would have to go through if they were to construct their own temple; they decide which deity the building shall be dedicated to, where the temple shall be built (the location in relation to the altar and the site orientation), which quarry is closest, what method of transportation shall be used for the heavy blocks (mules or ships, depending on the kind of stone that shall be utilised), the type of temple (amphiprostyle, peripteral, etc), the size of the building, and the order to be used. According to the availability of funds and craftsmen (who can be invited from another ancient city of the pupil's choice), the amount and type of materials to be used in the sculptural decoration will be decided and investigated (cult statues, pediments, Doric or Ionic frieze, acroteria, subject matter; cymatia, roofs, the number of doors and openings and their locations), colours and bronze fittings explored; finally the pupils are urged to calculate how much money and time their project will require.

'A Day Restoring the Acropolis': this programme is the most sophisticated and is addressed to older pupils. Through it they are initiated into the restoration philosophy and problematics that the Centre feels should inform the thoughts of every educated and responsible citizen and taxpayer who lives alongside the ancient monuments and cares about his heritage. The pupils are further initiated in the construction of the Classical monuments, their later history, the damages they have suffered, and the history of the restorations, whether older or ongoing. They are then invited to take part in and present their opinions on the given subjects with the help of the original records and studies. The goal of this programme is to encourage criticism through well studied arguments, the educational programme representing only a first stage in the initiation of the pupil.

As the Acropolis is an integral part of Greek school curricula, the interest in participating in these programmes far exceeds the potential of the Education Department. Thus the orientation of the Department was very early turned towards the training of teachers of every specialisation.

As the greatest achievement of the Classical world, the Athenian Acropolis represents an architectural, artistic, and cultural prototype for Western civilisation. The Centre for the Acropolis Studies feels that it is necessary to find ways to activate what is surely a huge educational potential. Our goal is to make the Centre render the maximum in educational proceedings and programmes that can have a general application the methods of learning about humanity through the brilliant spectrum of the Classical world.

Pupils' model illustrating the process of transporting building blocks to the Acropolis in Classical times

CURRENT PROBLEMS OF
RESTORATION ON THE ACROPOLIS

Charalambos Bouras

The interventions on the Acropolis monuments were a necessity. On the one hand the cracks and damages on the marble architectural members due to the oxidation of metal elements from earlier restorations, and on the other the rapid surface wear and corrosion caused by atmospheric pollution made action *urgent and unavoidable*. After four years of studies and research, work commenced in 1979 with the express intention of eliminating these two major problems.

In general lines the works have been divided as follows:

a) The replacement of the metal elements from older interventions (most of which have rusted) with new ones made of titanium, a material which does not corrode, following the dismantling of a significant part of the upper structure of the monuments.

b) The removal of sculpture in order to protect it from the effects of atmospheric pollution. The time-consuming and costly work of dismantling and repositioning of architectural members has been completed at the Erechthcion and on the east side of the Parthenon and is now in progress at the Propylaea and the opisthodomos of the great temple.

It should be obvious that while the first problem is being solved in a satisfactory way, the second (concerning the effects of pollution) remains unsolved and is being avoided by means of an action that is no doubt unfortunate for the Acropolis monuments.

The optimists hold that the removal of the sculptures from the Erechtheion and the Parthenon is temporary; that they should be able to return to their original positions once the dangers of atmospheric pollution are eclipsed or when a way by which to treat the surfaces of the marble elements is found which will definitively protect them from corrosion. But the removal of the rusted and expanded metal elements from the restorations of Balanos (1899-1933) and the dismantling of large sections of the temples brought to light a series of new problems: many architectural members were fragmented or did not sit securely on supporting stones because of the massive explosion of 1687 and subsequent earthquake activity. This situation made the buildings even more vulnerable to new earthquakes. The methodical joining of the fragments and the restoration of the original relationships between the course joints became the subject of intense work on the Erechtheion and the Parthenon for months.

Other problems with theoretical and practical dimensions inevitably surfaced and are, unmistakably, the result of the poor reassembly of the lateral walls both on the Erechtheion and the Parthenon during the older restorations. Because the sizes of the stones that make up the walls of the major standing monuments is roughly equal, Balanos did not hesitate to reincorporate fallen material anywhere he felt necessary. Once those elements were studied systematically and their positions on the lateral walls determined beyond a shadow of doubt with the help of a computer, the true possibilities of an accurate new restoration emerged, as did, alas, many discrepancies – as a number of stones were shown to have, in fact, been lost. So during the reassemblage some of the lost stones were necessarily replaced with new ones,

carved out of freshly excavated Pentelic marble, in order to restore the continuity and structural integrity of the walls.

The new study of the scattered architectural members over the entire surface of the Acropolis did not at first appear to be urgent. Never before had such a systematic study been initiated and naturally things had been left pretty much as they were after the excavations of the last century. But when the process of accurately measuring and recording every stone began, together with the careful taking-apart of the various stone piles and the cataloguing of hundreds of marble pieces, for the first time it was possible to recognise and rejoin countless architectural fragments, many of which, it emerged, could be safely repositioned. At once it was obvious that this rediscovered material was equally in need of protection and care, and that this could best be achieved if it was returned to its original position on the walls. The new project did not, therefore, merely create the right conditions for restoration work, but also highlighted a new need and urgency to proceed.

A large part of the interior colonnade of the Pronaos of the Parthenon has today been collected on the ground in front of the temple. Dozens of fragments from the coffers of the marble ceiling of the Propylaea have also been matched and may be repositioned. At the same time bases of monuments of the sort which in ancient times adorned the Acropolis have been restored, and architectural members have been correctly identified as belonging to the small temples of Athena Nike and Roma, which is a valuable step in the efforts to accurately document and project the buildings.

All this has stirred up serious theoretical problems. To what degree may one reconstruct Classical monuments, even when reusing original building material? Is it possible to change the fixed and familiar appearance of monuments (indeed the facades of the famed temples on the Acropolis) without negatively affecting their historic value or their symbolic meaning? How might we be able to maintain the character of a ruin when the reconstruction involves the restoration of the original shape of the building?

These issues are continually under discussion at the Committee for the Restoration of the Acropolis Monuments, as well as the Central Council of the Greek Archaeological Society, with results that are most certainly positive. The problems, in particular, relating to the restoration of the peristyle of the Parthenon Pronaos which collapsed during the great explosion of 1687 were discussed and finally focused on the question of the amount of new marble that would be necessary in order to complete the ancient architectural members as well as the need for continuity in the formal and structural elements along the peristyle.

A better understanding of all these questions becomes possible only through a systematic analysis of the primary values which contemporary civilization projects onto the monuments of the past. In other words the artistic values (the monument as a work of art), the scientific, historical and archaeological values (the monument as a mirror of knowledge), the functional values (the monument as shelter for ritual or as simple exhibit) and finally the environmental values (the monument as an integral element of the environment). A positive analysis along those lines brings out the unavoidable conflicts regarding what needs to be done regarding conservation, the restoration and the general handling of monuments. The promotion of restoration work is positive for the aesthetic values and the functional values of a Classical temple when seen as an exhibit, but it lowers its historical value. The effects, for example, of the gunpowder explosion of 1687 will not appear to the uninformed visitor on the Acropolis to have been so catastrophic after the restoration of the north colonnade and the planned restoration of the Pronaos.

FROM ABOVE: The Propylaea work-site with the Erechtheion in the background; the northern half of the east portico of the Propylaea covered in scaffolding

The restorers of monumental buildings are accustomed to handling such conflicts. It is obvious that the success of a restoration lies in the achievement of a balance between the 'musts' in every category of values, in the most efficient achievement, in other words, of a positive result with a minimum of capitulations. It would be a mistake, therefore, if these conflicts on a theoretical level led us to the abandonment of an effort and the limiting of our activity to salvage work or mere conservation. Monuments are cultural and social goods and their upgrading and upkeep constitutes a duty, at least in our age.

Another serious problem faced by the Acropolis is that of the replication of Classical sculpture. After the removal of the Caryatids, the pedimental sculptures, the metope reliefs and the figures on the west frieze, a substitute copy takes their place. Besides the purely technical problem of the material out of which the copy is made (which must be resistant to atmospheric pollution and aesthetically acceptable in the general appearance of the monument), there is always the theoretical question of limits: up to what point may one substitute sculpture with cast replicas without affecting the authenticity of the whole? The efforts to render ancient monuments appreciable and to increase their didactic value favours the placement of even more copies of known sculptural and architectural elements that are housed in foreign museums. But the problem always remains. The repositioning of the sixth column of the east portico of the Erechtheion (currently in the British museum) in the form of a concrete cast completed the elevation and significantly improved the general appearance of the temple, but at the same time provoked serious objections. The commitment to the principle of reversal, mentioned above, assures us that in any case a possible failure or miscalculation is reparable.

Besides the above, the Committee for the Conservation of the Acropolis Monuments must still deal with other, running problems: fiscal problems, administrative problems, problems relating to the organisation of working crews, the selection of personnel, and so on. But there is no need to examine these in the context of this presentation.

The Caryatid Porch with the newly-cast Kore reproductions in place. New marble infill pieces are visible in the south cella wall; OVERLEAF: Crowds surging through the Acropolis site on a typically busy day

STRUCTURAL INTERVENTIONS ON THE ACROPOLIS MONUMENTS

Costas Zambas

T he lay world is generally under the impression that the extensive interventions of the last twenty years on the Acropolis monuments are due to the destructive effect of atmospheric pollution. This is only one of the reasons, however. The installation of large scaffolds and heavy machinery for so long aims chiefly at amending the various types of structural damage that has been sustained by the buildings during the long course of their existence. Some of this damage is recent and is due primarily to the oxidation and expansion of the iron ties and cramps that were incorporated into the marble members during the restorations of Balanos at the beginning of the century. Most of the rest of the damage is ancient, and as it continues to worsen, requires calculated intervention.

At the Erechtheion structural damage that was dealt with by the Committee for the Conservation of the Acropolis Monuments (CCAM) was almost exclusively caused by the rusted ties from the restorations of 1902-09, and the recent activity largely concerned the previously restored parts of the building. It amounted, in other words, to nothing less than a restoration of a restoration. At the Parthenon, besides repairing the ties from the 1898-1932 interventions, the CCAM had to deal with ancient damage which had become critical following the great earthquake of 1981. For this reason the dismantling of members for restorative purposes extended to many parts of the building that were still *in situ* or untouched by modern activity.

The disturbance of the 'eternal' balance of the Parthenon marble members by the CCAM, even in their already altered state, was a difficult decision and demanded firstly exhaustive multidisciplinary research. Though damage tends to be the exception in new constructions, it is the rule in virtually every ancient Greek monument. The issue is therefore not one of recording and repairing all the damage, as this would mean the total alteration of the character of the monuments. In the case of the Acropolis this would result in the complete dismantling of the buildings.

Diagnosis and appreciation of damage

The most up-to-date methods of structural analysis of buildings offer an invaluable assistance in determining and appreciating the damages on the Acropolis monuments, but are utilised critically and with respect to the behaviour of the monuments, the understanding of which is a primary objective of the CCAM.[1] The ancient temples are not just bearers of artistic and historical values, but are also tireless venues of gravitational pull and seismic activity, having suffered over the centuries endless exertions in a satisfactory manner. The Acropolis monuments are living proof of their design as near permanent creations, something which is conspicuously absent in modern buildings. This fact alone deserves the attention and respect of the researcher. The interventions are being effected in the areas which have been most affected structurally. At the Erechtheion the dismantling of members included a small number of stones that had been until then *in situ* above the north entry because they had suffered grave damages from the effects of fire and the oxidation of ties. Interventions were not extended, however, to the adjacent areas, despite the fact that

OPPOSITE: Work in progress in the west peristyle colonnade of the Parthenon, looking through the Opisthonaos

here, too, there are shifted joints and consequently ancient ties that have 'failed'. These particular damages are not critical for the structural behaviour of the building and there are no indications of progressive deterioration. Equally, during the process of restoring the east elevation of the Parthenon the architrave blocks were not dismantled for repairs, though the shifted material also indicates imperfections in the ancient joints. Here too there is no indication of progressive damage.

Planning the structural repairs

During the erection or repair of new buildings it is desirable to design or redesign the structure in such a way as to permit it to behave in a manner selected by the architect or engineer, thus facilitating interventions should these be necessary later. In the case of ancient monuments the same, unfortunately, cannot hold. The design of the structural repairs must take into account the behaviour to date of the building and to aid it through the proposed intervention.[2] As such, comprehensive changes to the structural system of the monuments are not effected. The principle of minimal intervention that has been employed is justifiable both on a theoretical level and as regards the specific structural/tectonic considerations. In those parts of the monuments that are dismantled for repairs there are two basic issues which the structural engineer must address: a) The joining of the broken fragments of the ancient members, which is done with fine Portland cement and ties that are made of titanium, a metal that behaves similarly to iron but which is much lighter and does not oxidise.[3] b) The joining of independent architectural members with ties and cramps of titanium, which are held in place with cement in the ancient tie-holes. In the diagram the methodology of restorations is clearly outlined. In the design criteria that have been adopted for contemporary buildings the CCAM has added criteria which concern the preservation of the artistic and historical evidence in each monument. From among the tested methods of structural design the most flexible one is used in order to check against the permanent forces on the buildings, and that of 'breaking-point' strength against 'accidental' activity (which is chiefly seismic). Finally as concerns the dimensioning of the ties and cramps of titanium, the design is generally that which corresponds to the determined strength of the ancient marble in each case, or the greatest projected strength. In no instance is a questionable structural condition allowed to exist if it is detected in any one ancient block.

The methodology that has been adopted by the CCAM for the design of structural repairs has significantly reduced the size of the metal elements that are incorporated by necessity into the ancient marble members. Consequently interventions have been kept to a minimum, with respect to the integrity and authenticity of the historical material.

The north porch of the Erechtheion following the restoration work by the CCAM. The intervention was extended to the area above the entry, but not to the lateral regions of the cella wall, where damage was not critical; OPPOSITE: East elevation of the Parthenon after the CCAM restorations. Interventions focused on the two corners of the elevation and the entablature, but not on the architraves, which were found to be in sound structural condition. The Erechtheion and the Propylaea are visible in the distance

Notes

1 A multi-faceted examination of the damages on the Parthenon can be found in: M Korres, C Bouras, 'Study for the Restoration of the Parthenon', Greek Ministry of Culture and Sciences, Committee for the Conservation of the Acropolis Monuments, Athens 1983.

2 See S Angelides, 'Structural Considerations in the Conservation and Restoration of Historical Monuments', TEE Discussions, Athens, March 1980.

3 The use of titanium was first proposed by Theodore Skoulikides in 'Détérioration des Matériaux de Construction et Notamment des Marbres par la Corrosion d'Acier Incorporé – Cas de l'Acropole', Le Colloque Intern. sur la Détérioration des Pierres en Oeuvre, Athènes, La Rochelle, 1972, Comptes-Rendus, p41.

DIAGRAM OF THE STRUCTURAL DESIGN FOR THE RESTORATION OF THE PARTHENON

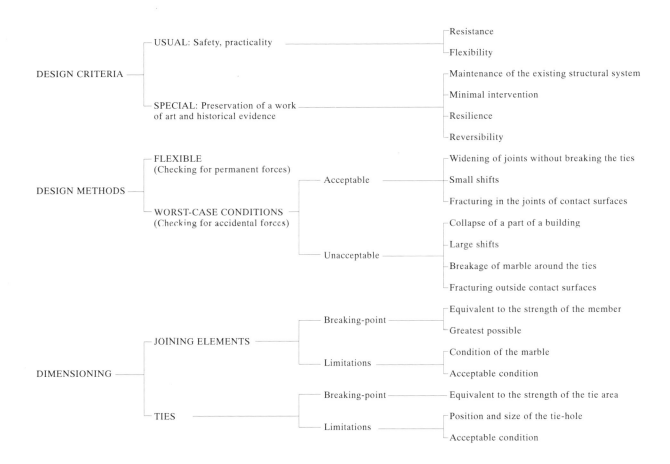

DESIGN CRITERIA
- USUAL: Safety, practicality
  - Resistance
  - Flexibility
- SPECIAL: Preservation of a work of art and historical evidence
  - Maintenance of the existing structural system
  - Minimal intervention
  - Resilience
  - Reversibility

DESIGN METHODS
- FLEXIBLE (Checking for permanent forces)
- WORST-CASE CONDITIONS (Checking for accidental forces)
  - Acceptable
    - Widening of joints without breaking the ties
    - Small shifts
    - Fracturing in the joints of contact surfaces
  - Unacceptable
    - Collapse of a part of a building
    - Large shifts
    - Breakage of marble around the ties
    - Fracturing outside contact surfaces

DIMENSIONING
- JOINING ELEMENTS
  - Breaking-point
    - Equivalent to the strength of the member
    - Greatest possible
  - Limitations
    - Condition of the marble
    - Acceptable condition
- TIES
  - Breaking-point
    - Equivalent to the strength of the tie area
  - Limitations
    - Position and size of the tie-hole
    - Acceptable condition

THE RESTORATION
OF THE PARTHENON

Manolis Korres

The job of restoring the Parthenon, like the works on the other Acropolis monuments, is a state programme and is being executed with funds from the Greek state and the European Community. Private donations, like the support coming from the Deutsch-Griechischen Gesellshaften, from the Rotary Club of Saint Cloud and from the English company Lansing Bagnall are welcome material and ethical contributions to the work.

Together with the interventions on the other Classical buildings that grace the ancient Athenian plateau, the restoration of the Parthenon is under the high scientific and organisational direction of the Committee for the Conservation of the Acropolis Monuments (CCAM). The tireless efforts and activities of the CCAM, which since 1975 has enjoyed the protection of a Presidential Decree, have resulted in the following: the continuing supervision of the works, the selection, hiring and further specialisation of the larger part of the scientific and managerial staff of the first Ephorate of Antiquities (which is responsible for the Acropolis), the compilation of the Archives for the works following the year 1975, the publication of scientific studies, the organisation of the Centre for the Acropolis Studies, the setting-up and co-ordination of four, until now, international scientific congresses (1976 for the conservation of the Acropolis and stone structures in general, 1978 for the Erechtheion, 1983 and 1989 for the Parthenon), the organisation of museum exhibits for the works (one of which was hosted in London and a few other European capitals) and the organisation of educational programmes for school children at the Centre for the Acropolis Studies and the archaeological site. In its current composition, the CCAM consists of Dr S Angelides, Professor of Building Structure, Dr A Delivorrias, Professor of Archaeology and director of the Benaki Museum, Dr G Despinis, Professor of Archaeology, Dr G Lavvas, Professor of History of Architecture, Dr V Lambrinoudakis, Professor of Archaeology, Dr T Skoulikides, Professor of Electrochemistry, Dr G Dontas, President of the Greek Archaeological Society and former (1967-81) director of the Acropolis, Dr I Dimacopoulos, Director of Restorations of Ancient Monuments, P Calligas, supervisor of the first Ephorate, and K Romiopoulou, director of Antiquities. The President of the Committee is Dr Charalambos Bouras, Professor of History of Architecture, formerly Director of Restoration and member of the Committee since its foundation, who is generally recognised as being the chief inspiration behind the works and the activities of the CCAM.

In full development since 1986, the restoration of the Parthenon far exceeds the older interventions on the monument (1834, 1842-44, 1872, 1898-1902, 1908, 1913, 1922-33) in its extent, quality, and total cost, and is aimed at conserving the existing structure and the stone surfaces, providing the best possible protection to the existing sculptures, the correct repositioning of stones that had been wrongly sited in previous works of restoration, and the filling in and partial restoration of certain portions chiefly through the reincorporation of existing fallen material that has been identified around the buildings. This work is being carried out on the basis of studies

OPPOSITE: View of the Parthenon from the northwest

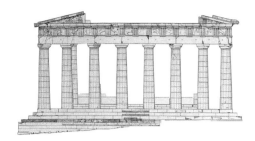

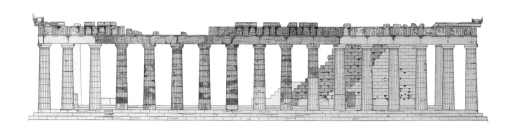

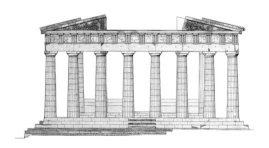

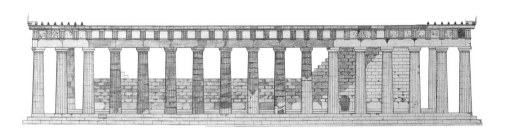

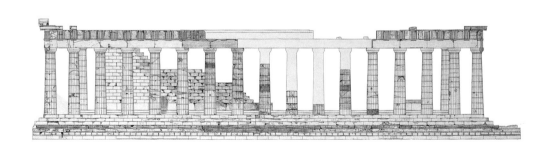

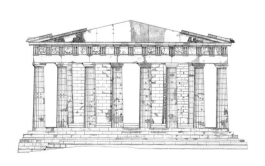

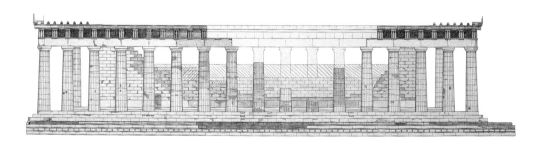

which have previously undergone critical scrutiny and have been approved according to the forecasts of the relative legal and scientific viewpoints by the CCAM and the responsible state services. Depending on the scope and the depth of these studies, they are categorised either as preliminary, general or special studies; as regards scientific focus the studies are divided into architectural and restorative studies, studies related to the organisation of the work site, structural studies, chemical studies, studies for the conservation of stone surfaces, etc. Until now three volumes of the ground-breaking *Study for the Restoration of the Parthenon* have been published (1983, 1989) as well as many dozens of specialist studies.

The first volume of the *Study* contains texts by Professor Charalambos Bouras in which the broader aims of the works are summarised, together with the theoretical principles behind the interventions. It also contains theoretical texts by this author, among which are the prescriptions for a system of codifying all the stones which has been in use until today. According to this system each stone carries an identity number which is used to track it on the building or in the storage site and to identify drawings, photographs, notes, and other pertinent material. To each stone corresponds a file in the archives which contains drawings of its existing condition at a scale of 1:10 or 1:5, drawn on A4 size sheets of paper, together with sketches, photographs and notes which describe the situation before and after every intervention.

A second series of files catalogues matters regarding the conservation of surfaces. The files in the Parthenon archives are to the stones what in a hospital archive the medical files are to the patients, and scientific research in general. The physical condition, various phenomena related to corrosion, cracks, older repairs, new attempts to join fragments, the positions and sizes of hidden metal reinforcements, medieval and later graffiti, traces of polychromy, dimensional and other material necessary for the verification of the original position of a stone on the building, details of sculptural decoration, and much more are included in the normal contents of each file. The number of files already surpasses two thousand and will be much larger when the work will have been completed. Because of the variety of information, in each file these are generally not complete but are added to from time to time throughout the duration of the studies and interventions. The system is so thorough as to permit one to say without exaggeration that for the complete survey of this large building, and at a level of detail that far surpasses all previous work, A4 size sheets alone are sufficient. For various other reasons, however, drawings are also made in larger formats. In general these consist of site drawings at 1:100 scale and detailed surveys of parts of the building at 1:20 and 1:10 scales, larger details often being drawn at 1:2.5 or 2:1 scales.

The compilation of the first studies which were necessary for the initiation and general organisation of the work was made by this author between 1980 and 1984. Subsequently the services of a number of scholars and scientists have enhanced the work. These include: Civil Engineer C Zambas and Architectural Engineers N Toganides and P Kouphopoulos, who undertook to carry out the larger part of the study and the supervision of structural interventions. Working closely with them is a photographer, a computer specialist and two draftswomen. The crew of marble craftsmen headed by chief craftsman I Arbilias, was originally organised in 1983 with six members who were instructed to proceed with the necessary preliminary operations; the team grew to a total of twenty-four by the commencement of works (1985-86). Two electricians who control the lifting mechanisms form an essential part of the group, as do two storehouse keepers in charge of the equipment and a few key helpers. For the production of cast copies of the sculpture and certain

OPPOSITE, FROM ABOVE L TO R: East and north elevations of the Parthenon, existing; east and north elevations, proposed; west and south elevations, existing; west and south elevations, proposed

L TO R: The east elevation of the Parthenon, with restoration work in progress; the west elevation of the Parthenon. The specially-designed crane is visible in the cella

L TO R: North peristyle colonnade of the Parthenon, east half; north peristyle colonnade of the Parthenon, west half

architectural details and surfaces the services of the casters from the Centre for the Acropolis Studies have been conscripted. The condition and conservation of the surfaces is indicated by specialist conservators A Galanou and G Dogani, who together with chemical engineer E Papaconstantinou oversee the conservation team.

The Parthenon work-site was organised between 1983 and 1985 in such a way as to serve any working requirement at any point on the building. To the south of the temple, where the ground consists only of recent level earth infill almost five metres below the stylobate, an area of 80 x 16 metres was isolated for the gathering of all Parthenon stone fragments from around the Acropolis, as well as for the establishment of the workshops. This location is better protected against the north winds, has the best exposure to the sun, and is the only one where the obstruction of visitor movement and the presence of foreign structures is somewhat tolerable both functionally and aesthetically. It is certainly no coincidence that the large ancient workshop which was used during the construction of the Parthenon was located in exactly the same place.

The obvious advantages offered by the interior of the temple for the development of a part of the work site did not, meanwhile, remain unrealised. From the beginning it appeared most sensible to place a single crane in the interior of the building that would be capable of reaching the larger part of the structure from one central position, rather than a mobile crane continually shifted about the temple or a number of smaller cranes located in various perimetric positions. The selection of this method satisfied demands for economy of space, and provided the possibility of quicker and more direct movement, without the need of reloading every stone to and from its position on the building or place in the workshop. At the same time it fulfilled requirements for a better handling of the negative aesthetic consequences resulting from the visible operation of a crane. This would not, however, have been possible if the ancient foundations were not so strong as to permit loads exceeding a hundred tonnes under pressures of ten tonnes per square metre to be applied at any point on the temple's floor without the least effect, or withstand the large and continual increases and decreases in pressure produced by the movement of loads of two to three hundred tonnes per metre together with the mobile part of the crane.

The necessary lifting capacity was rather modest – only ten to fifteen tonnes, as much, in other words, as the weight of the largest marble members from the temple – but the need for the provision of such a capacity at any radius (even above twenty metres) from the rotational centre and the importance of ensuring the greatest possible stability and rigidity of the crane during the removal or positioning of the stone elements led to the design of a very strong crane along the lines of the old *stiffleg derrick* type, which has microspeeds of forty centimetres per minute for the moment of positioning of a marble member and electric and electronic systems to check the load and motion of the crane arm. For even more precise manoeuvres of the loads hydraulic jacks and levers can be brought into motion. The movement of the marble elements in the work site and the workshops is facilitated by a bridge

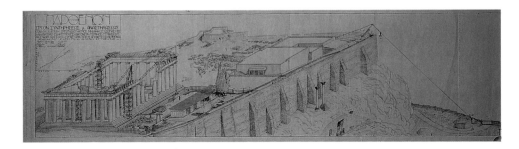

FROM ABOVE: View looking west down the Parthenon cella, with the specially-designed crane in operation; the Parthenon work-site; OPPOSITE: View down the west colonnade of the Parthenon, with the Opisthonaos columns to the right. The damages to the column surfaces due to bombardment, fire and atmospheric pollution are clearly visible

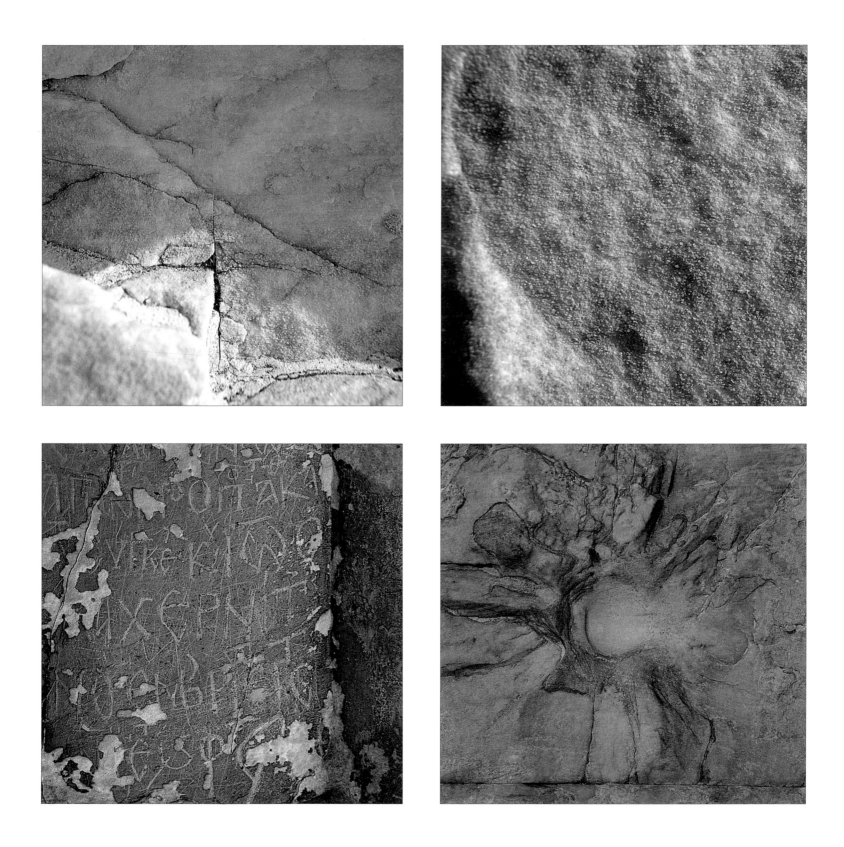

Examples of surface damage to the Parthenon. FROM ABOVE, L TO R: A stylobate joint after the most recent earthquake; crumbling marble surface due to atmospheric pollution; Byzantine graffiti standing out against a burnt, sooted column drum; close-up of the impact crater of a red hot cannon ball that found its target in the nineteenth century; OPPOSITE: View of the southwest corner of the Parthenon

which were prepared in the workshops of the Centre for the Acropolis Studies were used in place of the authentic metopes and the copies which were made in 1931 (Helios, two horses, Dionysos and a horse). The older proposal by the author of this paper to position copies of the other existing sculptures in the pediment (Iris, three goddesses, Selene) has not been accepted until now.

The new clamps and dowels were made of titanium and were placed as a rule in the original positions of the removed ancient elements. The selection of the thickness of each clamp or reinforcement rod is subject to a general rule which for the first time is being applied to such work: the thickness of the clamps must be such that in case of excessive stress the clamps alone break, and not the marble blocks (as a thread must break first before the button or shirt fall apart).

The structural intervention on the east side of the building was completed in 1991 and the large scaffolds were subsequently removed. Nevertheless conservation work on the building's surfaces continues with the help of a small moveable scaffold. The removal of the black pollutant crust will take place a little later.

On the south side of the temple the restoration of the fifth column and its superstructure was carried out in 1991-92; without doubt it was one of the most difficult structural interventions. During the explosion of 1687 the column had moved outwards in its entirety together with its superstructure, and one third of the first column drum had been destroyed. The 1981 earthquake had worsened its dangerous condition and the possibility of collapse in a future earthquake was obvious. As only the first drum needed repair it was judged preferable to effect an intervention without dismantling the column, so as to avoid even the smallest departure from the column's perfection and authenticity of construction. A decision was finally taken to temporarily lower the architraves directly above the column, together with the triglyphs, etc; to move the entire column intact by two metres to the interior of the building; to repair and complete the first drum in the workshop; and finally to reposition the drum, column, and superstructure. The work was carried out with the help of the special mechanism which we have already described together with the other mechanical tools of the project. During the intervention the column was initially raised only by one millimetre and shifted by the hand of ten men with a speed of one metre per hour. The completion of the ruined drum in the workshop with fresh white marble followed the most perfect ancient surfaces by one twentieth of a millimetre. Prior to the final positing of the column on top of the completed drum the column was raised temporarily by about another seven millimetres and the opening of the joint was steadied with three iron spacers of eight millimetres. Immediately afterwards a special tool eight millimetres thick designed by the author of this paper was passed into the joint, which precisely transferred the most minute variations from the overlying ancient surface to the new one. After the removal of the marble dust and the spacers the column was repositioned definitively and the joint closed over the greatest part of its surface with an accuracy of two hundredths of a millimetre.

The salvage work concerning the lowering and transport of the existing stones of the Panathenaic Frieze to the museum began with various preparatory activities in the summer of 1992 and was completed in the first months of 1993. All the stones of the sculptural masterpiece have been lowered under the supervision of P Kouphopoulos. Previously it had been necessary to lower the marble ceiling beams of the west wing together with many dozens of stones from the course of the sub-beam, which are adorned with Doric and Lesbian cymatia. Except for the difficulty in removing the most ancient and recent metal ties it was important to face the difficulty arising from the countless cracks which exist on the back of these stones which were caused by

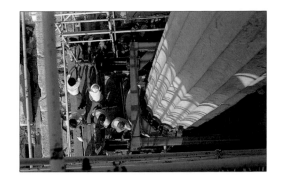

FROM ABOVE: Shifting the fifth column of the south side of the Parthenon; an old oxidised iron tie from the Parthenon next to its new titanium replacement; close up of a new titanium tie in a reused tie-cutting; OPPOSITE, FROM ABOVE: View of the southeast corner of the Parthenon; view of the east elevation of the Parthenon. The famed horizontal curvature of the building is visible along the north peristyle colonnade

129

the ancient fire in the building (third century AD). It would have been virtually impossible to remove these stones intact without the danger of fragments collapsing. It was decided therefore to remove most loose fragments on the spot, before any attempt to move the larger blocks. This approach was also applied during the lowering of a few backing blocks and the frieze itself. In order to avoid any damage to the highly sensitive relief surfaces along the ancient cracks, preventive protection was provided by the conservators under the supervision of G Doganis.

The programme is expected to continue as follows: the stones of the frieze, which are already being positioned in room VIII of the museum, shall undergo systematic conservation. The architraves which carried the frieze, fifteen ancient ones and six new ones which were positioned in 1900, will be lowered so as to allow structural conservation of the ancient and a partial substitution of the new members with ancient architraves that had been lowered in 1900 as they were believed to be structurally unsound. These are now judged to be salvageable if they are submitted to the right structural conservation. The temporary removal of the architraves will allow the structural conservation of the columns and especially the completion of the capital of the southernmost column. The complete destruction of a large part of this capital by the ancient fire had caused the subsidence of the superposed architraves to a point where they were held up purely by virtue of their interlocking joints. This resulted in sequential settling of the overlying stones and the appearance of many fractures in these, which extended over the entire thickness of the entablature and had even spread to the respective corner stones of the frieze. The repositioning of all the stones will take place as it did in the eastern side of the building, on the basis of minute calculations of their regular positions. Cast copies shall be positioned in the place of the frieze and all the new connections will be made out of titanium.

Salvage work has also progressed along the length of the side walls of the cella. Some three hundred stones that had been repositioned at random in 1842-44 were lowered, many of those conserved and all the metal elements that were causing damage to the stones and the wall were removed under the supervision of N Toganides. The structural salvage work will be completed with the dismantling of the restored portions of the north and south peristyle colonnade (programmes two and three) and the removal of all the later metal ties and reinforcements from the western facade (programme four). The interventions which follow the urgent salvage work consist in the correct repositioning of the temporarily removed ancient stones and the other ancient members which until now have remained on the ground. The total number of these members is much larger and permits the quantitative improvement of the form of the ruin. The available stones for the new restoration of the side walls are more than seven hundred and for the restoration of the Pronaos some three hundred. The study for the restoration of the side walls was completed at the beginning of 1994. The full study for the restoration of the Pronaos was published and discussed by the specialists who took part in the conference of 1989. From the records of this conference it is clear that the large majority of specialists have positioned themselves in favour of the more extensive restoration of the Pronaos. Similarly more members of the CCAM initially supported this view. However out of deference to the minority of objectors these members in the end went along with a more moderate intervention. This accommodating attitude did not positively impress this minority of objectors, but on the contrary encouraged them to fight the proposal by cultivating negative impressions and delaying the procedures. In the end it was decided only a few stone members were to be repositioned on two of the columns. In the view of the author of this paper the approved part of the initial

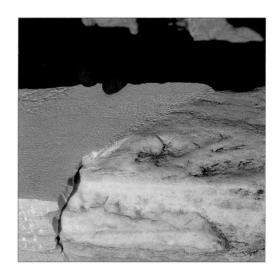

FROM ABOVE: The dismantling of the previously restored (1842-44) section of the south wall of the Parthenon; close up of a newly positioned marble infill piece; OPPOSITE, FROM ABOVE L TO R: Specialist masons working on marble blocks; view of the mechanical crane in operation in the Parthenon cella; stone mason at work; re-fitting a broken marble fragment

THE RESTORATION OF THE ERECHTHEION

Alexander Papanikolaou

T he recent works of conservation and restoration on the Erechtheion (1979-87) constituted the first organised attempt to restore the Acropolis monuments by the Greek state after the Second World War. The new interventions on the Acropolis monuments are not the result of a more ambitious restoration programme; they are due primarily to the need to amend and revert the devastating consequences of the Balanos restorations of the end of the nineteenth and beginning of the twentieth centuries which were precipitated by the incorporation of iron beams and joining elements in the ancient material. Balanos' unqualified methodology inflicted terrible damages on the ancient architectural members with the passage of time. Referring to a single example may perhaps best describe the magnitude of the destruction: the exposed iron elements that were incorporated in the architraves of the famous Caryatid Porch had so rusted by the time the CCAM intervened that they had shattered the stone members that make up the roof of the porch. One of the formerly monolithic architraves was removed during the course of the recent works and was found to have been broken into no less than 137 independent fragments.

Only seventy years after the completion of what was meant to be the definitive restoration (1902-08) of the Erechtheion it was necessary to completely dismantle the restored parts in order to remove the iron from the surfaces and the mass of the reconstructed ancient marble pieces. The restoration procedure applied by the CCAM was of a very calculated nature. At the Erechtheion a comprehensive study was carried out which identified the problems and posited the necessary proposals for their solution. Subsequently an international meeting of specialists was held in order to further analyse and examine the problems. The conference participants unanimously approved the study and its recommendations, which were then authorised by the responsible government bodies, leading to actual interventions on the building.

The new work on the Erechtheion lasted for a total of eight years. A primary goal was the removal of the Caryatids and their placement in the Acropolis Museum in order to protect them from the disastrous effects of atmospheric pollution. The sculptures were transported to a specially arranged hall of the Acropolis museum and placed inside a glass enclosure. Immediately afterwards the main task of dismantling the restored members was begun, extending as far as (but not including) the areas which had not been disturbed since antiquity. On the whole about 720 members of the marble structure were removed with the help of cranes, the majority of which were fractured in two or more places. The stones weighed between one and seven tonnes. More than 1,250 tonnes of marble were removed, mostly in a poor state of preservation. All of the elements that were restored by Balanos were thus removed from the south wall, the south porch, the upper courses of the west wall, the roof of the north porch, and the north wall. It was also deemed necessary to replace and consolidate the lintel of the entrance in the north porch. This had been broken in the middle and presented an angle of declination of about thirty millimetres.

The restoration of the individual members was a slow and careful process. Those

OPPOSITE: The northeast corner of the Erechtheion with the newly positioned copy of the north corner column. The entablature with new material completes the elevation and stabilises the portico, the columns of which were purely self-supporting prior to the CCAM restorations; OVERLEAF: The south elevation of the Erechtheion with the casts of the Caryatids, and the new marble that fills in the gaps in the south wall resulting from the removal of blocks that were wrongly positioned in older restorations

The new interventions on the Erechtheion included the restoration of the stones from the north and south walls, the coffered slabs from the roof of the north porch, the stones from the cornice of the Caryatid podium, and, in part, the stones of the superstructure of the west wall.

With the replacement of the ancient fragments in their original locations, the Erechtheion has become significantly more intelligible as a building. In contrast to the appearance of the monument just before the recent restoration, today it is possible to accurately discern the later historical interventions on the building, namely those from the period of Roman occupation, the phase in which the structure was transformed into a tripartite Christian basilica, and the subsequent phases during which the various additions on the interior and exterior left distinct traces.

It would be possible to characterise the previous restorations of the Erechtheion as an essentially scenographic approach. Certainly the available original material that was not *in situ* was sufficient to supply such an exercise; however this material was used merely as a means, regardless of its original function, to achieve the main objective of the day, which was the raising of the ruinous building in height. In very many instances marble members from other, unidentified, monuments were transformed by means of cuttings and reworked surfaces into infill material for the Erechtheion. Many stones which were found *in situ* on the monument were also cut in random ways in order to allow the positioning of the infill pieces.

All material that was foreign to the Erechtheion has now been entirely removed from the structure and replaced by accurately sculpted elements. Objections are raised today regarding the high number of small and large surfaces of new marble on the Erechtheion, but it should be kept in mind that this was the inevitable result of the removal of the foreign material from the building.

A substantial visual discrepancy is evident at the Erechtheion, and is the only truly significant one, in our opinion. This relates to the extent to which the new infill pieces harmonise with the ancient elements on the interior of the building. In order to make this question more clear we shall point out that the interior surfaces of the stones of the Erechtheion acquired their irregular egg-like profile due to the effects of intense heat produced by at least two fires that destroyed the interior of the temple in historical times. The new infill pieces could not possibly be made to replicate the natural effects of thermal fragmentation, and were therefore treated on their interior surfaces with shallow point marks. The visual antithesis between the ancient, naturally damaged material and the contemporary stone surfaces is certainly pronounced. The alternative, however, of mimicking shattered blocks in an artificial, random manner was not considered to be a valid solution. It was decided that the antithesis was a preferable and more honest effect.

One thoroughly restorative intervention was included in the CCAM programme for the Erechtheion, namely the reconstruction of the northeast corner of the east porch. As is generally known, the northeast (or sixth) column, including its capital, the architrave of the porch facade, and the capital of the anta of the north wall, are currently in the British Museum together with other architectural elements from the Erechtheion. Exact copies of the original elements were therefore placed in their respective positions during the recent restorations. The reasons which led to this intervention were: a) the need to augment the didactic value of the monument by completing its ruined image, and, more importantly, b) the need to fasten the porch entablature to the two nave walls in order to give this part of the building a greater resistance to seismic activity.

It is well known that this reconstruction was effected with copies and not the original material. We are however of the opinion that in a future Europe of federated

Panoramic views of the restored interior of the Erechtheion. Where new marble blocks had to be incorporated, their inner faces do not mimic the older damaged block surfaces but restitute the original face of the walls; OPPOSITE: View of the north porch of the Erechtheion, with the newly restored Ionic portal

states the need to return this material that is an organic and inseparable part of the Erechtheion shall finally be appreciated. After all, according to the Charter of Venice the monument is 'inseparable from its historical and actual context'. As the removal of the northeast corner of the Erechtheion by Lord Elgin in 1802 was carried out under assumptions and considerations other than a true respect for the nature and integrity of the monument, it is our view that the return of the original material will one day be considered to be the only just course of action.

The principle of reversibility that was incorporated into every restored element at the Erechtheion and the Acropolis monuments as a whole shall permit the relatively easy dismantling of the restored parts of the structures in order to replace them with the original material, whenever this can be secured. In the case of the Erechtheion the possible reincorporation of the absent parts of the east porch would help greatly in restoring the image of the building to the state it was in at the beginning of the nineteenth century.

The Erechtheion seen from the southwest. The elaborate west half of the building is set off dramatically against a plain eastern section, the visual continuity of which has now been correctly restituted; OPPOSITE: View of the north porch of the Erechtheion, looking west. Note the ominous blanket of atmospheric pollution that covers the city of Athens in the distance

THE RESTORATION
OF THE PROPYLAEA

Tasos Tanoulas

When the Committee for the Conservation of the Acropolis Monuments was formed in 1975, the shape of the central building of the Propylaea was the cumulative result of the restorative interventions of Nikolaos Balanos, which were performed between the years 1909 and 1917, the restorative and stabilising interventions conducted by Anastasios Orlandos through his associate Stikas from 1946 until 1957, as well as various works that had been effected after the Second World War for the securing of broken fragments from the roof of the Balanos restoration. As the initial goal of the Committee was to deal with the serious problems of the monuments stemming from the work of Balanos, it is crucial that, before passing on to the description of current restorations on the Propylaea and the problems that are being dealt with, we review what exactly Balanos restored at the Propylaea and how. This will be based on his own testimony and the study of the interventions before and after their recent reversal, which shall be discussed later in this paper.

The Balanos interventions were limited to the central building. The drums of the three south columns of the east stoa were repositioned in their original locations, as were the stones of the respective east anta of the south wall. A new capital was placed on the second column from the south, the original having been taken away by Lord Elgin and currently on display in the British Museum. The remaining capitals, of which the eastern side was damaged, were rotated 180 degrees in order to show the better preserved face, and were completed with new marble. At the time only the central part of the entablature with the architrave backing-block which connected the south column with the respective anta remained *in situ*, as well as the central portion of the second architrave from the north and the north end of the architrave of the northeast corner. Balanos restored the face of the southern architrave in the eastern stoa, while in the central intercolumnar space he restored the entire width of the architrave and the face of the frieze as well as the north half of the respective cornice. In the two north intercolumnar spaces of the east stoa, he completely rebuilt the entablature, roof and tympanum of the pediment, together with a portion of the raking cornice. Specifically, the part of the coffered roof which was restored consists of a half-beam, in contact with the backing-block of the north architrave of the stoa, the two beams to the south and the twenty coffered slabs which covered the respective spaces between the beams. A part of the roofing of the northeast corner was also restored, with corresponding parts of the sima.

In the west hall the entire easternmost column of the north Ionic colonnade was restored, of which only the base and the two lowest drum sections had been preserved *in situ*. The western end of the Ionic architrave was placed on the reconstructed column, while the eastern end was positioned on the inner wall. The southern ends of the two beams were in turn positioned on top of the Ionic architrave, while the two spaces between the beams from the flush beam on the wall and the beams themselves were filled with twenty-six coffered slabs. In order, of course, to restore the ceilings in the

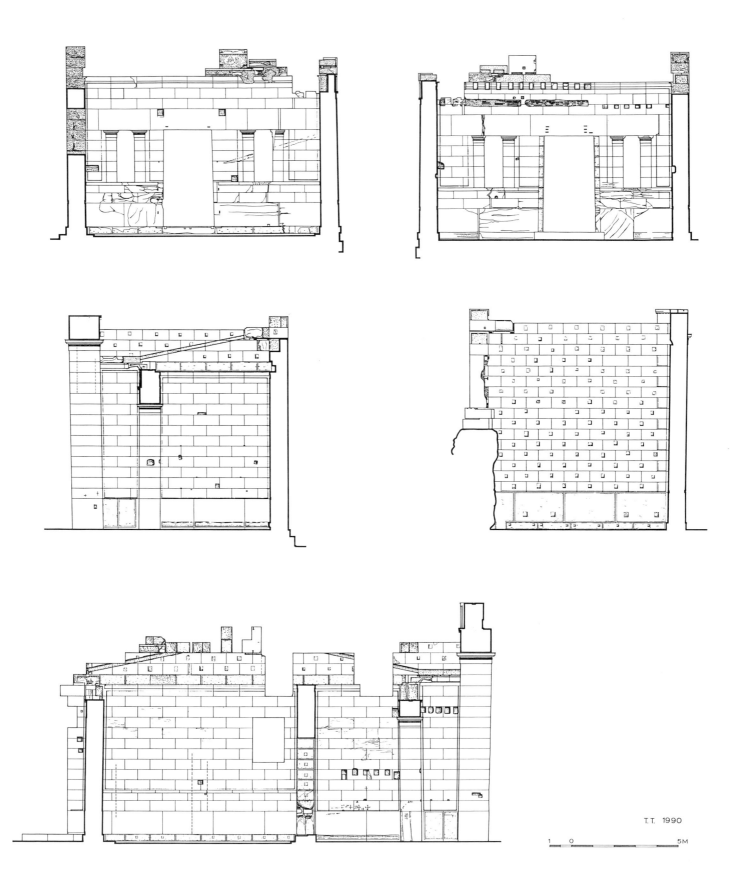

T. T. 1990

1 0   5M

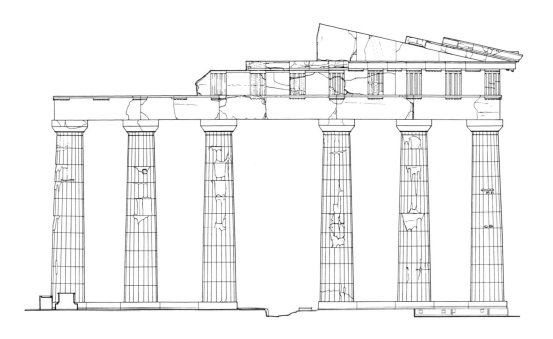

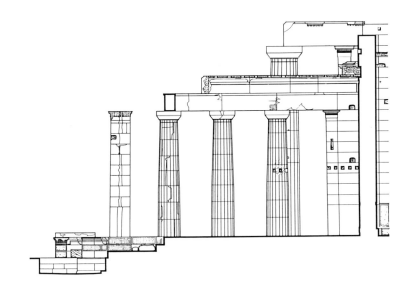

FROM ABOVE: The eastern facade of the central building of the Propylaea as restored by Balanos; the inner face of the colonnade of the southern wing, the western part as restored by Orlandos and Stikas; western facade of the northern wing, at the very top the Classical blocks as moved by the Franks, in order to make room for the windows of the added floor (drawings by T Tanoulas); OPPOSITE, FROM ABOVE: The two faces of the door wall of the northern wing, with the crack caused in 1687, showing the top cornice pieces built in the wall of the added floor, and the lower part of a door; the inner (left) and outer (right) face of the eastern wall of the south wing of the Propylaea – the cuttings for the wooden ceiling and roof are visible; western face of the eastern wall of the northern wing, the cuttings for the wooden ceiling and roof at the top courses (drawings by T Tanoulas)

155

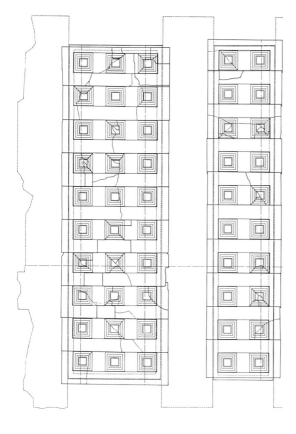

FROM ABOVE: *An inside view of the eastern portico entablature, showing the modern inner part of the capitals. The picture is taken after the 1982 restoration indicated by the white pieces of marble (1988); eastern portico, view of the restored ceiling coffer slabs, showing the fragments of which they were composed. Continuous line: fragments belonging together, dotted line: fragments not belonging together (drawing T Tanoulas)*

eastern stoa and the western hall the respective stones in the upper parts of the north and main walls had to be rebuilt as well.

In order to reunite the shattered fragments that made up each one of the restored beams, long channels of trapezoidal section were cut along the upper surfaces of the beams, into which Balanos then fitted iron I-beams. Furthermore, a system of suspending the marble beams from the encased iron beams was worked out. The space between the contained structure and the walls of the channels were filled with a strong cement mix which completely covered the iron beams.

The way in which the Ionic cymatia, or crown mouldings along the top of the beams were restored is especially characteristic of the work of Balanos. As long stretches of the cymatia were found to be broken or in ruinous condition, they were completed with new marble pieces or ancient fragments of similar cymatia which had preserved the crispness of their profile. As a rule, the main body of the beams and the newly-added stone elements were carefully carved and adjusted so that their junction coincided with the base of the cymatium and was unnoticeable even from a short distance.

Each restored coffered slab was the result of the combination of numerous fragments which in most instances did not belong to the same original slab. Occasionally new marble was used as a filler. In order to secure the pieces that were assembled for each coffer, Balanos carved channels of square section along the sides of each reconstituted slab, into which he placed iron bars. The ends of each bar were bent to form right angles, allowing them to be inserted into sockets that had been cut at the ends of the channels. The spaces between the bars and the channel walls were filled with lead. In most of the slabs additional reinforcements were used: on top of the slabs and along their longer dimension iron I-beams were positioned, from which the various fragments were suspended by means of screws. Each screw hole was effected to great depth in the marble slabs, often just 1.5cm from the lower, visible surfaces. The fragments that constitute the inter-beam vertical slabs were joined with bars similar to those which had been used on the sides of the coffers. In addition, common cement was used to join the fragments that constitute the restored architectural members of the east stoa. When the assembled pieces were found not to belong to each other, Balanos chipped and smoothed the damaged surfaces which he had decided to join, creating level surfaces. This tactic has rendered the precise identification of fragments used by Balanos extremely difficult.

The method by which Balanos joined the fragments that constitute the beams, the inter-beam vertical slabs, and the coffered slabs from the ceiling of the west hall was almost identical, but rather than using cement, this time he chose reconstituted marble with inserted fragments of new marble and, in discernible places, I-beam connections covered in lead. Almost the entire restored ceiling of the west hall was covered with concrete, lime mortar, and stone slabs. Only the northern ends of the beams and the slabs between these were covered with protective glass roofs.

Balanos placed a second iron I-beam on the south side of the Ionic architrave in order to fasten the assembled pieces of ancient and new marble to each other. In order to reconstitute the existing Ionic capital he used fragments belonging to four different Ionic capitals from the Propylaea, the broken surfaces of which he cut back to allow closer fits between the diverse pieces. To join them he used numerous I-beam connectors and cement.

Much iron is contained in the other restored parts of the building as well, but as there are no records of these it is not possible to prepare a detailed description before their removal.

A complete picture of the situation at the Propylaea in 1975 requires a brief account of the interventions that have taken place on the building subsequent to the completion of the Balanos restoration.

Oxidation of the densely distributed ironwork from the Balanos restoration began to create problems soon after the completion of the works, causing concern among the authorities, which had to contend with dismal conditions under German occupation. In a paper written on March 15th, 1943, Orlandos called for the immediate replacement of the ironwork of the roof of the east porch of the Propylaea with copper and cement, or lead. The archaeological service acted ten years later when, in a paper written on October 14th, 1953, Meliades records the collapse of two marble fragments almost half a metre each in length from the restored Ionic architrave. A committee consisting of the architects Orlandos and Stikas, the archaeologists Meliades and Karouzos, and the civil engineer Solomonides recommended, after an on-site autopsy on October 14th, 1954, the reinforcement and repair of the Balanos restoration work on the Propylaea. Despite the urgency of their appeal, the iron beam was reinforced only eleven years later, in 1965, with the joining to the beam of a sheet of stainless steel, which soon proved to be disastrous. At the same time the joints between the coffered slabs of the eastern stoa were provided with insulating material and the glass roofs which protected the north part of the restored roof of the eastern stoa were made good again.

In 1943, the same year of German occupation in which Orlandos issued his warnings about the problems stemming from the restoration work of Balanos, he announced that further restoration work would soon take place in the south wing of the Propylaea. Indeed, the following year a cornice was repositioned on the south wing. Systematic work by Orlandos and Stikas in this part of the building did not commence, however, until 1946, and this was continued until 1954, at which time activities were interrupted up to 1957. During the course of these works most of those parts of the building which had been razed in the fifteenth century for the construction of the tower in the south wing of the Propylaea were reconstructed, making use of the material that had been retrieved during the demolition of the tower. The western column and the pillar of the west elevation were restored, together with the architraves that connected them and the freestanding pillar which turns the corner at the westernmost end of the north elevation. In order to join the fragments, which included pieces of new marble, stainless steel was used this time instead of iron. Orlandos expected that the restoration of the south wing would soon be complete, but his hopes were never fulfilled.

The north wing is the only one of the three parts of the Propylaea complex in which no restorative interventions have taken place. On September 20th, 1948, Kotzias, who was at the time director of the Acropolis, commenced a correspondence in which he asked that the conspicuous plaster foundries, stone workshops, wood warehouses, etc, be removed from the Pinakotheke in the building's north wing. On October 29th, 1948, Orlandos agreed, suggesting that the equipment be transferred from the Pinakotheke to the new storage house next to the Acropolis museum. It was not until 1954, after the combined dispatches of the then Director of the Acropolis Meliades and the then Curator of the Acropolis George Dontas, that a significant intervention was effected on the Pinakotheke. In a paper prepared on December 9th, 1954, Meliades proposed the roofing of the Pinakotheke for the housing of research equipment (models, plans, etc), while Dontas, in an essay of December 14th, 1954, described the critical condition of the Pinakotheke, the northwest corner of which was damp and particularly the limestone foundations which contained stones in a state of impending collapse. In a paper of October 24th, 1955, Orlandos ordered the transfer and use of iron bars from the storage house of

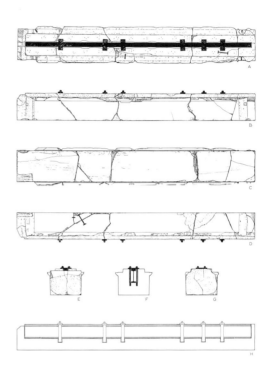

FROM ABOVE: Upper part of the Balanos restoration. Ceiling of the eastern portico of the central building, view from the southeast. Note the iron frame of the protective glass roof (1984); drawing of a typical beam restored by Balanos; OVERLEAF: The east portico of the Propylaea under restoration

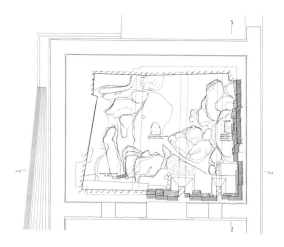

FROM ABOVE: Detail of the restoration by Balanos, the coffered ceiling in the eastern portico. Note the breakage caused by the iron bars (1989); marble fragments not belonging originally to one coffered slab, as cut and put together by Balanos, after the removal of lead, iron and cement; the reinforced concrete structure inserted in the Pinakotheke foundations in 1955, plan (drawing T Tanoulas)

the Direction of Restoration in order to strengthen the Pinakotheke foundations. Unfortunately there is no other record concerning this intervention in the interior of the Pinakotheke. These works, for which Orlandos and Stikas were responsible, can now be confirmed to have taken place as follows: a floor of reinforced concrete was positioned in the Pinakotheke in order to strengthen the western part of the north wing, of which the pronounced westward lean was continually increasing. In order to do this the packed earth and rubble between the Pinakotheke foundations was removed, deep wells along the width of the north and west wall foundations were opened and subsequently filled with reinforced concrete, and one third of the inside surface of the foundations was covered with concrete. This intervention has very little to commend it, as the Pinakotheke foundations consist of porous limestone architectural members from older buildings, and there was not even an attempt by the architects to record the material which they covered.

In 1979 the Acropolis Committee decided to study the special problems at the Propylaea. The result of this work was the publication *Study for the Restoration of Part of the Entablature of the East Stoa of the Propylaea*, compiled and submitted to the Acropolis Committee by architect A Tzakou and civil engineer M Ioannidou. On the basis of this paper the following work was effected in 1981 and 1982: the second from south architrave of the east stoa was removed, together with the cement and the iron pieces from the Balanos restoration. The iron elements were replaced by titanium while the spaces that were filled with cement were filled in with new marble. Of course in order to make possible the removal of the architrave it was necessary to dismantle the last to the south restored portion of the Doric frieze and its backing block, which was filled in with new marble pieces.

Subsequently the Acropolis Committee decided to proceed with the study of the technical problems which had emerged in the area of the coffered ceilings of the central building which had been restored by Balanos, together with the north wing. In 1987 the author of this paper submitted the first synoptic exposition of the problems of the Propylaea, entitled *The Problems of the Propylaea and their Possible Solutions. An Exploratory Approach*. In 1989 the author (in his professional capacity as architect) together with civil engineer M Ioannidou submitted a study for the removal of the restored roofs of the central building of the Propylaea. The study recorded the tragic condition of the coffered slabs and beams that had suffered because of the densely distributed ironwork, and proposed the immediate removal of the roofs in order to pre-empt the further cracking of the marble and the collapse of portions of the building.

Before moving on to the description of the works that have been effected until now on the central building of the Propylaea, we ought to mention the organisation and construction of the work-site. Unlike the Erechtheion and the Parthenon, which are surrounded by open spaces in which the various building facilities might be located with ease, the Propylaea are situated in an area where the rock presents dramatic changes in level and are surrounded by the ruins of buildings of great archaeological importance, made mostly of porous limestone, a particularly sensitive, fragile material. Furthermore the Propylaea provide the only access to the ancient sanctuary of the Acropolis, which means that the area of the work-site is crossed daily by thousands of visitors. These factors imposed serious problems which needed to be solved with the study of the work-site.

The selection of the location for the workshops and the work surfaces was made in such a way as not to burden the fragile ancient remains. Firstly it was decided that the new temporary constructions should not bear down on the north wall of the

Acropolis, because the structural balance of this wall was not perfectly sound. Furthermore, the construction of workshops on the periphery of the wall would make them visible from the city. The first workshop was constructed on top of two rows of iron foundation piers arranged along the length of the two south sides of the limestone foundation of the northwest building. The piers to the north of the limestone foundations were secured to the rock, while the piers to the south were secured in a new earth infill which is dated to the period after the completion the excavations of Kavvadias, in other words after 1890. None of the new constructions come into contact with the limestone blocks. Both before and during the construction of the workshop careful documentation of the unearthed material was made, as well as of the artefacts which would cease to be accessible during the Propylaea restoration works (see *New Discoveries at the Propylaea*).

Next, a work-surface was constructed above the Justinianic reservoir. This reservoir had been preserved intact and was in use until the excavation of Kavvadias, who in 1885 destroyed the vaults that covered it and tried to remove it entirely in order to examine the older layers beneath it. The strong plaster surfaces of the reservoir, however, made the attempt extremely difficult, and the findings were not encouraging; Kavvadias did not, in the end, destroy the entire structure, of which the portion which lies below the level of the plinth of the Propylaea's western chamber and north wing remains untouched. In this part of the reservoir Kavvadias collected fragments of architectural members from different periods and of a few sculptures which he considered not to be of particular value, and created a floor surface on the level of the *euthynteria* of the western hall and the north wing. As the area of the reservoir was essential for the execution of heavy work, it was decided to empty the reservoir of archaeological material and to construct a wooden horizontal work surface supported on metal foundation piers. In this way both the collected archaeological fragments and the reservoir itself would be protected from the activities of the building site.

The emptying of the reservoir was an enormous enterprise which began in April 1988 and ended in June 1989; the total mass of the material which was removed was around three-hundred cubic metres. The material was divided into the following categories:

a) Marble fragments from the Classical period, many of which belong to the Propylaea and were collected separately; b) marble fragments from the Hellenistic, Roman, and Byzantine periods; c) porous limestone fragments, mostly Archaic and Classical; d) roof tile fragments; e) non-architectural, archaeological material, in other words terracotta sherds, inscription fragments, sculptural fragments, etc; f) earth and stones from modern quarrying work.

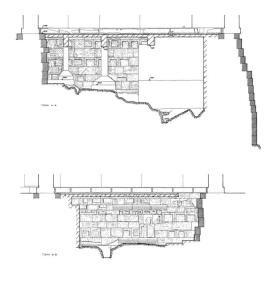

The greatest part of the architectural members was recorded by the crew of the Propylaea and the whole was arranged in groups to the east and southeast of the northwest building. The earth and modern stone chippings from the quarrying work were transferred in a small electronic windlass to the area of the ancient Peripatos just north of the Propylaea, from where they were subsequently removed. The non-architectural material was recorded by the curator of the Acropolis Ephorate C Vlassopoulou and was taken to the storage rooms of the Acropolis Museum.

The reservoir was subsequently drawn and photographed in detail, together with the portions of the base of the Propylaea that were uncovered. The iron foundation posts were secured on the strong pavement of the reservoir, which consists of three layers of dense terracotta slabs held in place with waterproof lime mortar. The work surface is now at a slightly higher level than the ground prior to the emptying of the reservoir earth deposits, so that it may oversail the Propylaea wall socle in this area.

FROM ABOVE: The surviving bottom of the Justinianic cistern, after emptying and cleaning, view from north (1989); the iron beams ready to receive the pavement of wooden planks (1989); the reinforced concrete structure inserted in the Pinakotheke foundations in 1955, cross sections (drawing T Tanoulas)

FROM ABOVE: The restoration of the Propylaea by Orlandos and Stikas. Superstructure of the southern wing, view from west (1988); detail of the restoration by Orlandos and Stikas. Western part of the southern wing showing the end of the stainless-steel bar (1993); view of the Propylaea from the east before building the work-site of the CCAM Propylaea project (1992)

The foundation of the piers was accomplished by embedding them in reinforced concrete footings, beneath which a damp-proof course of heavy plastic sheets was laid.

Between the northwest corner of the central building of the Propylaea and the Arrephorion a ground crane was constructed for the moving of architectural members and heavy loads in connection with the extensive joining-work. In the area of the Propylaea superstructure where the roofs were restored by Balanos, two systems of cranes which move in a north-south direction were positioned on scaffolds in order to facilitate the dismantling and depositing on the ground of the restored elements. A sturdy wagon was installed on rails which commence from the reservoir's new wooden floor and are directed east, allowing the transport of heavy architectural members that are lowered from the cranes to the surface at the north of the central building. The planning and supervision of the work-site was done by structural engineer M Ioannidou and the author of this paper; its implementation was successfully and efficiently accomplished, however, by the working staff headed by George Arbilias.

Six coffered slabs were removed in June 1990 from the roof of the east stoa in order to complete the upper part of the scaffolds supporting the sky-crane. The remaining fourteen slabs were dismantled and removed in December of the same year. As the fragmentation of the coffered slabs was at a very advanced stage, due to the method by which Balanos had joined them, and it was certain that if we followed the ordinary procedure of dismantling every architectural member separately there would be many accidents and losses, it was judged best to dismantle the coffers at once *en masse*. A strong metal grill was constructed for this purpose on top of which a surface of wooden beams was arranged. This surface was vital during the transportation of the coffered slabs and the slabs from the two inter-beam spaces of the stoa.

Following their transposition to the ground surface the coffers were placed along the northern section of the wooden floor which covers the area of the large reservoir, and were protected with sheets of plastic. The moving of the coffered slabs on the surface was done with great care and proved our original suspicions that in reality they were much more broken and damaged than what was visible when these were in contact with and supported one another. Between the fragments bronze hooks were discovered, mostly rusted and dissolved, the existence of which could not possibly have been surmised prior to the dismantling of the roof.

In the first months of 1991 the dismantling of the protective layer above the restored ceiling of the western hall was commenced. This layer consisted of the following strata: a) a lower layer of cement, lime and pumice-stone; b) a middle layer of lime-plaster; c) a layer of stone slabs. Because of the great depth of the space between the restored parts of the roof of the east stoa and the western hall, Balanos filled it with earth, positing at the top a layer of cement and stone slabs. The dismantling of twenty-six coffered slabs from the roof of the west hall was effected in October 1991 with the same method which was used in the dismantling of the coffered slabs from the east stoa.

In February and March 1992 the dismantling of the two restored beams in the western hall of the Propylaea was effected. In order to do this a metal support grill was used and the total duration of the operation, from the moment at which the beam was lifted until its positing on the ground to the northeast of the Propylaea, lasted exactly twenty-three minutes. Subsequently the slabs from the spaces between the beams and the flush beam above the main wall were dismantled. In September of the same year the Ionic architrave and capital that had been restored by Balanos were dismantled; in November and December the two beams of the east stoa of the central building of the Propylaea were taken apart. In each case the beams were brought to the area of the ground crane to remove the cement and rusting iron. The Ionic capital was immediately carried to the workshop in order to protect it from the effects of atmospheric pollution.

The dismantling, cleaning and maintenance of the parts of the Propylaea that had been restored by Balanos provided many new insights concerning that operation, the most important of which have been listed at the beginning of this article. The removal of the cement and iron from the beams was particularly difficult and time consuming. The cement was incredibly hard and practically fused to the marble. In order to avoid damaging the marble surfaces it was decided not to remove the cement unless it was necessary for the excision of the rusting iron. The amount of iron was very large, because in most cases the ends of the beams had been reinforced by one or more iron sheets. The removal of the iron and cement made the poor results of the Balanos joining methods even more apparent, exposing the fractures that had been caused by the oxidation of the iron elements.

From the summer of 1990 surface repair work has been proceeding concurrently. This was necessary because of the serious problems encountered in extensive sections of the building's surfaces. To date the entire surface of the orthostate on the interior of the Pinakotheke has been repaired and work on the surfaces of the Ionic column drums in the central building has advanced significantly. In March 1993 the joining of matching fragments from the dismantled coffers of the Balanos restoration was commenced, using rods of titanium and white cement.

The difficulties of an intervention on the north wing of the Propylaea are compounded by diverse factors: a) the first and most serious is that this area of the monument has never been restored – all the imperfections in its appearance are the result of the behaviour of the structural fabric of the Classical building according to natural laws in events like earthquakes, explosions, bombardment, etc. Nevertheless the detailed study of these imperfections, which include the shifting of stone blocks and the exposure of most of the ancient metal ties to oxidation, show that an intervention in this sector of the structure is crucial; b) the second factor is that the walls and colonnade of the north wing can only be restored fully by utilising the remains of an architecturally and historically important phase, namely the Frankish period; c) the third factor is the reinforced concrete floor which was built in 1955, leaving negative and irreversible effects on the porous limestone foundations: a strong fusion of the concrete with the worked surfaces of the limestone Archaic members which were used by the architect of the Propylaea Mnesikles as the main building material of the building's foundations; 'wells' that were opened in the mass of the porous limestone foundations means that reinforced concrete remains locked in place and threatens to cause significant structural damage once the metal begins to rust and corrode; d) a fourth factor is that the largest number of architectural members from the superstructure of the Classical building which do not remain *in situ* are in excellent condition, and with the introduction of a small amount of new marble may be used for a full restoration of the superstructure. The study of both the fixed and movable parts of the monument led to a full graphic reconstruction of the wooden ceiling and roof of the north wing, something which would allow the covering of this part of the building with a ceiling and roof identical to the ancient ones; e) today a part of the material lies on the ground surface, and another part crowns the walls of the north wing as it was transfigured in the middle ages. The dismantling of these last elements in order to use them in the restitution of the classical shape of the building would essentially consist in eliminating the last surviving portions of the medieval phase of the north wing.

FROM ABOVE: Part of the northernmost row of coffered slabs of the eastern portico lifted from their place to be taken to the ground (1990); after the removal of the adjacent slabs, the fragments of each slab became loose, revealing their bad condition (1990); one side of the new fracture due to Balanos' iron hoisting elements, just after the separation of the two fragments. The complete disintegration of the marble is conspicuous (1990)

 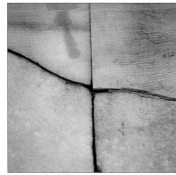  

FROM ABOVE: View of the south exterior elevation of the Propylaea, from the east. Note the atmospheric pollution (nephos in Greek) that blankets Athens in the distance behind the temple of Athena Nike; examples of older attitudes in restorative interventions, showing how ancient members were cut and levelled to match the surfaces of new infill pieces. On the far right an early twentieth-century capital completes a column which has been cut to receive the new addition

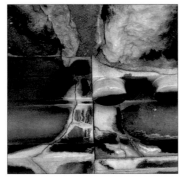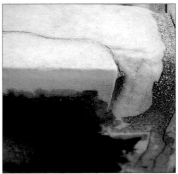

FROM ABOVE: The east portico of the Propylaea from the southeast; black pollutant crusts on the Propylaea, as seen under the cornice eaves, around guttae, triglyphs and the corona

168

THE TEMPLE OF ATHENA NIKE
A BRIEF DESCRIPTION

Built by the architect Callicrates between 427 and 423 BC, the temple of Athena Nike (Victory) was conceived as one of the four primary structures in the Periclean quartet, or *tetras*, that grace the Athenian Acropolis. Like its companions it is made of Pentelic marble, a material which substituted the Hymetteian variant as the preferred medium in post-war Classical Athens. It is an amphiprostyle, Ionic temple, and the most westerly in its location on the Acropolis. It therefore is the first structure to be perceived in the round by visitors making their way from the city through the Propylaea. For this reason, and because of the constraints of its site, it is also the smallest of the standing buildings, being conceived as an *agalma* or votive sculpture with chiefly symbolic functions. Most obvious of these was the projection, for the benefit of approaching parties, of the divine protection that was afforded by the gods to the city of Athens.

The Classical building is known to have replaced an earlier limestone temple, also dedicated to Athena Nike. The construction of the new temple and the extent of its sanctuary is one of the factors that influenced the eventual shape and size of the Propylaea, as it required the architect Mnesikles to adjust his more ambitious plans for the latter to accommodate access to the new temple and its altar. The conspicuous disalignment of the temple of Athena Nike with the Propylaea served a number of purposes: firstly, it placed the building's northwest corner in alignment with the north edge of the Propylaea's southern wing, thereby masking its asymmetry; secondly it directed the main western axis of the temple toward the Pnyx, which was the most important place of assembly of the Athenian deme, and the eastern axis toward the Parthenon's western facade, thus visibly linking the democratic process which unfolded below the Acropolis to the city's divine protectress, Athena, whose *oikos*, or home, was the Parthenon; thirdly it set the temple off as an independent object against the taller datum of the Propylaea. Another possible symbolic function of the temple was to remind visitors that Athens was an Ionic city – its inhabitants being descendants of the first Greek settlers in Hellas, and not the later Dorian invaders who, though Greek as well, overwhelmed their Mycenaean cousins and forced them to flee across the Aegean or accept serfdom.

The temple survived almost intact until the eve of the Venetian attack under general Morosini in 1686, when the Turkish garrison that occupied the Acropolis entirely demolished the building and incorporated its pieces into a new gun bastion. During the dismantlement of the bastion in 1835 (following the Greek War of Independence) the temple was entirely rebuilt and remained unchanged until settling in the foundations required yet another reconstruction, this time by Nikolaos Balanos, whose work was completed by Anastasios Orlandos. Recently the temple has been the subject of an exhaustive study by the architect Demosthenes Giraud, who has been commissioned by the CCAM to identify problems stemming from the second reconstruction and put forward proposals for a new intervention. This will be the third in a series of restorative efforts on this most important structure, one of the jewels of the Periclean age.

OPPOSITE: The east elevation of the temple of Athena Nike. An exhaustive study and restorative proposal has just been prepared by Demosthenes Giraud

FROM ABOVE: The temple of Athena Nike seen from below its tower, looking north; the temple in its context against the Propylaea; view from the east, with the port of Piraeus in the distance; OPPOSITE: The modern industrial city versus ageless equilibrium. The temple of Athena Nike as seen from the east against the Athenian nephos, *the notorious pollutant haze*

fragments of small marble equestrian compositions from the end of the sixth century BC (in the store rooms of the Acropolis Museum and the National Museum) came from the pediment of an up-to-now unknown Archaic temple on the Acropolis. Other research by Evi Touloupa led to the graphic restoration of very significant bronze dedications of the early Archaic period. During the intervention on the east side of the Parthenon it was determined that in the fourteenth metope the horses of Helios were not two but four, and that the corner acroteria were gigantic marble Nikes and not fine floral compositions.

During the course of work on the krepis of the cella, numerous other reused stones of the first Parthenon were uncovered, most of which had suffered surface damage through intense thermal activity. This observation constitutes further proof for the dating of the first Parthenon to the period just before the Persian invasion. The study and detailed drawing of most of the stones of this earlier monument revealed many interesting architectural details. Its columns would have been lower than those of the Pericleian building by one drum but its capitals would have been about twenty centimetres larger.

During the study of the scattered stones it was determined that the Pronaos differed in many more places from the Opisthonaos: the east door was a little narrower than the west and on both sides of the door there were two large windows for the enhancement of the statue's lighting. Inside the north window, built into the thickness of the wall, was a staircase which led to the interior of the roof. The roof of the Pronaos was much richer than that of the Opisthonaos. Its underbeam contained a unique for the Parthenon Lesbian cymation relief and its coffers were not double-graded but triple-graded. Evidently these particular characteristics of the Pronaos were later used as prototypes for the Ionic Erechtheion. The detailed study of the pavement over the entire surface of the temple proves the existence and conservation in Classical times of the temple's oldest shrine inside the north wing. As far as the plan of the Parthenon is concerned, it has been shown that the numerous differences that appear between the east and west porches are not characteristics of the original design but the result of a series of changes it underwent during the process of construction. These changes were dictated by a continually increasing demand for a large narrative sculptural embellishment of the cella wall of which the final result is the famous Panathenaic Frieze (see *The Sculptural Adornment of the Parthenon*). This more recent discovery justifies to a large degree two older theories according to which the original plan of the cella must have foreseen metopes in the place of the executed frieze (Doerpfeld 1884, Wesenberg 1983). As regards the four lost columns of the west compartment of the Parthenon it has recently been held, on the basis of good argumentation (P Pedersen, 1989), that these were not Ionic but in all likelihood Corinthian, possibly even archetypes of this order.

The detailed study of the ancient pavement and the traces that various later uses and interventions left on it allowed the compilation of the most complete until now body of knowledge regarding the form, the interior arrangement and the function of the Parthenon from the fourth century AD (after the fire and the crude attempts to repair the building) and especially after the sixth century as a Christian church. The north part of the western chamber contained the baptistry, which was rectangular, and had low walls and two entries. In the main church there were low divisions along the columns and across the width of the cella, which defined a central space and the *presbyterion* in the eastern sector. The circular *ambon* was placed on five colonnettes in the central space. Initially, however, it was lower, with a compact lower part. The arrangement of the *presbyterion* and the existence of two building phases in the apse of the church are a few of the new discoveries regarding the Christian Parthenon.

The hundreds of stones from other monuments that were used for the great repair work on the Parthenon in the fourth century AD and during the various phases of the Christian rebuilding are now a broad field of study. The examination of this material has already produced very satisfactory results, even if it has been conducted only in connection with the works of conservation. The surviving stones from the later phases of the Parthenon were picked out of thousands of other stones over the entire surface of the Acropolis, and were identified following a case-study for each individual fragment. These stones were interpreted in a way which determined on the one hand their original provenance from other ancient monuments, and on the other the position and the way in which they were reused in the Parthenon. A few were shown to have undergone numerous reuses in the Parthenon as well as elsewhere. The scientific value of this foreign material is great not only as it sheds light on the historical phases of the Parthenon, but also as it helps us toward a more complete understanding of the monumental landscape of the Acropolis and the city of Athens in general.

The most significant new discoveries are the following: in the third and fourth centuries AD the many smaller ancient buildings and structures on the Acropolis were demolished, leaving only the ones which survive to this day. The Hellenistic columns that were used for the reconstruction of the interior colonnades of the Parthenon (fourth century AD) come from a single-storey stoa in the city or perhaps two similar stoas totalling around two hundred metres in length of which at least one was a single-storey structure. Monolithic Ionic columns from the interior of these stoas were turned into beams for the repair of the Parthenon. During the middle Byzantine period various damaged marble elements from the demolished Panathenaic Stadium and the Temple of Olympian Zeus were hoisted onto the Acropolis to use as common building material for various projects.

In the thirteenth century the side walls of the monument of Philopappos (on the hill facing the Acropolis) were demolished and its stones were used together with a few stones from the Propylaea for the construction of the tower near the Parthenon cella. A few more stones from the Philopappos monument were used for the tower at the southwest corner of the Propylaea. From marble blocks which were used in the older apse of the Parthenon church it has been possible to restore the original form of the honorary monument of general Kefissodotos and its original position near the entrance of the Brauroneion has been confirmed. For the original pulpit of the Christian Parthenon, stones from a large circular pedestal of a colossal bronze statue were used, as well as from the circular base of a gigantic tripod, the krepis of a small temple or a large podium, and from the honorary monument of generals Konon and Timotheos. The inscription of this monument has now been restored, as well as its form. The upper course of this podium was of black Eleusinian stone. From the stones that were used for the repair of the west door of the Parthenon it has been possible to fully restore the form of the base of a bronze dedicatory four-horse chariot from the middle of the fifth century BC. The ascertainment that on either side of the chariot stood two male figures as in the podium of Agrippa is valuable as it has given us certain hints as to the restoration of the famous four-horse chariot of Delphi.

It has also been ascertained that the northeast corner of the Parthenon was occupied (and a part of its architrave was hidden) by a Hellenistic four-horse chariot on a very tall podium – not the chariot dating from the Classical period, as was previously supposed. By all indications this monument was later re-dedicated to the emperor Augustus. Many dozens of stones from this podium survive, together with hundreds of smaller fragments. The study of stones older than the Parthenon has shown that the so-called Hecatompedon temple was built in the same position as the

Parthenon and not near the Erechtheion as was supposed. The concentration of fragments from the base-blocks of the acroteria on its roof showed that these acroteria were sphinxes in the corners and large anthemia at the peaks. The east anthemion was flanked with statues perhaps similar to the acroteria on the temple of Aphaia on the island of Aegina. The four similar small heads of horses in the Acropolis museum do not come from a single dedication but from a metope of this temple: a four-horse chariot of Zeus from a gigantomachy scene, similar to a metope on temple C at Selinus or the pediment of the temple of Athena and the Archaic temple of Apollo at Delphi. Other smaller but extremely important finds are a few fragments from the monument of Callimachos: the lower part of the column, which has allowed us to calculate the column's dimensions, and its rectangular base, which permitted the search for a cutting in the face of the rock with respective dimensions. There is only one such cutting, a few metres north of the Parthenon, at the highest point on the Panathenaic road. The joint examination of all the fragments of the monument has confirmed the old theory of professor Raubitschek. The Ionic capital which Hansen first drew and the Nike No 690 of the Acropolis museum both belong to the inscribed column in the Epigraphic Museum. From a historical, artistic, and archaeological point of view this monument can be compared only with a handful of other structures, and as such the need for a unified museum display of its surviving pieces is obvious.

The studies of A Papanikolaou at the Erechtheion and its immediate surroundings led him to a restoration of the small Ionic stoa of Pandrosos on the strength of his observations that the slit windows of the Erechtheion are not Christian, as it has been generally held, but original elements of the ancient building; Papanikolaou also determined that the ruins northwest of the Erechtheion which have been considered to be either Mycenaean or medieval constitute the remains of a defensive enclosure which was put up hurriedly by the Athenians before the Persian onslaught in 480 BC. Many other observations were made possible during the conservation work at the Erechtheion. The interesting technical details of the way in which the repairs to the north door took place were recognised, the older comments of Stevens regarding the unusual constructional nature of the west wall were completed, and the original positions and sequence of the stone blocks was ascertained. The architectural study of the stones of the south wall of the Erechtheion and the ascertainment of the original position of each one by civic engineer C Zambas allowed the most accurate possible restoration of this wall and the extraction of valuable conclusions about ancient and modern methods of construction.

At the Propylaea Tasos Tanoulas conclusively studied the later phases of the building and numerous new observations were made about the later history of the monumental complex. The changing form of the complex in the various periods from the Frankish occupation until the gradual removal of the medieval additions (until 1888) has been documented in a series of drawings and a scale model. Tanoulas concentrated especially on the complex internal function of the structure as a palace and as an autonomous fort. The defensive system of the complex which consists of multiple successive fortifications and gates was analysed and interpreted in a very enlightening manner. In the meantime the research by Tanoulas regarding the ancient building and its immediate surroundings have continued with very interesting results. A special study was even dedicated to the Archaic cistern. The study of the form and structure of the famous coffered roofs of the Propylaea is of particular theoretical interest as well. Its first part concentrates on identifying the scattered and randomly assembled pieces of beams and coffers.

At the temple of Athena Nike Demosthenes Giraud studied the various historical phases and many new identifications were made of fragments belonging to the temple, its tower-like base, and its altar. Thanks to this study the new restoration of the temple projected by Giraud will be as accurate as possible.

Studies have been made during the last years for the smaller structures as well. Of these it is worth noting a study of the Brauroneion (RF Rhodes – JJ Dobbins, 1979) and one for the Chalkotheke (L La Follette 1986).

The structural situation and the historical phases of the Acropolis walls are the subject of a special study which is being carried out by P Kouphopoulos. Many interesting observations have already been made, but much more time is required before the completion of this project.

A programme of great value, of which the first part has already been completed by A Mattheou and his collaborators, is the study and assembly of stone inscriptions. This programme will contribute not only to the planned protection of inscriptions in museum displays, but also to the promotion of epigraphic studies for the Acropolis and its monuments. It is also worth mentioning the developing research of D Harris regarding the treasury documents of the Parthenon: *Inventory of the Treasures kept in the Parthenon*.

The above historical research in architecture and topography is being carried out largely in the context of the national works of conservation of the Acropolis monuments and comprise the greatest guarantors of the archaeological correctness and conciseness of the executed or planned works of correction and completion of the older interventions on the monuments.

The northeast corner of the Parthenon at the end of the first century BC, with shields in place on the architrave and the large tower-like pedestal with the four-horse chariot

179

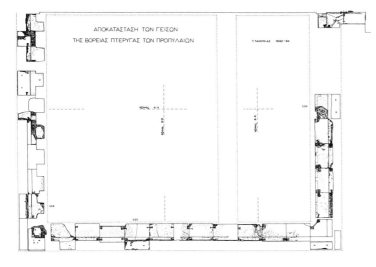

APOKATASTASH TΩN ΓΕΙΣΩΝ
ΤΗΣ ΒΟΡΕΙΑΣ ΠΤΕΡΥΓΑΣ ΤΩΝ ΠΡΟΠΥΛΑΙΩΝ
Τ.ΤΑΝΟΥΛΑΣ 1992-94

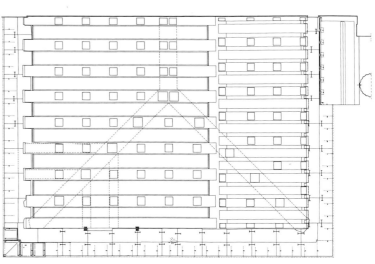

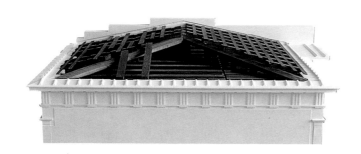

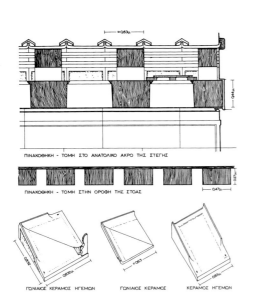

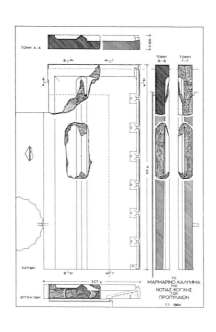

ΠΙΝΑΚΟΘΗΚΗ - ΤΟΜΗ ΣΤΟ ΑΝΑΤΟΛΙΚΟ ΑΚΡΟ ΤΗΣ ΣΤΕΓΗΣ

ΠΙΝΑΚΟΘΗΚΗ - ΤΟΜΗ ΣΤΗΝ ΟΡΟΦΗ ΤΗΣ ΣΤΟΑΣ

ΓΩΝΙΑΙΟΣ ΚΕΡΑΜΟΣ ΗΓΕΜΩΝ   ΓΩΝΙΑΙΟΣ ΚΕΡΑΜΟΣ   ΚΕΡΑΜΟΣ ΗΓΕΜΩΝ

ΤΟ ΜΑΡΜΑΡΙΝΟ ΚΑΛΥΜΜΑ
ΤΗΣ ΝΟΤΙΑΣ ΚΟΓΧΗΣ
ΤΩΝ ΠΡΟΠΥΛΑΙΩΝ

Τ.ΤΑΝΟΥΛΑΣ 1994

180

NEW DISCOVERIES
AT THE PROPYLAEA

Tasos Tanoulas

The present work on the Acropolis, which was inaugurated in 1975 with the constitution of the Committee for the Conservation of the Acropolis Monuments, has provided the opportunity to enormously advance our knowledge concerning the several structural phases of the great Classical monuments and the various structures between them. This is due to the full documentation of all of the interventions on the buildings or in their vicinity, as well as everyday contact with them and the ability to study parts of the buildings that were not regularly accessible to scholars in older times. Many of the new discoveries concerning the successive structural phases of the Propylaea and their vicinity during the Middle Ages and the period of Turkish occupation have been included in the relevant chapter in this issue. Here attention will be drawn to discoveries which could not be incorporated in that chapter.

The Pre-Mnesiklean cistern

It is interesting to note that many of the discoveries were the result of exhaustive documentation of the ancient vestiges which were to be temporarily covered by parts of the work-site. In summer 1987 while clearing the area to the northeast of the Propylaea for the foundation of a workshop, two blocks of a Pre-Mnesiklean cistern were found, that had been unnoticed before.[1]

Considerable parts of this cistern had been discovered in 1886 but, as the relevant documentation and publication had not been thorough, during the last few decades the very existence of the cistern was ignored or disputed. The rediscovery of the two blocks prompted a new examination of the vestiges in this area, which led to the following important conclusions.

Some of them concern the actual function of the cistern, which consisted of two rooms of unequal capacity. A conduit was cut in the rock in order to direct the rainwater on the surface of the Acropolis rock to the southeastern corner of the cistern. A wall of reused *poros* blocks, built along the eastern wall of the cistern, formed an inside continuation of the conduit, which led the rainwater to the northern area of the cistern's eastern room; in this area the living rock had been dressed in order to increase the depth of the cistern. The purpose of the inner conduit was to conduct dirty water to the northern lower parts of the eastern chamber of the cistern, which served as a settling tank; this procedure would force the particles of dirt to the bottom of the deeper northern side, while at the upper levels the water would be cleaner. When water reached a certain height, it would flow over the top of the dividing wall and into the western chamber of the cistern. It would then trickle down the western surface of the dividing wall and fill a trench that was carved along the latter. The dirt particles still contained in that water settled in the trench, and ran its length down to its northern end. The sediment gathered at this corner in the form of mud; in order to clean the chamber after the cistern was empty of water, one had to conduct the mud through a hole at the northern end of the dividing wall and into the northwestern corner of the eastern chamber; then, through a hole at the lowest part of the northern wall of this chamber, the mud of both

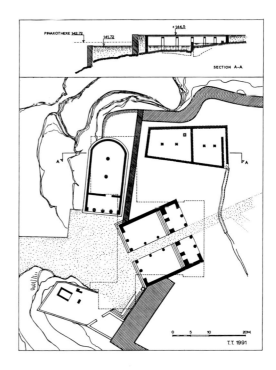

Restoration of the entrance of the Acropolis before 480 BC. The section above shows the relation between the level above the cistern and the level in the terrace occupied by Building B, which made the intermediary retaining wall necessary. The plan, below, of the whole, shows the relationship between the Old Propylon, Athena Nike temple's predecessor, Building B and the Pre-Mnesiklean cistern; OPPOSITE, FROM ABOVE L TO R: North wing of the Propylaea, restoration of the surviving blocks of thee upper courses of the east wall; cross section of restored ceiling and roof against the west surface of the east wall; north wing of the Propylaea, restoration of the cornice fragments; north wing of the Propylaea, restored plan of the ceiling and roof; scale model of restored roofs and ceilings of the north wing of the Propylaea. View from the southwest and view from the west; restored details of the roof and ceilings of the northern wing, section looking north, with the characteristic marble roof tiles; the huge marble tile that covered the area between the central building and the southern wing; axonometric of the same marble tile

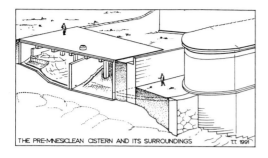

THE PRE-MNESICLEAN CISTERN AND ITS SURROUNDINGS   T.T. 1991

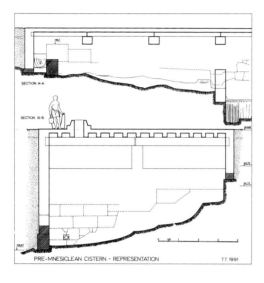

SECTION A-A

SECTION B-B

PRE-MNESICLEAN CISTERN - REPRESENTATION   T.T. 1991

FROM ABOVE: Restoration of the Pre-Mnesiklean cistern and its surroundings before 480 BC, bird's-eye view from the northwest. The northern wall of the cistern has been removed, while the retaining wall and the Mycenaean wall further to the west appear in cross section. The broken lines, below, signify the upper outline of the rock at the bottom of the Mycenaean northern Acropolis wall. To the west, Building B and above it the northeastern corner of the Old Propylon; restored sections of the Pre-Mnesiklean cistern

compartments could be conducted northwards, outside the cistern. This whole operation was designed to ensure healthy drinking water for the Acropolis.

Another group of important conclusions concern the relations of the cistern with the other buildings around the Pre-Pericleian entrance to the Acropolis. The cistern was covered with a horizontal wooden structure, which formed the ground inside the western end of the northern Acropolis wall at about the same level with the present stylobate of the eastern portico of the central building of the Propylaea. The direction of the southern wall of the cistern indicated by the two newly discovered blocks make clear that the Pre-Mnesiklean terrace (the lowest courses of which are incorporated in the foundation of the northern wing's western wall), the so-called (after Wiegand) Building B which was standing on this terrace, the Pre-Mnesiklean rock-cut conduit which conducted the water to the cistern, the Old Propylon and one of the predecessors of the Athena Nike temple belonged to the same building project for the entrance to the Acropolis. This project dates from the period between 510 and 480 BC.[2]

The preparations for the installation of the work site for the Propylaea project brought to light more elements which, until now, had escaped scientific observation. Their study led to the important conclusion that the foundations of the Northwestern Building, the foundations of the eastern wall of the Pinakotheke and those of the eastern wall of the northeastern wing of the Propylaea, the Mnesiklean drain channel, and the Acropolis wall to the north of these structures were constructed in the same period of building activity, which must be 437-432 BC, while the Mnesiklean Propylaea were being built. The Northwestern Building must have started being built with the intention of including a portico along its southern front, but soon Mnesikles added the existing courses of the foundation of the northeastern wall of the Propylaea, thus curtailing the original plan. It seems that building activity in this area stopped rather abruptly, and that the substructure for the Northwestern Building never attained the anticipated levels. On the incomplete substructure a new superstructure was installed, obviously not as originally planned. On the top of the wall bordering the building to the north, the superstructure of the northern Acropolis wall was extended, employing a masonry of the sort used for the latest part of the northern Acropolis wall. The irregular courses of the substructures and the *toichobate* of the superstructure must have been buried in the ground, which would have been level with their upper surfaces, and the built superstructure of the Northwestern Building must have enclosed no roofed spaces but a single open-air court. This superstructure was extended only to a part of the area which was intended for the portico. On the *toichobate* of the northeastern wall of the Propylaea a sort of wall was built, corresponding to the western side of the portico area. The *stylobate* or *toichobate* of the southern side and of the southeastern corner of the Northwestern Building were never built. The area intended for the portico was levelled with earth and the same was done in the area between the southern side of the Northwestern Building and the northern side of the eastern portico.

The area in front of the southern wall of the court – to which the Northwestern Building was finally reduced – was given a water outlet by cutting a new drain in the natural rock, leading the rainwater from the pre-Mnesiklean rock-cut drain to the Mnesiklean drain channel, the northern end of which still survives inside the northern Acropolis wall.

The Mnesiklean Propylaea

The study of the architectural members of the superstructure of the lateral wings of the Propylaea led to a detailed reconstruction of the wooden ceilings and roofs which rested on them. The ceiling of the Pinakotheke had a total of nine horizontal wooden beams (0.44 metres high and 9.44 metres long). The proportions of the beams and the spaces between them were almost identical to the ones of the marble ceiling of the eastern portico of the Propylaea. The gaps between the beams were covered with a wooden coffered structure. The ceiling of the portico consisted of eighteen beams. The narrow slots between the beams of the portico were probably covered with wooden planks. We now know that the roof of the southern wing of the Propylaea was similar to the roof of the portico of the northern wing. The roof of the northern wing abutted the eastern wall of the wing, and sloped to the east, west and north; the ridge beams had considerable dimensions: the top one was 0.87 metres wide and 0.46 metres high, while the two diagonal ones were 0.84 metres by 0.44 metres. The weight of the marble tiles, the ridge-beams and the rafters must have been partly supported by means of the horizontal ceiling beams and vertical posts.

These are but a few important observations concerning structural details and techniques used on the Mnesiklean building. Because of their specific character, it is almost impossible to go into any further depth in the space of this essay.

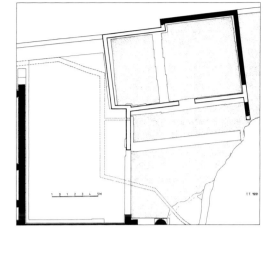

Notes

1   For a detailed study on this discovery, see: Tasos Tanoulas, *The Pre-Mnesiklean cistern on the Athenian Acropolis*, Mitteilungen des Deutschen Archaeologischen Instituts. Athenische Abteilung, 107, 1992, pp129.

2   For a detailed publication of these discoveries see: Tasos Tanoulas, *Structural relations between the Propylaea and the NW Building of the Athenian Acropolis*, Mitteilungen des Deutschen Archaeologischen Instituts. Athenische Abteilung, 107, 1992, pp199.

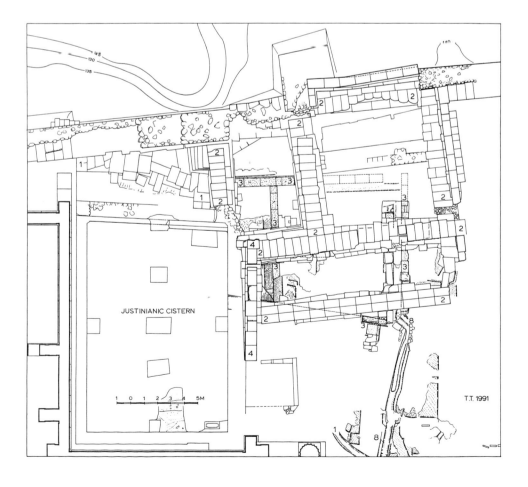

JUSTINIANIC CISTERN

FROM ABOVE: Conjectural plan of the area to the northeast of the Propylaea after the end of the Mnesiklean building activity in 432 BC. Solid black: surviving parts of classical superstructure. Dot-and-dash line: surviving parts of classical drains; plan of the area to the northeast of the Propylaea

The Parthenon as viewed from the Propylaea

THE INTERNATIONAL DEBATE
THE CURRENT INTERVENTIONS
Viewpoints and Opinions

Peter Calligas
Ephor of Antiquities; Director of the Acropolis Ephorate, Greek Ministry of Culture

There can be no question that it is a historical moment for the Acropolis monuments. Those of us who have visited the ancient site have seen the condition of many of the unrestored parts of the buildings, and will appreciate the urgency of the situation. The restoration of the monuments is directly related to the increasingly dismal atmospheric conditions in Athens and the many flawed interventions of the recent past. A solution to the problems that have accrued is necessary, indeed it is a duty.

To do nothing is not an alternative. Until the recent interventions the Pericleian monuments were in a state that may be characterised as accidental, as they had been reduced to ruins and endangered by a series of accidental mishaps and miscalculations. We must therefore proceed bravely in our efforts to restitute the structures. The existence of a new body of identified ancient material is not something anyone can ignore.

We must move ahead even more efficiently in our research and restorative actions, including conservation and the protection of the buildings against the destructive effects of the present environment. We must also ensure the existence and activity of the Committee for the Conservation of the Acropolis Monuments for a long time to come. Without our generation's active concern for the Acropolis we place the very fundaments of our civilisation at risk.

(Excerpt from the Proceedings of the Third International Meeting for the Conservation of the Acropolis Monuments, Athens 1989)

Charalambos Bouras
President, Committee for the Conservation of the Acropolis Monuments

No one can underestimate the value of dialogue for a subject as important as that of the interventions which are now being carried out on the Acropolis Monuments, and most significantly on the Parthenon. Those of us who have been dealing directly with the problems of the ancient buildings know that there have already been prolonged discussions both inside the Committee for the Conservation of the Acropolis Monuments (CCAM) and outside it; the debate has been certainly time consuming but not always useful or beneficial. There is a lively concern from good-intentioned people (including members of the press) with programmed interventions in general, but at the same time complete apathy regarding the indecision that has marred the progress of interventions, many of which finally never occur, and by extension for the slow but certain wear and denigration of our architectural heritage.

The dialogue that has been conducted through the press has not proven to be particularly helped by the media, because the need to inform and concoct sensational news regarding well known matters (among which the Acropolis of Athens figures prominently) leads to hurried judgements and invariably to the adoption of impressive but unrealistic views, as was, for example, the idea of creating a glass dome above the entire Acropolis in order to protect the monuments from atmospheric pollution. A constructive dialogue needs, I think, a minimum of theoretical and specialist knowledge, good faith, and an appreciation of the importance of the time that is lost through cancellations and false problematics – time that works against the necessity and urgency of effecting the interventions. Contrarily, in the Committee the antithesis of viewpoints has almost always been helpful.

In issue 21, 1990, of the yearly periodical *Art and Design in Greece* (which is published in Athens), one may find the opinions of four or five specialists who apply a severe critique on the works currently under way on the Acropolis and more generally on the philosophy of the CCAM. On the basis of these published views I express the following thoughts.

Firstly concerning the critique of the methods in use: it is claimed that the international conferences that the CCAM has organised (there have been four until now and more are planned) have been useless, given that views of numerous eminent foreign restorers or conservators have not been heeded. The matter has two sides, the typical and the objective. Greek law requires that decisions for the restoration of architectural monuments are taken by the Minister of Culture, to whom the responsible committees and other collective bodies express an opinion in each case. Objectively speaking the participants in international conferences do not constitute a specific decision-making entity – their constitution is entirely incidental. Despite this, international conferences are very useful as they allow the CCAM on the one hand to listen to the opinions of a host of people with different specialities and significant experience, and on the other hand to inform the general opinion of the specialists involved in the works in progress and related studies. The views of the foreign participants and conservators can be said often to be heeded, as they undoubtedly influence the Greek side.

The declared intention of the CCAM to increase the didactic character of the ruins through restoration work (involving the reincorporation in the ancient monuments of the fallen architectural elements) was confronted cautiously, if not in a downright hostile manner. It has been said that models, drawings, and films can provide the same didactic content and that the current restorations are a form of banal populism which destroys the 'beauty of comprehension' sought by sensitive visitors. For the rest of the visitors the results are the same, whether the buildings are restored or not; for the average person is deemed unable to comprehend, one way or the other, the significance of ancient art.

The issue connects directly to the social role of architectural monuments and to other serious contemporary problems, such as the educational potential inherent in touristic activity and the wider initiation of the general public in Classical humanist education and ancient Greek cultural values. Unfortunately we lack figures from social studies and polls which might throw some light on these issues. It is paramount, however, to stir greater interest in the Acropolis monuments and to increase the numbers of people immediately conscious of their artistic, primary values. The ongoing restoration work is on the verge of spanning the great divide between the specialist's appreciation and that of the general public, and stands, in fact, at the antipodes of populism (which normally seeks to flatter the uneducated) because of its educational intent. Models, drawings, or films cannot recreate the direct experience of the space, nor of the perfection of the details contained in the architectural work, namely the structure itself.

Accusations have been laid as well against certain scholars involved in the interventions on the Acropolis, that they are motivated and led astray by their personal scientific interests and make proposals which are aimed at projecting the results of their research at the expense of a logical series of priorities. A personal 'stamp' branded onto any restorative intervention would be unacceptable to anyone with an interest in and appreciation of the monuments, but the accusation holds no water: true, there are many new insights regarding the Parthenon and the other Acropolis monuments, but these are confined to details and are separate to the programmes in motion on the Acropolis.

There is a continual criticism regarding the quality of the cast copies which have taken the place of original sculptures on the Acropolis, particularly at the Erechtheion. It is true that there was little experience in producing high-quality copies in Greece when the CCAM interventions commenced on the Acropolis. The copies that were produced were meant to be exposed to the elements and to the negative levels of atmospheric pollution in Athens and not in closed spaces, something which precluded from the beginning the use of most contemporary materials. At any rate, the means by which the Caryatid copies were incorporated or fixed to the Erechtheion allows for their easy replacement, if this is deemed necessary, by better copies.

It is also said that the principle of reversibility has only a theoretical value and cannot be applied fully, given that any two fragments of marble are normally joined with the help of titanium rods, the cuttings for which are effected on the ancient marble members in an irreversible manner. Indeed, cuttings of all shapes and sizes that are effected on the original material during their conservation are irreversible. However these are never carved through to the visible surfaces of the blocks; they are always effected on fractured surfaces. In any case the systematic study of this matter has led to the reduction, where possible, of the titanium rod diameters (including the width of the respective cuttings that are effected), as well as to the reuse, as much as possible, of cuttings that had been made during older interventions, especially those of Balanos. Thus there is no damage to the appearance of the rejoined architectural members; new cuts are limited to the inside mass of each piece of marble, and in this sense the intervention may be regarded as reversible.

Finally, the manner in which the CCAM has worked until now has favoured dialogue and precluded the enforcement of personal views during the decision-making process. In the internal functions of the Committee, dialogue has indeed been very useful and ultimately constructive.

Demetris Fatouros
Greek Minister of Education

The Acropolis in Athens is a rich spatial complex with various types of enclosure, all of which served strong ritual purposes. The experience of moving up to and through the ancient *temenos* was one of a continuous interplay between temples, courtyards, narrow passages, open spaces, smaller shrines, and a myriad of votive offerings. To a significant degree this experience remains unchanged. Even the Parthenon, by far the largest building on the Acropolis, was meant to be perceived as a part of a larger delicately co-ordinated urban whole.

Within this whole, the numerous enclosures and courtyards subdivide the plateau and continually restructure the visual and perceptual axes. A complicated hierarchy of larger and smaller architectural manifestations, whether solid or void, is established by the temples and their constituent parts, and the walled sanctuaries, traces of which surround them. The rigorous, resolute character of each building is offset by the overall spatial complexity of the site, inciting an exploratory mood in the visitor, who is called to commence a journey of discovery that leads not only to architectural certainties but to cultural revelations through the art and symbols that are an integral part of every structure.

In ancient times the brilliant colours from the polychromatic schemes of the buildings combined with the sculpture and precious metals to further enrich the experience of movement through the sacred grounds. The constantly changing quality of sunlight and the processional torches and sacrificial fires that we know accompanied the rituals added yet another element. This now-lost reality is essential in understanding the Pericleian monuments, and more generally Classical architecture.

There is no question in my mind as to the significance and quality of the current works of restoration that are being carried out on the Acropolis by the Committee for the Conservation of the Acropolis Monuments. My concern is that the complexity of the ancient Athenian *temenos* remains part of the experience of each visitor. We ought to avoid reinforcing the misconception of Greek Classical architecture as one concerned primarily with rigid symmetries and stiff axiality in which formal references and styles are all-important. Through selective restoration of secondary edifices like the sanctuary of Artemis Brauroneia, the Pandroseion, or Arrephoreion, we may help to re-establish a level of complexity that better approximates the original urban

character of the Acropolis. Thus restoration will not emphasise the late Classical and eclectic interpretations of the Acropolis, that prevail among certain scholarly circles today.

One reason I feel the extensive restorations by the CCAM are significant is that by coming closer, through the reincorporation of fallen material, to the original appearance of the monuments, we are less at risk of enduring fanciful or arbitrary interpretations.

I shall end by recommending that large models of the Acropolis be installed on site for the benefit of the visitor, who must at all costs be adequately instructed about the complexity of the experience that the monuments once helped to create.

Manolis Korres
Architect, Co-ordinator of the Parthenon Restoration Work.

Thanks to the groundbreaking work of J Ruskin and A Riegl and to various new contributions in the field of architectural history it is well understood today that the overall value of a work of architecture, and more particularly a monument, consists of the sum of different, specific values. Among these the most significant are the sacred nature of the structure, its material value, its usage value, artistic value, historical value, value as a memorial, and architectural rarity. It is obvious that monuments differ substantially among themselves not only as concerns the magnitude of their total value, but also as concerns the percentage by which the specific values participate in their overall value. Very often certain of these specific values are entirely absent in a monument. Some monuments lack a sacred character, others a historical value, yet others lack the uniqueness that gives great buildings their cultural weight. It is easy to see that the Theseion temple in Athens has a lesser artistic value than the temple of Apollo Epicurus at Bassae, but has greater historical value and significance as a monument. The temple of Apollo is characterised by a typological (plan) and stylistic (use of Ionic and Corinthian orders on the interior) inventiveness and, consequently, uniqueness. Its short history, however, was interrupted in the Roman period and was revived only as a consequence of certain events during the last two centuries. The so-called Theseion remained in use as a church during the early Christian and Middle Byzantine periods. Its columns bear medieval inscriptions, and numerous important Athenians and foreigners were buried under its floor slabs between the Byzantine period and the nineteenth century. But even as concerns the value of their respective historical phases, monuments differ substantially. At the Theseion the form assumed by the Byzantine building was far less important architecturally than the form of the ancient structure. On the contrary the basilica of Santa Maria degli Angeli in Rome, designed by Michelangelo as a transformation of the ruinous tepidarium of the Baths of Diocletian, is far more significant than the Roman structure on which it is founded.

It would be wrong to rebuild part of a defensive structure that has been destroyed by bombardment and siege operations, no matter how limited the intervention might be. In doing so we would be removing all indications that this building lived out its historical purpose, and with them all those things that most stir out emotions when visiting a military monument. It would be best if we left it in its most current state, as Ruskin and his followers would have wished.

At the Parthenon, on the other hand, despite the intense presence of historical significance and the highly moving reminders of wars and barbarism that are etched into the building's surfaces, the predominant value is the *aesthetic* one. As such, the benefits acquired from the restoration of the form of any semi-destroyed column weighs heavier than the loss such an action would inflict on the historical value of a ruinous structure. In reality this loss is not even a full loss, as the new elements and infill material are always perceived as such and therefore do not impede the careful observer from discerning the extent of the previous destruction. Despite the fact that they are comprised chiefly of the authentic ancient drums, the eight restored columns (1923-30) of the north side of the Parthenon are obviously different from the surviving ones because of the damages they sustained during their collapse in historical times. Only a completely indifferent visitor will not perceive that these eight columns have been repositioned after a destructive fall. Consequently this side of the building, restored a full sixty years ago, does not weaken the historical value of the monument. The ruinous state of the temple that came from the explosion of 1687, which of course is not as evident as before 1930, nevertheless coexists with the restored building, the restoration itself constituting a historical event which ought to be counted as a significant part of the recent history of the temple. If the proposed repositioning of the original fallen material back onto the structure is approved (Pronaos and side walls), the degree of its self-protection shall increase and the ruin itself shall augment in size by about nine per cent without altering its perimeter and without a serious reduction in the effect of its originality, as the visible new material behind the peristyle will not be more than two per cent. The various spaces between walls and columns will regain something of their original relationship.

As concerns the proven scientific correctness of the proposed repositioning of the authentic marble members in their original places, it should be said that never before has such an undertaking been realised on a building as large as the Parthenon. The precision which guaranteed the situating of every stone in the exact location where it had stood until its collapse resulted in yet another gain, which proves wrong those who believe dogmatically in the (elsewhere true) argument that the restoration of the Parthenon will destroy important historical evidence. Ten years ago the vague conception of history that was held by certain theorists contained no more than an image which was recognisable only to their own and their fathers' generations. This celebrated 'historic image' incorporated little of the Roman Parthenon and practically nothing of the Christian Parthenon. Thanks to the exhaustive study of all the material remains of this most important structure, these traces have now been rediscovered; large sections of the Roman east entrance, characteristic elements of the Early Christian apse and Baptistery, the Middle Byzantine apse, all of the Christian *ambon* and many other ancient and later elements from the historical phases of the monument are now ready to be repositioned.

Finally, if despite all that and for whatever legitimate reasons it becomes necessary in the future to undo any part of the current restorations, the CCAM has ensured that this be possible through the principle of reversibility that was first stipulated by Professor Charalambos Bouras in 1962 and subsequently introduced into the Committee's programmes. Detailed drawings at 1:10 scale chart every new addition, metal tie and hidden titanium rod, and provisions have been made to permit the future removal of these elements. After the above discussion my position can be summarised as follows: the various arguments in favour or against the completion of ruined architectural monuments are relative and in any case useful and applicable depending on the specific case under consideration. What matters more, however, is the strict scientific archaeological/architectural/technical documentation and daily presence of specialists whose interests and abilities are not limited to immaterial, evolving philosophical and theoretical questions, but are applied much more towards the solution of organisational, mechanical, technical, historical, archaeological, artistic, geological, economic and other tangible problems. This pragmatic disposition, which is apparent in the descriptive chapters that chronicle the new interventions, is dictated by the actual working conditions. After all the purpose of the interventions is the securing and preservation of the physical state of the monuments.

Unfortunately the outlook regarding the problem of atmospheric pollution in Athens remains rather bleak, having improved only fractionally recently; the optimism that accompanies the actions of the Committee relates only to matters of structural conservation and formal restitution of the ancient buildings (which is the domain of architects and civil engineers) and not preservation of marble surfaces. For the moment, then, the only radical measures that can be taken against the effects of atmospheric corrosion is the selective removal of sculptures and their placement in the protected environment of the museum. I think, however, that a number of fine architectural members ought to be included in the same programme, together with their replacement with marble copies (which in the case of simple Doric elements are far more appropriate than cast replicas).

Tasos Tanoulas
Architect, Co-ordinator of the Propylaea Restoration Work

According to *The Concise Oxford Dictionary*, 1982, to restore means: '1 Give back, make restitution of. 2 . . . bring back to original state by rebuilding, repairing, repainting, emending, etc, . . . ; make representation of supposed original state of (extinct animal, ruin, etc). 3 Reinstate, bring back to dignity or right; bring back to or to health etc, cure (person). 4 Re-establish, renew, bring back into use. 5 Reinsert by conjecture (missing words in text, parts of extinct animal, etc). 6 Replace, put back, bring to former place or condition.'

Applied to a monument, each of the above six definitions of the same verb defines a wholly different sense, a different essence and an individual *raison d'être* for the act of restoring a monument. In every case the meaning has positive connotations. Numbers two, four, five and six concern technical aspects of restoration, the manner in which it can be achieved. Numbers one and three elucidate the social-moral aspects of conservation. The social-moral implications of restoration are inevitable, as buildings always carry the ideological weight of the periods which produced them.

For the verb *reconstruct* the number of definitions is very restricted, and their sense is always very concrete: 'build again; restore (past event) mentally; reorganise'. These definitions make it obvious that reconstruction is a term with a mainly technical meaning that describes one of several ways to practice conservation.

But restoration must also be defined in relation to other terms introduced in our days, which correspond to different ways of intervening on historic buildings. The actual choice of intervention is always one laden with ideology, even when those who have selected it claim that it has been arrived at by the specific needs of the monument itself: understanding these needs is, *a priori*, the application of a pre-existing ideology.

Where ideology gets involved, things inevitably become relative and dependent on the corresponding historic environment. Therefore, before starting a debate about restoration vs reconstruction, we need to define the historic environment of our days and the ideology it generates. Bearing in mind the current dramatic upheavals in the political and economic scene around the globe (and the length allowed to this paper) it would be better to confine ourselves to the field of contemporary architectural currents and the conception of our built environment in a wider sense.

Modernism continues to exert influence through the rearrangement of the triadic hierarchy Function-Structure-Form, the elements of which in the last decades have been altering positions of priority in a bid for attention according to the specific branch of the movement employing them, eg Neo-Rationalism, Functionalism, High-Tech, Post-Modernism, Deconstructivism. Each of these movements is supported by a theoretical background which does not fail to refer, even if obtusely, to the architecture of the past and which, inevitably, influences the way we think of an architectural monument today.

Modernism rejected direct inspiration from monuments, considering them merely under the scope of form and structure; in the field of restoration, the tendency to stress these elements led to partial reconstruction (in Greece see Balanos' and Orlandos-Stikas' restorations). Some of Modernism's *epigoni* (particularly Neo-Rationalism and Post-Modernism, which have had a great and most immediate impact on the taste of the general public) initiated an interlocution with the architecture of the past and, very often, combined monumental forms that were openly influenced by examples of historic architecture with modern materials, modern technological icons and contemporary morphology. This led to the consideration of historic monuments as raw material which could be used as components of architectural compositions, that were otherwise 'contemporary' (see the Cortile di Simeone del Pollaiolo in Palazzo Strozzi, the Louvre Pyramid, the Musée d'Orsay; also, the often suggested idea of a glass or Plexiglas roof in the Pinakotheke of the Propylaea). Neo-Rationalism, Post-Modernism and more recently, New Classicism, tend to encourage the identification of extant historic monuments with their original complete shape, favouring their total restoration, in other words reconstruction (an example of this tendency can be found in the interest of the general public and elements of the press in wholesale reconstruction of the Acropolis monuments); another related conception is that of didactic

FROM ABOVE: The western access to the Acropolis from the southwest; the Parthenon from below the Acropolis rock

reconstruction: parts of the monument are reconstructed so that characteristic elements of its original architectural form or of its structural phases are discernible by an informed eye.

Deconstructivism, which is the most recent modernist tendency, has not developed a consciousness that is able to engage a meaningful debate about restoration vs reconstruction. In considering the philosophical background of Deconstructivism, I cannot avoid thinking: in an age which goes as far as proposing deconstruction, what *could* we think about reconstruction?

In the beginning of this discussion we saw that although the attitudes towards restoration involve social-moral considerations, reconstruction refers primarily to practical features. After the Second World War, theoretical approaches to the monuments showed increasing attention to the problems of preservation: restoration was now considered to be a possibility after an extremely careful and specialised procedure. This was the result of the changes in the natural and built environment due to industrial development, the disasters of the war and vehement building activity; all this caused the scientific world to realise how quickly valuable monuments of the past can be seriously or fatally damaged. The new approach was epitomised in the Charter of Venice, which went a step further than the Charter of Athens in appreciating the social-moral values relating to monuments.

Today we are in danger of leaving this consciousness behind, many priceless monuments of the past already having been sacrificed in the name of 'development'; the care shown for some of the better known monuments seems almost an alibi for crimes done to other historical treasures. Under the pressures of a public taste informed by a new sensitivity, as well as political and financial pressures, reconstruction stands today as the token of ultimate care, under our present circumstances, for a monument.

The observations expressed above, though in a rather sketchy manner, lead me to the next point, which is that while most monuments were meant to last forever, our interventions today are inevitably influenced by temporal factors. A monument links us not only with the past but also with the future; for while we are informed by the past, the future depends on us. We must be extremely careful, when dealing with monuments, to respect both their physical and spiritual substance (by the latter I mean their aesthetic, social, moral and informative values). Preservation of a monument is our duty. Restoration is preferable. Reconstruction is a possibility; sometimes it can be objectively identified with restoration, but there is always great danger that it will be only the projection of the subjective vision of an individual, or of a specific age. The kind of intervention one ultimately selects is the result of a procedure special to each monument, not only demanding deep knowledge of all the facts concerning its structure and history, but also loaded with moral implications; one has to go further and develop a deep consciousness of oneself and of the influences one is subject to, a deep consciousness of the *data* and the *desiderata*, and a moral strength to make a decision as objectively as possible, for the benefit of the monument, and of humanity.

Alexander Papanikolaou
Architect, Co-ordinator of the Erechtheion Restoration work

After the completion of the CCAM restoration works on the Erechtheion, a group of experts wrote a number of critical commentaries on the aesthetic quality of the results. Their critique centred around several points: the restoration of the missing corners of the exterior stones; the discrepancy between the appearance of the interior surface of the ancient burned stones and the new stones; the quantity of the new material which joins the two long walls of the cella; and, finally, the addition of the replica of the northeast column and a section of the entablature, the originals of which can today be found in the British Museum.

It is worth noting that the criticisms come from those who, throughout the restoration project, participated and still participate in the decision making. They therefore were aware from the beginning of all the formal decisions and judged (and continue to judge) the final result as if they had no idea of what was going to happen. Yet they had the opportunity to intervene before and even during the execution of work, in order to prevent the 'failure' of the final result. From this viewpoint, their criticisms seem to be a critique for critique's

sake, perhaps as a means of excusing themselves from the fact that they did not actually comprehend the analytical description initially outlined in the realisation of the study.

Their critique is twofold. First, it is concerned with the comparison of the older restoration with the present one – with the critics evidently preferring the previous restoration; secondly, it is concerned with the distortion of the original image of the monument itself as a result of the addition of new Pentelic marble.

The previous restoration by Balanos is regarded by the critics as satisfactory because it diminished the opposition between the old and the new. Thus the aesthetic result of this particular restoration was more in keeping with the structure, precisely because it corresponded with the ruined, fragmented nature of the monument. I would agree that this is partly true – it arose by making use of the ancient material as a *set piece*, independently of what had been its intended use (north and south walls). In other parts of the monument however, such as the north portico and the west wall, the restored parts and the additions to them presented, at the beginning of the century, the same colour contrasts between new and the old, and the same discrepancies between stones which had aged naturally and stones which had been added recently, as can also be seen today in the new restoration of the Erechtheion.

The eventual blending of old and new in the Balanos restoration itself was a result of the corrosion and ageing of the surface of the new additions. Critics of today's restoration do not take into account the fact that a colour homogenisation had already occurred on the older interventions.

In response to the second aspect of the critique, it could be argued that if one wanted to be absolutely strict in respect of the original state of the monument, then the Erechtheion should never have been restored since the formerly scattered material did not allow for an accurate vertical repositioning unless adjoining material were added in between the newly placed pieces. Therefore the monument should have remained in the state it was immediately after the 1821 Revolution. However, no one dared to propose this in relation to the Erechtheion, and the reason behind this can probably be found in the *set-like* restoration made at the beginning of the twentieth century, and the concomitant visual representations which seemed to have satisfied the tastes of the experts.

If one accepts the necessity for restoration in the light of the large amount of dispersed material, then there are only two ways in which to proceed. The first is the accumulative and arbitrary Balanos restoration, which, if resumed, would be a very easy and practical solution, and in which case it would be unlikely that anyone would come forward with criticisms since the existing state of the monument would provide a perfect alibi. The second and more difficult procedure would be to reposition the various parts of the Erechtheion according to a specific original scheme, as the CCAM has done. The solution which was actually taken up was considered to be an extreme kind of restoration. However, it did establish a more honest approach to the monument and to the originality of its parts as compared with the previous restoration by Balanos.

Since it is impossible to develop the whole of the argument in such a short passage, let us, then, limit ourselves to one aspect of it, one that poses a dimension to the problem which has not yet been addressed. The notion of beauty had a particular significance in ancient times. Pausanias refers to the temple of Epicurus Apollo as being a building '[that] could be granted the first place amongst all temples because of the beauty of its marble and the harmonic articulation of the whole synthesis' (VIII 41 8).

In ancient Greek music, the word harmony meant the synthesis (concordance) of musical notes; and in architecture (structure), it meant the correct adaptation or the perfect articulation of the parts of a building.

The Erechtheion today accommodates a correct order in its remaining parts, as these had been positioned in ancient times and not as they had previously been restored. From this viewpoint, then, the monument has a 'harmony' according to the ancient Greek conception and terminology.

However, at the same time, due to the inevitable addition of new material, a visual 'disharmony' has also been effected, between the naturally aged original material and that which has been artificially added.

Therefore perhaps we can now understand the contradiction that occurs today between the sense of beauty based on perception and that of an imaginative and intuitive appreciation leading to a more profound sense of beauty permitted in the recent past in the Erechtheion and more generally on the Acropolis in Athens.

Evi Touloupa
Former Director of the Acropolis Ephorate.

In questions of restoration all viewpoints today appear to be acceptable, depending on the group focusing on the subject. To a degree these questions are really matters of taste; some people prefer to look at 'intact' ruins and others would rather see them restored in varying degrees. The debates that have been generated by these questions are indeed very interesting, and criticism, particularly when it is scathing, is generally well received. Things are different, however, for those who bear the actual responsibility for the conservation of the monuments, especially when they have been commissioned by the State to protect the ancient structures.

I have the good fortune to have been Director of the Acropolis Ephorate for eight consecutive years and great luck in having had excellent collaborators; archaeologists, architects, engineers, conservators and technicians. I shared responsibility for the conservation of the monuments with the scientists who constituted the Committee for the Conservation of the Acropolis Monuments and who had previously organised work carefully and systematically. The committees of the CCAM convened as a rule on a weekly basis, the discussions lasting many hours and often ending up in disagreement. I believe that all of us benefited from the different viewpoints that were expressed; we learned at least to be sceptical and cautious before taking any decision.

In the beginning even those who had been left with the impression that work would be limited to conservation (ie the dismantling of those parts on the monuments that had been restored in older interventions and developed the known problems of oxidation in the exposed iron connectors, the replacement of the metal ties with titanium, the joining of broken members and the repositioning of these elements on the buildings) had no objections to the reincorporation of ancient fragments or members that had been found lying about on the site or in the storage rooms. The disagreements began when the use of new marble became necessary to help fit the ancient stones in place. The chief bone of contention, therefore, is the percentage of new marble required for the reincorporation of the ancient material. The difference in chromatic tones that resulted from the use of fresh marble only inflamed the protests. Another serious disagreement emerged when it was recommended that the remaining sculpted metopes and frieze of the Parthenon be removed to the Museum and replaced with copies.

Let us examine each one of those points around which so many seemingly endless discussions were held and repeated every so often, resulting either in delays in the progress of operations or the circumventing of decisions. Initially all parties had accepted that new marble would have to be used, as they had agreed that those parts of the buildings that had been completed in concrete by the chief pre-war restorer Balanos would have to be replaced in marble. Thus the 7.5 by 7.5 marble member that has already been transported to the Acropolis from the quarries of Dionysos will replace the concrete lintel of the western door of the Parthenon. Another example: the cornice of the northeast side of the Parthenon which had been completed in 1930 in marble and was now found to have been ruptured by the oxidised iron clamps used in the earlier interventions, was agreed to be replaced in new marble. The dimensions of this block are 2.5 by one metre. Yet there were serious objections to the replacement of one of the guttae from the regula of the first architrave block on the north side with a piece of marble just twenty centimetres in length. This little piece was intended to hide the connecting tie that would secure the adjacent architrave block. Even though it was not vital to the structural integrity of the architectural member, this infill piece nevertheless would have provided the reading of solidity and security demanded by the monument's aesthetic. What harmonious balance was achieved at the Erechtheion with the reconstruction of the northeast column and corner portion of the entablature from copies of the originals now in the British Museum!

And how many petty comments were aired about this new little intervention, and only from a handful of people!

If it may be permitted of me in this context I shall express my view here on a rather controversial subject, as I happened to be absent and it was not recorded when discussed by the CCAM. It regards the much-debated and till now undecided restoration of the Parthenon Pronaos. I believe that the restoration must proceed in stages and am certain that all concerned parties shall be convinced that the third or even fourth alternative solution put forward by the scholar in charge of works on the building is the proper one. Why should I be disturbed by the completion of the columns in new marble, when I thus gain the ability to perceive their continuity up to the original capitals and their entablature which currently remain on the ground and continue to deteriorate? Why shouldn't a beam that fell and broke into five pieces not be joined into one piece again and repositioned on the building? Is it not unreasonable to leave so much ancient material unused when it can give us a more complete impression of the monument? Despite the numerous proposed additions, the Parthenon shall not lose its character as a ruin.

Archaeologists regularly reassemble the fragments of vases and complete the vessels' shapes in plaster. Completing a ruined statue is far more risky, and yet we dare to add plaster if by doing so we might reposition the severed head or the limbs on the torso and thereby allow the sculpture to stand intact. In architecture restoration is even more necessary, as the large dimensions involved do not allow us to appreciate the mass or volume of the structure unless its primary vertical and horizontal readings are reinstated. What would our appreciation of the Treasury of the Athenians at Delphi or the temple of Athena Nike be if these had not been restored earlier in this century? Certainly the use of new material ought to be restricted, but what some people consider to be restricted others claim is exaggerated.

It has been said occasionally and has finally been agreed by practically all those concerned with the new Acropolis interventions, that the monuments must not lose the form they have assumed over the last forty years. What a narrow-minded opinion! We forget that we are discussing monuments that have already been restored, in some places successfully and in others with technical and aesthetic faults. And yet objections have been raised even as concerns the amendment or reversal of those faults, whether it involves the repositioning of one stone member in its correct place, as at the Erechtheion, or the dismantling of the prosthetic works that were effected at the Propylaea with the cutting and levelling of ancient architectural members. According to this attitude we accept the Balanos restoration as far as it was executed, while we reject the planned intervention which may today be carried out under the direct supervision and control of a multi-disciplinary scientific committee consisting of mature scholars and marble craftsmen whose skills have reached a level of technical perfection.

The objections to the addition of new marble were expressed primarily after the restoration of the south wall of the Erechtheion, when the chromatic difference between the old and new marble was finally apparent. This came about after the decision to move the older infill pieces used by Balanos on the south wall back to their original ancient positions on the north wall. Those who disagree with the results of the new intervention would have preferred either not to do anything at all at the Erechtheion, or to remove the Balanos material and leave the long south wall full of gaps (veritable 'lacunae'), or to complete the wall in pink marble (even that was proposed). If the whiteness of the new marble pieces is so bothersome, what could be simpler than applying a patina on their surfaces to make them correspond more closely to the hues of the older building members? In any case time has already softened the chromatic difference. And why should the proposed new columns not stand out and thereby allow the visitor to witness the liveliness of marble as opposed to the concrete replacement that was incorporated at the Erechtheion? Is not the clear differentiation between originals and copies one of the principles stipulated in the Charter of Venice?

However bitterly, we all accepted the removal of the architectural sculpture from the Acropolis temples. We were convinced, however, some sooner than others, that there was no other solution if we were to save what remained of the Classical sculpture from the effects of the elements. If only that had been done with the west frieze of the Parthenon at the beginning of the century, when the matter was first discussed! Only those who have seen the sculpture, now that we can, at last, closely examine the damage and wear that this masterpiece by Phidias has suffered (it has recently been placed in a special hall of the Museum), can appreciate just how disastrous the indecision and delays in proceeding with the protective measures were. All the proposals to protect the sculpture *in situ* proved unrealistic, unless we wished to transform the Parthenon into a kind of banal, high-tech laboratory and hide the sculpture indefinitely behind thick glass.

When it was decided to replace the Parthenon frieze with a copy, new warnings were sounded and accusations of 'dismemberment' and 'falsification' were put forward. What is strange is that when this happened with the Erechtheion Caryatids and the Kekrops complex from the west pediment of the Parthenon, nothing similar took place. The criticism was aired without serious counterproposals for what might replace the originals. Perhaps 'antiquated' marble copies treated to match the ancient stones' ruinous condition? Smooth, unsculpted slabs which would give the building a false appearance? Or perhaps nothing at all, leaving gaps at the temple's most harmonic and complex architectural junction? The chosen solution of using fine, cast concrete copies with the right constitution and the appropriate chromatic tones is certainly the best, and despite some criticism regarding the quality of the copies, it is now apparent that following many experiments a significant improvement in the technique of producing the copies was achieved; naturally it is important to continually co-operate with foreign experts in order to achieve the best in this area.

The philosophical considerations regarding the problems of conservation and restoration are useful, but naturally will never cease. Specialists and lay people like to discuss and write about and repeat the same things over and over again. Someone must act in the end, however. Restorers must by all means consider opposing views, explore them, put them to the test, and finally decide on the relevant course of action after detailing why they chose this and not the other solution to a particular problem. And they must proceed with the execution of the measures before it is much too late.

Fani Mallouchou-Tufano
Archaeologist, Historian

The restoration of the Acropolis monuments has long been a subject of intense discussion, disagreement and problem-casting. The latter, which has centred chiefly around the Parthenon because of its particular ideological connotations, actually concerns the restoration of any ancient Greek monument, Classical or other. In each case it reflects the most current ideological and aesthetic preferences of the age as well as the specific level of scientific knowledge concerning ancient Greek architecture.

The 'Question of the Parthenon Restoration' first appeared in the nineteenth century, at the same time as the first works of conservation on the monument. These works, which were to a large degree improvised, empirical and incidental, focused the criticism of the first European 'scientists' who had started in this period to research the Acropolis monuments. At the same time they were scrutinised by the first 'tourists' who began to visit Greece, who often were left with negative impressions. Most of these early visitors were British, and they brought with them aestheticist and spiritualist attitudes which urged them to view ruinous antique structures romantically, finding value primarily in their picturesque nature and harmony with their natural surroundings, rather than in their potential as restored monuments with restituted original forms and unity of parts. At the start of the twentieth century, on the occasion of the First International Archaeological Congress in Athens in 1905, a question was raised regarding the nature and the limits of the restoration of ancient monuments and particularly the Parthenon. To this question the European scholarly world, especially the French, answered by passionately condemning as unholy any thought of restoring the monument. The reasons put

forward were the need for respecting this most celebrated ancient ruin, the presumed contemporary inability to fully comprehend the thinking and vision of the ancient builders, and consequently the inability to match, through modern techniques, the constructional perfection achieved by the ancient Greeks. By condemning the real possibility of restoring the Parthenon the entire field of restoration in nineteenth century Europe was condemned, together with the wholistic stylistic restoration of its own monuments. The 'Question' flared up for a third time in 1922, on the eve of the programmed restoration of the north Parthenon peristyle colonnade. This time the critique was concentrated around the criteria and the intent behind the planned restoration, the aesthetic results, and most importantly the scientific accuracy, method of intervening, and the available techniques and materials – a sign of the new demands of the more scientifically-oriented age and the maturing that had occurred in connection with questions of principle behind interventions on monuments. The need to prepare careful studies prior to interventions and the establishment of a multi-disciplinary scientific board of supervision in each case was stressed for the first time. The various desiderata relating to restorations were established gradually in the international charters that focused on the restoration of monuments, first in Athens (1931) and later in Venice (1964).

In these days there is a revived international interest in the works of conservation, restoration, and, more generally, restitution that have been in progress on the Acropolis since 1975. These are without question interventions which take into consideration the messages and perceptions of our own times; they are based on the established principles of restoration set out by the Charter of Venice, but are enriched with complementary provisions and stipulations that have emerged out of the specific nature of ancient Greek monuments. The restorative part of the works responds to the new social demands of a more immediate appreciation and enjoyment of the monuments and their surroundings, as well as the growth of mass tourism and global mobility. As regards the scientific side of the works, it should be said that this not only seeks to amend older flawed interventions but promotes the research and studies that are being carried out prior and during the restorations. These have resulted in a wealth of new information and knowledge about the ancient world and its achievements.

Finally, the certainty that has built up around even the smallest intervention due to the exhaustive surveys and records that are produced by the CCAM, together with the knowledge that at any time it will be possible to a large degree to undo the current works, all this covers the psychological repercussions of actual responsibility for monuments of such importance.

The ongoing restorations on the Acropolis have already been nationally and internationally recognised and lauded. Indeed, certain entirely original aspects of the works, as is the use of titanium for the joining of broken building fragments or the support of parts of the monuments, have begun to be applied internationally in similar interventions. However the 'Question of the Restoration of the Acropolis Monuments' continues to exist and nag the scientific world. Aesthetic concerns have been expressed regarding the percentage of new marble infill pieces, their chromatic contrast and visual imbalance. The 'Question' now assumes the form of philosophical discussions around the results of the removal of architectural sculpture from the buildings or, contrarily, the repositioning of cast copies of elements that for a long time have been absent in museums around the world. It is also expressed as concern for the effect of the new restorations on the internationally established image of the monuments as ruins – even if this has largely been artificial and accidental. This objection sometimes gives the impression of having emerged from the depths of the past, but it is in any case part of the fluid, contentious, antithetical age we live in.

The 'Question of the Restoration of the Acropolis Monuments' essentially represents the continuing interest in the ideas and values which these unique monuments represent. Let us, then, hope that it shall continue to enrich the scholarly world into the next century.

View of the Parthenon Pronaos from inside the cella

COMMITTEE FOR THE CONSERVATION OF THE ACROPOLIS MONUMENTS

QUESTIONNAIRE TO THE PARTICIPANTS OF THE THIRD INTERNATIONAL MEETING FOR THE CONSERVATION OF THE ACROPOLIS MONUMENTS (ATHENS 1989)

In March 1989, on the occasion of the Third International Meeting for the Conservation of the Acropolis Monuments, the CCAM distributed a series of proposals for the restoration of the Parthenon Pronaos, the methods of structural reconstruction of the temple and its architectural members, the preservation and restoration of the marble surfaces of the building, and outlined the programmes for the restoration of the Parthenon cella walls, and the ceilings of the Propylaea and the temple of Athena Nike. Conference participants were asked to respond to a total of four Pronaos proposals, indicating their areas of agreement and disagreement in each case. The contents of the questionnaire are reproduced below and are followed by selected responses by internationally known and respected scholars, architects, and archaeologists.

The Committee for the Conservation of the Acropolis Monuments invites specialists and scholars from all over the world to participate in a fruitful dialogue on the current Anastylosis (Restoration) project and to contribute their views and opinions on the various proposals presented to it. These views shall be taken into consideration by the authorised bodies prior to arriving at their final decisions; these bodies being the Committee for the Conservation of the Acropolis Monuments and the Central Archaeological Council. However the said Committee must stress that members of this Meeting cannot share responsibility for any decision the Committee may arrive at concerning the Anastylosis proposals. With the above in mind, the Committee has deemed it preferable that those specialists and scholars who have been invited to express their views should do so individually by submitting written answers to specific questions which appear below. The Committee will later submit its own conclusions to the Central Archaeological Council which constitutes the legally competent body in this instance.

1)   Four alternative projects for the restoration of the six-columned portico of the Parthenon Pronaos (east side) are hereby presented in summary form (see illustrations). A fifth alternative proposal would be the absence of any intervention.

   Please formulate your opinions on the proposal which you consider has the most to offer, noting possible advantages and, conversely, whatever disadvantages it may have. It would also be appreciated if you could express your views as to the fate of the scattered ancient material belonging to the Pronaos in the event that it is not re-incorporated into the Parthenon.

2)   Two alternative projects for the restoration of the south side of the Parthenon Pronaos have been formulated in summary form (see illustrations). To these a third alternative proposal would be the absence of any intervention. As with the previous question, we request that you outline your opinion on the proposal you feel to be the most appropriate.

3)   Two alternative projects for the restoration of the Parthenon east wall (between the Pronaos and the Naos proper) have been drawn up in summary form (see illustrations). Again, a third proposal would be the absence of any intervention. Please outline your opinion on the proposal you feel to be the most appropriate.

4)   On pages 131-150 of the CCAM Study Document the proposals for the methods of structural reconstruction of the Parthenon and its architectural members are presented. We request that you express your views on these proposals.

5)   On pages 151-187 of the CCAM Study Document proposals are laid out for a 'Pilot Programme' aiming at the preservation and restoration of the marble surfaces of the Parthenon. Please outline your opinion regarding this proposal.

6)   Concerning the programmes for the two long sides of the cella of the Parthenon, the coffered ceiling of the Propylaea and the small temple of Athena Nike, please indicate whether you agree with their being dismantled with view to carefully studying the constituent members, systematically preserving them, and ultimately reassembling them in improved condition.

   The answers that follow were first published in the Proceedings of the Third International Meeting on the Restoration of the Acropolis Monuments (Athens 1990).

Brian F Cook
Former Keeper of Greek and Roman Antiquities, British Museum
Ian D Jenkins
Department of Greek and Roman Antiquities, British Museum

The ultimate responsibility of our generation is to hand on to future generations the artistic and archaeological heritage of the past, if possible in better state and certainly not in a worse state than we received it from our predecessors. In considering the proposed anastylosis of part of the Parthenon, priority must be given to the consolidation of the monument and the conservation of individual members: nothing must be done that would endanger either of these fundamental purposes. It is clear from the admirable exposition by Manolis Korres that these factors have been fully taken into account throughout.

To restore the Parthenon to the state it was in at any particular period in the past is not only impossible but unnecessary and undesirable. The Parthenon has seen many changes of form in its long history, and further changes are

The Parthenon as seen from the Propylaea

unavoidable, if only because earthquakes and other natural causes will destroy the building if we neglect its care. The immediate question is whether to leave the Parthenon as a picturesque ruin, appealing to a romantic but outmoded taste, to be interpreted as a monument only by the

expert, whether archaeologist or architect, or rather to attempt to present it as an intelligible structure for the millions of ordinary people, Hellenes and philhellenes, who are drawn to visit it each year. Some degree of anastylosis is therefore essential.

If the Parthenon is to remain a picturesque ruin, then the fifth option must be adopted: no restoration at all. If some restoration is to be undertaken, the first option (minimum anastylosis) might satisfy the purists and the romantics, but it will do little for the ordinary visitor. If an attempt is to be made to revitalise the building for the people, rather more anastylosis must be undertaken.

The second option (full restoration only of the south side) seems to lack courage and conviction. It will satisfy no one. The third option (completion to architrave level) has the merit of presenting a balanced appearance, at least in the drawing of the elevation. Since a large part of the original architrave is available it makes sense to continue the restoration at least to this level. At this point it is essential to consider whether the incorporation of new material is justified, and whether enough of the original members survive to maintain the integrity of the building as an ancient monument rather than a modern pastiche. There is a certain danger that the quantity of new marble required for the anastylosis of the columns on the north side might seem to overwhelm the original blocks in the eyes of an observer on the ground. This danger would be particularly acute if the restored blocks remain in the stark white of newly quarried marble.

This introduces the question of the surface treatment of the marble restorations. Recent investigations into the extant surface coatings of the Parthenon and its sculptures show that the temple was, at various times in its history, treated to a protective wash, which both tinted the marble and protected its surface. Indeed the original surface only survives where this coating has protected it from the weather. A similar tinted wash, applied to the new marble after anastylosis, would enhance the appearance of the building while being consistent both with authenticity and the demands of conservation.

Restoration above architrave level requires particularly careful consideration, especially as it involves the use of casts of the frieze. It is necessary to try to anticipate the likely reactions of influential but uninformed people (journalists, politicians, etc) and if possible to forestall them. The great virtue of placing casts of the frieze at the original height is that it enables the visitor to see the sculpture at the height and angle at which it was seen in antiquity, and indeed as it was originally designed to be seen. From time to time

criticisms continue to appear in the press about the height at which the original sculptures are exhibited in museums (both the British Museum and the Acropolis Museum). Such criticism could be more easily refuted if a substantial length of the frieze were available in the original position in the form of casts, which experience with the west pediment has shown to be indistinguishable from originals at this height. Casts here would balance those in the west frieze when the originals are removed, as is desirable, to the safety of the museum environment.

The best solution to the problem of how to care for the scattered blocks is to incorporate them into the anastylosis. In this way they will not only be protected from further deterioration of the ends and upper and lower beds, but will also be displayed for all visitors in an intelligible context. If they are not so re-used they will need to be protected from the elements and to be accessible to specialist archaeologists and architects. Since it is inconceivable that the general public would have any interest in an exhibition of isolated blocks, the concept of a special 'museum' is nonsensical. Removal of the blocks from the Acropolis is probably unacceptable and there is evidently no available space for their storage within the existing Acropolis Museum. A low, open-sided shelter on the south side of the Parthenon, on the site of the present temporary structure, would be practical but unsightly. An ideal solution would be excavation of that area to provide a subterranean extension to the existing store rooms of the Acropolis Museum, but this would be very expensive.

The treatment of the south face of the Parthenon depends on the same principles as those for the east face. To disregard this opportunity for discreet anastylosis based on the detailed examination of the surviving blocks recently undertaken by Manolis Korres is to condemn the Parthenon to remain as a picturesque ruin. The first option (anastylosis to architrave level) presents a minimum requirement. The second option (anastylosis to the level of the beams) should be undertaken if the east face is restored above architrave level, but not otherwise.

The east wall, being solid, seems in general to require a different approach

The north peristyle colonnade of the Parthenon

to anastylosis from that appropriate to columns, which are separated from one another by spaces. In this particular instance the case for more rather than less anastylosis seems weaker than in the case of the columns of the portico, which are needed to support the restored architrave. The

benefit of showing more of the original doorway hardly seems to outweigh the disadvantage of using a smaller proportion of original blocks in option two. Partial anastylosis of the Christian apse is desirable to illustrate a long and important phase in the history of the building.

The methods of structural reconstruction must be consistent with the overall technical aims of the proposed anastylosis: protection of individual blocks from further damage and stability of the structure as a whole. To determine whether the particular proposals are likely to achieve those aims requires expertise in architectural construction and engineering that we cannot pretend to possess. We do, however, have great confidence in the ability of Professor Bouras and the Committee for the Conservation of the Acropolis Monuments (CCAM) both to assess the problems and to evaluate the advice of the appropriate technical experts.

The future treatment of the surface of the marble calls not only for consideration of the technical aspects of treatment but also for a detailed study of former treatments. Evidence exists for the application of protective coatings in the past. Provided that any proposed future coating meets the appropriate technical standards, the archaeological precedent for such a coating should override any mistaken objections on merely aesthetic grounds. At the same time, before any new coating is applied, it is essential to conduct a full survey of all traces of ancient polychromy, including where necessary the removal of samples for analysis and microscopic examination.

It seems desirable that all blocks that have been replaced on the long sides of the Parthenon cella from time to time should again be removed with a view to study, conservation, and, if possible, reassembly.

Regarding the coffers of the Propylaea and the temple of Athena Nike: in principle it seems best to dismantle all previous restorations for conservation purposes (including the removal of old iron dowels) and for study with a view to reassembly. The sculptured friezes of the temple of Athena Nike should be removed to the protective environment of the museum and replaced with casts.

William D E Coulson

Director, American School of Classical Studies, Athens.

Regarding the east side of the Parthenon Pronaos: as Director of the American School of Classical Studies at Athens, I am influenced by the philosophy of complete restoration, as has been done with the Stoa of Attalos in the Athenian Agora. Accordingly, of the four plans proposed I prefer plan

four which proposes complete anastylosis up to the wall crown and the beams and includes cast reproductions of the frieze. Plan four has the advantage of providing the most complete picture of how the Parthenon looked throughout its long life in antiquity; more importantly, it restores

Parthenon triglyph and metopes

to its original position the frieze which is arguably the most significant part of the Pronaos. Without the frieze, the symbolism of the east side of the Parthenon is lost.

Plan two has little advantage to it. There is little advantage to restoring completely the south half of the Pronaos and not the north half (if one half, why not the other also?). Likewise, plan three has little advantage to it, since it omits the frieze. The two most serious proposals, therefore, are plan one and plan four; the difference between the two is really a difference in the philosophy of restoration. To recapitulate, plan four provides the most complete picture of the Pronaos of the Parthenon in antiquity and as such is to be preferred.

In the event that the scattered ancient material of the Pronaos not be reincorporated into the Parthenon, it should be collected, catalogued, drawn/photographed, and stored in a nearby *apotheke* or storage space, but not out in the open where it is subject to deterioration by acid rain.

Regarding the south face of the Parthenon: in accordance with my philosophy of complete restoration, I prefer anastylosis up to the wall beams. In fact, if complete anastylosis up to the wall crown and beams is performed on the east side, then it follows that for aesthetic reasons and for the reasons expressed above, similar restoration must be done on the south face of the temple. For both the east side and south face, the architect has proposed a very sensible scheme of incorporating the ancient material where possible and supplementing it with newly cut blocks where necessary. He has managed a restoration whereby the ancient blocks do not have to carry much weight, thus avoiding the imminent danger of collapse.

Regarding the east wall: in the final analysis and despite the problems the architect outlines, the more complete proposal is preferable since it is in keeping with the aesthetics of restoration that I have outlined.

As concerns the structural reconstruction: the overriding concern here should be the stabilising of the building against further damage, especially seismic activity. This writer is not an expert on the chemical properties of the materials proposed for use in the reconstruction of the building, but feels that concern should focus on the strength and durability of the materials, ie that they cause no damage to the ancient blocks and that they last for a significant period of time in the future.

Regarding the Pilot Program outlined in the CCAM's study: it seems to have been well conceived and formulated and, accordingly, should be started as soon as possible.

Concerning the two long sides of the cella of the Parthenon, the coffered ceiling of the Propylaea, and the Temple of Athena Nike I agree with the proposal that they be dismantled for careful study, preservation of the individual architectural members, and reassembled. This work, however, should be accomplished expeditiously in order to preserve the aesthetics of the Acropolis.

Karl Schefold

University of Basel, Switzerland.

I shall begin by saying that the CCAM restorations are in my opinion outstanding in every respect. The work of Manolis Korres on the Parthenon is of such quality and integrity as to deserve our encouragement; the scholarly world must facilitate by every means possible his plan to restore the east facade of the temple. The interventions are doubly beneficial as, through their proposal to reincorporate the scattered fragments that belong to the Parthenon they provide the best means of preserving the ancient material.

It would be desirable, for both aesthetic and iconographic reasons, to place weatherproof casts of the sculptures that are now housed in museums abroad in their original relationship to the buildings on the Acropolis. The didactic value of this kind of restoration is evident at the Sculpture Museum in Basel, where Ernst Berger brought together all the casts from the Parthenon frieze and metopes that were until recently displayed in the Basel Museum of Casts.

I would like to point out, as a means of illustrating the significance of the CCAM activities in related areas, the results of the collaboration between Manolis Korres and Professor Gottfried Gruben: together they were able to ascertain that elements of the Pre-Parthenon, which was burned by the Persians during their invasion, were reused in the construction of the Classical Parthenon. It was also shown that the temple with the gigantic pediment that was built by the Peisistratids replaced a much smaller temple dating from the seventh century BC – the so-called 'Ancient Temple', of which two bases and possibly an iron acroterion survive. Furthermore, the fragments from the colossal pediment showing Heracles battling the lioness and the bull were

proved to belong not the Pre-Parthenon, as had been assumed until recently, but to an even earlier building, the foundations of which E Buschor was the first to discover. This original Parthenon, judging from the style of the sculptures, dates from the time of the Athenian lawmaker Solon,

Model of the Archaic Acropolis

and not that of the Peisistratids.

The recent investigations that were initiated by the CCAM have shown that the original Parthenon must have been built to house the oldest Attic representation of an armed Athena (this assumption parallels Herbert Cahn's evidence that the oldest Attic coins portraying the helmeted head of Athena date back to Solon's currency reform of 594 BC). The significance of the era of Solon for the Acropolis is described in my book *Götter und Heldensagen der Griechen in der Früh-und Hocharchaischen Kunst (Geschichte der Griechischen Sagenbilder 1)*.

Our knowledge of this era and subsequent periods has been broadened significantly through the new research and interventions on the Acropolis, which is a reminder of the broader benefits of architectural restoration when it is effected with respect to the history and archaeological documentation of a site.

Homer A Thompson

Professor Emeritus, The Institute for Advanced Study, Princeton.

Having read the text of the CCAM's 'Study for the Restoration of the Parthenon, vol 2A', 1989 and having looked closely at the accompanying drawings (vol 2B) I favour anastylosis four for the east side of the Parthenon Pronaos, anastylosis two for the Parthenon south face, and anastylosis two for the Parthenon wall.

My opinion depends on the assumption that the materials and techniques which the CCAM is now employing will assure sufficient strength in both the horizontal and vertical planes of such elaborate restoration.

Permit me to say that in assessing the various aspects of the whole programme of anastylosis (restoration) I attach great importance to the desirability of making the ancient monument more readily intelligible not only to the scholar but also to the many thousands of non-scholarly but intelligent and interested visitors who see the Parthenon each year. In observing the reaction of visitors over the past thirty years to the restored Stoa of Attalos I have been much impressed by hearing innumerable expressions of gratitude for the fact that this great building has been made readily intelligible through a *complete* restoration in which the ancient evidence for all members is clearly visible.

I am also influenced by the practical consideration that much the best way of displaying and preserving the innumerable fragments that have now been

attributed to this part of the building is to incorporate them in the anastylosis.

Despite the aesthetic objections that may be raised to the inclusion of so much cast sculpture, I would favour the insertion of copies of the whole east frieze. This is the best possible way of relating this so very significant part of the frieze to the whole building, and of encouraging the visitor to compare the east frieze with the west frieze. Even if the original marbles should one day be returned to Greece they should undoubtedly be placed in the shelter of the new museum while the casts could remain indefinitely on the building.

The Stoa of Attalos

One of the very few criticisms I have heard of the work on the Erechtheion has to do with the unhappy colour contrast between the ancient and the new marble. The same problem will arise in still greater scale if the complete anastylosis of the Parthenon Pronaos is adopted. I am aware that the specialists are trying to devise some way of reducing the contrast in colour. If I may express a personal opinion I would resist the temptation to tint the new marble and would recommend patience. Once again I venture to refer to my own experience with the Stoa of Attalos. There nothing was done to change the tone of the modern marble. At first the striking contrast between old and new was admittedly painful. But after more than thirty years of exposure the contrast is much less marked; it is now just enough to enable one readily to distinguish the new from the old.

In closing I wish to express my warmest admiration for the work that the Committee has done to facilitate the study for the next, and perhaps most vital, stage of this great project.

George Dontas

President of the Greek Archaeological Society, Honorary General Ephor of Antiquities.

In reading the proposals for the interventions on the Acropolis following the work that was done a few years ago at the Erechtheion I must confess that the questions I had then have come back to me: what is the reason for these restorations? Is it only because there is an available amount of original material that lies scattered about the Acropolis plateau?

Let me explain by making the following supposition: assume, for argument's sake, that the British government decides to return the Parthenon ('Elgin') marbles. Would we, in this rather unlikely event, reposition them on the ancient temple? Proposal number four for the restoration of the Parthenon Pronaos foresees the positioning of copies of the Parthenon East Frieze (that is now in the British Museum) in its original location on the building, including extensive reconstructions. Would we dare to use the authentic material in place of the copies if it were in our hands? After the removal of the metopes from the East facade of the Parthenon at the insistence of the CCAM's

chemical engineers who warned about the dangers of a total deterioration of the marble surfaces if exposed to the high levels of atmospheric pollution in Athens, and following recommendations, for the same reasons, that the West Frieze be removed from the structure, I wonder if anyone would go as far as proposing the repositioning of the original Frieze over the Pronaos. Certainly not. We know all too well that should this happen, the sculptures would suffer the same fate as those that have remained on the building – they would be destroyed. The damage shall spread to all those parts of the monuments that are exposed, both sculptures and architectural members, despite the fact that this shall occur sooner for some and later for other elements (sculpture generally being more easily affected because of the delicacy of its surfaces); the only other scenario would be the sudden imposition of tough new measures to eliminate atmospheric pollution or the discovery of protective methods that have a lasting effect on the exposed sculptures and architectural elements. How, then, can we seek to reposition original architectural members on a building which is as seriously ill as the experts tell us it is and so long as no effective measures are being adopted by the government for the atmosphere, or, for that matter, for a fully convincing structural strengthening of the buildings? Perhaps the politics of 'removing to save' applies only for one part of these ancient structures which we deem so worthy of our rescue efforts; what, then, is the real criterion for this selective process, and what is the general syllogism that led to the decision to reposition original elements on the monuments?

An explanation is put forward regarding those ancient members that lie scattered around the monuments that they shall continue to be damaged by the elements unless they are repositioned on the buildings. This justification seems to me rather weak; for, though the State certainly has a duty to protect the fallen fragments, it cannot be argued that their repositioning on the buildings is the sole method by which to safeguard them. If anything, the simple erection of a roof or shelter above these fragments is guaranteed to be effective.

One of the main arguments that are advanced in favour of the new restorations is the enhancement of the 'didactic' nature of the monuments. This, too, seems to me to be a weak point to make – largely because in order to truly achieve this goal the structures would have to be fully reconstructed, whereas the proposed restorations fill only a small fraction of the gaps in our appreciation of the ancient buildings. I should point out that I was not initially against the repositioning of ancient material, but felt it should address two basic prerequisites: firstly that this material would be positively protected from corrosion and exposure to the elements.

The Erechtheion at sunrise

Secondly that the restored fragments would be those that preserve a continuity in the surviving walls of the buildings and would not require to be embedded in an extensive area of new marble merely to satisfy a desire to reincorporate whatever we can of the available material. A careful and very restrained use of new marble would have been a better approach, as the current restorations basically falsify the character of the monuments. The Parthenon did not need to be completed beyond the state it was in before the CCAM interventions in order to show its architectural value. As the smallest fragments from this masterpiece show, its value is above all immanent. Even if we were left with only one Parthenon column we would not have to restore a part or the entire peristyle in order to show the architectural value of the one member. In later ruins which need to reaffirm the relationship between their component parts and the overall architectural composition only a small amount of new material is allowed, but in Classical monuments and especially the Parthenon with its unrivalled aesthetic qualities the incorporation of extensive areas of new material only in order to reposition certain fallen pieces and thereby create the impression of an 'improved' structure is a violation of the value and honesty of the monument. Instead of imposing a 'didactic' experience on the visitor by intervening on the buildings themselves, the state ought more properly to do so in the halls of the museum through good models of the complex and the components of the buildings.

I would like on this occasion to bring your attention to something else: the CCAM is in danger of losing sight of its original stated intentions with the new restorations, intentions which are summarised in its very name. The chief concern of the Committee ought to have been the *conservation* and not the restoration of the Acropolis monuments – the protection of the ancient structures from the thousands of dangers of erosion and corrosion, particularly that of atmospheric pollution. This is being confronted, if I may say so, in a somewhat resigned manner by the CCAM, except as concerns certain elements that were already heavily affected. Now that the appearance of this most holy archaeological site has been so dramatically affected through the new additions and the enormous scaffolded enclosures that have isolated the buildings for decades, we must reappraise the entire position of the Committee regarding this attempt, to save the monuments before the interventions go to such extremes as to make any such revision impossible – though I fear we are already at that point.

These are, in a few words, the main objections I have to the restorations that are proceeding on the Acropolis. I have confined myself to the broader comments as I feel that so long as the CCAM continues to avoid addressing them there is no point, really, in getting involved with specific issues.

Olivier Picard
Director, French School of Athens.

I must commend the CCAM for the wonderfully successful conference it organised; it made a very strong impression on the French participants both as regards the quality of the research that has been done by the architects in charge and the precision and beauty of their survey and reconstruction drawings.

I have chosen not to provide a point-for-point response to the CCAM questionnaire as I do not wish to oppose those involved in the new efforts who position themselves according to the Latin maxim 'ne ultra crepidem, sutor'. But it does seem to me that certain reservations, indeed hostile reactions to the current restorations have not given sufficient attention to the special character of the Parthenon and the grand nature of Greek architecture in general. We are habituated today through attitudes in contemporary or modern art to expect a radical separation between architecture and sculpture, and our studies and manuals of archaeology perpetuate this division. This division was not at all natural to the Classical Greek spirit. Phidias, Scopas and the master craftsmen who produced the Siphnian treasury were artists who were well versed in the problems associated with carving in marble; as G Roux has noted, the Classical temple is in its entirety an *agalma* or sculptural offering to the particular god.

When Manolis Korres graphically reconstitutes the succession of column drums or restores the cella doorway, it is more a geometrical sculpture

A Caryatid's view of the Parthenon

than a work of architecture in the modern sense of the word that he is projecting. This position allows me to happily accept the restoration work he is proposing.

After all, if we were to rediscover a statue with a broken head, could we imagine a situation in which we did not allow ourselves to replace the broken part under the pretext that the two pieces were recovered separately or that the headless body or dismembered head create aesthetically moving impressions – or that a restoration of this sort is not permitted according to the Charter of Venice?

Jordan Dimacopoulos
Head of the Department of Restoration of the Greek Ministry of Culture.

I would like to begin with an enjoyable scene from Lucian's Symposium: Instead of embarking, after their dinners, on the expected interesting discourse, the wise participants exchanged heavy remarks and soon afterwards were involved in a tempestuous brawl. The reason for this passionate engagement with each other, in which guests went as far as hurling the remains of their dinners at each other, was the reading in public of a sophist's letter of disagreement. I hope, in recalling this passage, that no such situation shall repeat itself here with what I am about to say.

First of all I would like to examine the proposals by Manolis Korres for the Parthenon Pronaos. I am of the general opinion, as concerns the four options that he presented, and of which he himself prefers the fourth (which would involve the greatest degree of intervention on the ancient building), that he has surpassed all previous researchers in the detail, beauty, and exactness

Scaffolds on the Parthenon

of his survey drawings and graphic reconstructions. These constitute the unquestionably positive side of things.

The negative side, in my opinion, consists of the nature of the proposals for the Pronaos. Both Korres and those of us who give the green light to interventions must abide by even stricter principles and assume a rigorous ethical disposition without which we shall be treading on thin ice. It is also important, I think, to examine opposed points of view with greater attention. Otherwise one shall continue to focus chiefly on the purely technocratic, admirably designed forms and tectonic nature of the Acropolis monuments, which are, nevertheless, above all spiritual. As such they cannot be dealt with merely through scientific analysis. On the contrary, it is a matter of preserving that immeasurable, calculated enchantment that overpowers every educated, sensitive visitor on the Acropolis. Even today's Parthenon, that perfect embodiment of beauty, continues in its old age, as Plutarch had already remarked, to charm the beholder with a balance and harmony that radiate in truly Olympian serenity. It is this balance that is forcibly disturbed, in my view, by the proposals to maximise interventions in the eastern area of the temple.

I shall venture to say that the entire methodology applied by Korres reminds me of an admirably programmed computer. He has engaged himself in nothing less than a quest to solve a huge three-dimensional puzzle (as he himself likes to say) consisting of the scattered remains of the Parthenon which he proposes to reconstitute with an accuracy of a thousandth of a millimetre. His graphic restoration of the temple's inner porch alone has earned him justly deserved awards. Yet both he and those who support him in his course proceed, in my opinion, with sole compass the scientific familiarity with the construction of ancient Greek temples.

A restored Pronaos without at least one of the two antae and without the wall behind the porch is simply not comprehensible to the average visitor. Furthermore it will be difficult for the visitor to appreciate the ordering of the Pronaos when its wall is many times lower than the hexastyle and completely restored porch. Instead of the consistent datum of the originally darkly shaded wall against which these columns once stood, they will now be perceived against the bright sky which is their sole background. Despite the obvious similarities, this criticism is by no means equivalent to that of Orlandos in 1922, who argued against the restoration of the north peristyle colonnade by Balanos. In that case not only was there a substantial surviving part of the cella wall along the westernmost half of the colonnade, but the approaching visitor could only experience the peristyle in dense perspectival arrangement – rendering the absence of the cella wall unnoticeable until one had at least passed the highest point on the Panathenaic processional road. In the case of the Pronaos the visitor moves frontally towards this part of the Parthenon during the initial stages of his approach from the Propylaea; consequently he will be forced to see the restoration against the sky. And even if he were to move along the length of the building's north facade, he would be able to discern, between the intercolumniations of the northeast peristyle columns, the back side of a restored pronaos colonnade. Thus, except for a colonnade of which five out of six columns shall be almost entirely made of brilliant new marble, the visitor shall have to look upon a completely unconnected colonnade which has no physical or visual connection to the (absent) wall of the Pronaos, or, for that matter, to the respective northeast anta. The educated visitor, therefore, shall associate options three and four, should they be executed, with the form of a lateral building – perceptually experiencing the restored section of the building as part of a stoa colonnade rather than of a pronaos. The elevation in height of the surviving five columns may thus reduce rather than increase the 'legibility' and 'didactic' qualities of the Pronaos, which in any event cannot be equally restored perimetrically due to the absence and ruinous nature of fragments from its north wall and respective anta.

A second point regarding the restoration of the colonnade is the extent to which it shall re-create the original subtle visual games at this location in the building. These refinements, which have been interpreted since the time of Vitruvius, concern both the Pronaos and the Opisthodomos of the Parthenon: the hexastyle colonnade, though smaller both in height and in the width of the columns to the octastyle peristyle colonnades on the pedimented sides of the temple, appear equal in size to those of the peristyle. Vitruvius atributed the phenomenon to the dark interior of the Pronaos against which

Parthenon, northeast corner

the columns stood. Choisy, however, explained it as the result of a sophisticated use of perspectival corrections: a reduction, in other words, of the columns of the Pronaos in such a way as to produce the sensation of two equal colonnades. Whatever the case, the dark background that was provided by the Pronaos interior played an important role in this illusion. The question, then, is to what degree this will be appreciable in the newly restored Pronaos, given that the building here shall not have a roof or a wall between the open cella and the Pronaos. The restored colonnade shall almost certainly appear to be smaller than the peristyle colon-nade when it is viewed from between the latter's intercolumniations. The visitor who shall approach the Parthenon from the east will see the Pronaos columns against the bright sunlight which will further reduce the columns visually.

Furthermore it should be pointed out that the morning and afternoon sun will cast shadows from the Pronaos across the octastyle facade of the temple, something which has never occurred in the long life of the building. I leave it to the responsible authorities to judge whether or not the points I raise should be examined prior to the restoration work. If there are questions regarding what I am saying the restorers need only construct a rough full-size model of the mass of the proposed restored columns and entablature and to study the results *in situ*.

I would like to bring to your attention another very important point with aesthetic repercussions regarding the proposed restoration work. This concerns the proposals by Nicholas Toganides to restore the long north and south cella walls of the Parthenon by filling in the thousands of large and small gaps that dot the surfaces with bright new marble.

The five columns of the proposed Pronaos restoration shall have some areas of original aged material only in the lower parts of the shafts. Necessarily, the restorers shall have to secure the numerous surviving fragments of the building by surrounding them in new marble. But will this 'patchwork' not be visible between the columns of the temple? Can it be seriously claimed that no negative impressions will be created in the appearance of the building? Furthermore, how do these interventions contribute to the maintenance of the ruinous aspect of the ancient structure? If the restorations go as far as

completing the lateral walls of the temple up to the sixth stone course, there can be no doubt that the myriads of marble 'patches' shall be visible even from below the Acropolis in the city of Athens. One need only look at the effect that was produced on the north wall of the Erechtheion: the (bothersome, in my opinion) marble completions are discernible from as far as Athenas and Aeolou streets.

If we concentrate for a moment on the implications of the new restorations on the interior of the Parthenon, it is clear that the contrasts shall be even greater. The almost complete destruction of the interior surfaces of the temple during the traumatic explosion of 1687 is proposed by the restorers to be entirely made good again in new marble. Thus one shall have a building which on its exterior is composed of an endless patchwork of old and new fragments, while the interior surfaces are as new. This shall be the impression of the structure regardless of the height to which the restoration shall proceed.

It should be mentioned that despite the polluted atmosphere of modern

Athens, the brilliance of the new infill pieces shall nevertheless create intense contrasts with the aged marble surfaces of the temple. Time will of course soften the contrasts, but not before the passing of at least a few decades. Another way around the problem would be to apply a patina to the new marble pieces, something that has already been proposed by Manolis Korres and researched by the project's chemical engineer, Prof Skoulikides, in connection with the Erechtheion restoration. Objections have been raised here, however, by scholars who warn against a 'falsification' of the new material. There is a solution

New marble on the Erechtheion

which foresees the use of a new material which does not have the brilliance of fresh Pentelic marble, but is of a natural coloration closer to that of the aged ancient temple surfaces.

At this point I would like to bring to your attention the rather soft, inoffensive chromatic contrast between the ancient marble surfaces and the reinforced concrete completions effected by Balanos in the north colonnade. At any rate the point made here is essential to the appearance and appreciation of the Acropolis monuments and deserves, in my opinion, further attention.

On the whole I feel that the new proposals shall have negative consequences regarding the aesthetic balance of the ancient buildings as well as the perception of their authenticity. I must say that I do not find, at least in Greece and Italy, a similar precedent. Even the temple of Vesta in Rome, that product of the famed Italian *restauro archaeologico* of the mid-war period, was not a standing, surviving monument like the Parthenon. The only similarity in the two examples is the use of even the smallest fragments from the original material in order to effect a 'didactic' anasynthesis.

In the case of the Parthenon the 'falsification' of the material becomes a 'falsification' of history. What else can the careful preservation of the traces of the ancient fire of AD 267 and the partial removal of the effects of the explosion of 1687 mean? I believe that the intentions behind the current restorations spring from a deeper tendency to view the monument as if it were a machine of which many parts are missing, and fragments of others survive. The restoration team is busy replacing the former and completing the latter parts, so that the visitor may be able to witness a pristine mechanical object that is as intact as possible. But nothing could be more alien to the nature of the ancient temples than this attitude. The supposed goal of protecting the surviving fragments that were collected from around the ancient buildings is negated by positioning them on the buildings a mere few meters above ground in the same polluted atmosphere – they would be far more protected if they were kept in a covered area.

In my opinion the restoration work on the Parthenon ignores two essential points, namely the intent enshrined in the Charter of Venice, which seeks to protect the authenticity and historical value of ancient monuments. The CCAM should concentrate on purely conservationist matters on the Acropolis.

Antonino Di Vita
Director, Italian Archaeological School, Athens.

I have expressed my agreement – in general lines – with the current work of restoration and conservation that is being effected on the Acropolis in Athens in the announcement I made at the conference 'The Athenian Acropolis: Conservation and Restoration' that was held in Napoli on February 8th-9th, 1984.

Regarding the CCAM questionnaire, I provide answers which I personally feel are more acceptable to the general visitor, the researcher and conservationist, but bearing in mind that this new intervention represents a new historical phase in the Parthenon's history.

Regarding the restoration of the Pronaos Stoa: mindful of the assurances given by engineer C Zambas as concerns the structural integrity of the proposed restoration, the solution that I prefer is the one listed as number two, though the frieze that is shown must, so long as the problems of atmospheric

pollution persist in Athens, be a cast copy. This solution permits the predominance of unique elements that give the visitor the opportunity to appreciate the full succession of architectural and ornamental features. Furthermore this solution structurally reinforces the south corner of the building, which, together with the frieze above the opisthodomos, facilitates the reconstruction, in the visitor's mind, of the entire frieze that wrapped around the cella perimeter.

Regarding the restoration of the south side of the Parthenon Pronaos: here, too, I feel that the most acceptable solution is that

North corner of the Pronaos

listed as number two. The same comments apply as with the restoration of the Pronaos stoa.

As concerns the restoration of the east wall of the Parthenon: despite the concerns regarding what might be interpreted as a 'diachronic restoration' (as pointed out by Manolis Korres), I nevertheless lean again to solution two, which allows the ancient doorway and the spaces that were meant to be delineated by the east wall to read clearly.

As regards the other points in the CCAM questionnaire (four and five), as I am not a specialist I can only say that the method that was used in the various departments of research appear to me to be correct and appropriate to the specific situations. After carefully reading the pages referring to the 'Pilot Programme', I feel that a positive response to the deterioration of the surfaces on the ancient monuments would be to give them the 'skin' and 'covering' that were proposed by the conservators. But is there really the possibility and courage to effect this?

I feel that the unused material from the Pronaos can be satisfactorily preserved in a special storage area and made available to researchers and conservators. As concerns the proposal to dismantle, for the purposes of cleaning and strengthening, the long side walls of the Parthenon cella, the roof of the Propylaea and of the small temple of Nike, my opinion is that such an intervention can be considered only for serious conservation problems – otherwise I do not find it justifiable.

JJ Coulton
Reader in Classical Archaeology, University of Oxford.

Reconstruction is not normally an element of the conservation of a building, and in other cases I would tend to argue against it, because any major movement of blocks involves some risk of damage, because blocks left on the ground can not fall further, and because there are bound to be visual problems in incorporating new material beside old. Having seen the present state of the Parthenon marbles, however, and having studied the careful investigations of decay and corrosion, I am convinced (i) that corroding iron, both ancient and modern, must be removed from the building, and (ii) that the large number of blocks on the ground is suffering serious and rapid damage from atmospheric

pollution and tourism. To maintain the status quo is not therefore a viable option. Since ancient blocks replaced have fewer exposed surfaces, reconstruction offers a substantial reduction in certain damage which outweighs the possible risks. The alternative is to remove a large number of ancient blocks to storage areas off the Acropolis, where they will be of no value to the understanding or enjoyment of the site or building.

None of the proposed reconstructions will change the distant view of the Parthenon significantly, and from close up they will help appreciation of the original form of the building, which is the fundamental reason for its fame. The existing state of the building is largely fortuitous, and results from many past interventions, including a substantial lowering of the 'historic' (early nineteenth-century) ground level. Of the reconstructions proposed I prefer number four since it protects most, and at the same time shows most. Proposal three is the least satisfactory. The use of casts of sculpture removed to a museum is in principle acceptable to me, but the appearance of the replace-

ment east metope is not wholly satisfactory. It would in any case be desirable to arrange any casts so that they can be removed without disturbing the building, in case opinion turns decisively against them, or a more satisfactory material becomes available.

For the reasons given above, the more complete proposal for the south side of the Parthenon Pronaos is preferable. Aesthetically it presupposes a substantial reconstruction of the south long wall of the Parthenon, which I favour, for the same reasons of protection of ancient material.

Again for the same reasons, I prefer the

The Parthenon from the Propylaea

more extensive proposal for the Parthenon East Wall. This has the added advantage that it removes any risk of people climbing on the east wall if, after the reconstruction, the public is again allowed into the cella (this would be desirable if appropriate walkways could be prepared).

My answers to the CCAM's questionnaire points one to three above are given on the understanding, which appears to me justified, that the competent structural specialists see no significant predictable risks in the methods proposed. Damage to the Parthenon from any conceivable earthquake can not be excluded, whether before or after reconstruction. A structural system as close as possible to the original one seems safest, and the principle of designing the titanium clamps and dowels to yield before the marble breaks is an important one. Care must be taken in completing fragmentary blocks to ensure that the holes drilled for titanium rods do not coincide with and intensify a pre-existing weakness in the stone.

Regarding point five of the questionnaire: some sort of surface consolidation seems urgently necessary. The research on causes and mechanisms of corrosion is thorough, but no final cure has been attained. Limewater seems an excellent temporary measure, while research is still continuing. White Portland cement, although chemically satisfactory, has in the past shown excessive strength; it is not clear how far that is being systematically dealt with.

The present condition of the long walls of the Parthenon, the coffered ceilings of the Propylaea, and the temple of Athena Nike, justifies their dismantlement and the removal of corroding iron. Careful study and systematic preservation will obviously be appropriate, but the possibility of reassembly must depend on their condition, which in the case of the Propylaea ceilings looks questionable.

John McKesson Camp
American School of Classical Studies, Athens.

On the question of the restoration of the Parthenon Pronaos, I lack the technical knowledge to assess the desirability of replacing original pieces in their correct location within the building. I defer to the experts on what can be achieved and what is best for the preservation of the fragments themselves.

Storage on the ground in the vicinity seems to me a bad idea.

Leaving aside technical questions, I feel that no restoration makes sense unless it helps enlighten the thousands of daily visitors to the Acropolis. Their needs seem to me paramount and, as a general rule, they seem to enjoy and appreciate sensitive restoration. One architect has called for the opening of the interior of the Parthenon to visitors. If this cannot be accomplished then it seems to me no restoration is desirable or necessary. If the building is to be opened to the public – and I strongly believe it should be – then I favour restoration number four or, failing that, restoration number two, for they both would help the visitor picture the original appearance far more successfully than either number one or number three.

For the same reasons, then, it follows that I favour also the full restoration of the south side of the Parthenon, to go with either restoration number four or number two on the east.

I would also favour the more complete restorations for the Parthenon

The restored southeast corner of the Parthenon

east wall, especially those parts which show later phases. Again, I lack the technical skills to comment or even fully understand the problems of the restoration and preservation of marble surfaces, though the movement of moisture and salts through marble makes me uneasy about the application of any foreign material, particularly any which might act as a sealant.

In some respects I feel that the vast effort and expense represented by the Acropolis restoration projects are undermined by the fact that the symptoms and not the cause of the deterioration are being treated. Unless a serious long-term effort is made to cleanse the air over Athens it seems to me that the extraordinary dedication and expertise shown by those working on the Acropolis monuments will have been in vain.

In closing, let me express my admiration for the work already done by the Committee for the Restoration of the Acropolis Monuments. The Greek people and all of us who love the monuments of Greece are greatly in its debt.

Robert Chitham

Architect, Chapman Taylor Partners, London.

The extent, if any, to which anastylosis (restoration) should be undertaken depends on the purpose for which it is carried out. During the conference of March/April 1989 three principal motives for anastylosis were discussed:

a) The present vulnerability of the fallen and dispersed material.

b) The potential for increased understanding of the monument.

c) The enhancement of its aesthetic quality.

The first and second motives were not in my view convincingly argued. Protection of the fallen material could be provided by its systematic storage either on or off the site, in a manner which would make it available for recording and research over an indefinite period, a facility not afforded by its reintroduction into the monument. With regard to increased understanding in an objective sense the impressive depth and quality of the research presented to the conference demonstrated that the process of anastylosis would be incidental, indeed almost irrelevant to the knowledge and understanding already gained by the research team. Moreover, the reincorporation in the walls of material at present available for inspection would limit future re-evaluation that the discovery of any further information might make desirable.

It is when the prospect of enhancing the aesthetic quality of the monument is considered that a different picture emerges. The conference found the issue of aesthetic quality difficult to discuss in purely objective terms. Partly, this is because the questions of our intellectual understanding of the monument and its innate aesthetic quality are most difficult to differentiate; partly because of the sheer impossibility of setting a meaningful quantitative scale of aesthetic value.

What the conference demonstrated beyond all doubt, however, was its near unanimous belief that the incomparable nature of the Parthenon transcends such analytical considerations. This conviction, expressed in different ways by speaker after speaker, was only possible because of the confidence generated by the high quality of the research and drawings presented to the conference. Furthermore, even beyond the competence of the research material itself, the love of and identification with the monument demonstrated by the research team in the quality of their results proved a source of inspiration to which this response was an eloquent testimony.

If the principle of anastylosis is accepted on this basis, it seems to me to follow that it should be as extensive as is practicable within certain bounds. I believe that any work of reinstatement must be governed by the following principles:

a) Reinstatement must be limited to that for which there is an incontrovertible factual basis, and should not be attempted where speculation is involved as to the original form.

b) Since the Classical orders embody a logical assembly of elements, which is necessarily diminished when it is incomplete, there is a case for the reinstatement of coherent structures rather than simply the disconnected fragments of such structures.

c) As against this, it is essential to maintain a very clear dominance of original material over new material. The amount of new material which can be incorporated without impairing the aesthetic integrity of the monument must be severely curtailed and this places strict limits on the extent to which reinstatement can be undertaken.

d) The introduction of cast, as opposed to carved, material would strike an unacceptably discordant note, as is demonstrated by earlier projects, and anastylosis should stop short of the introduction of castings.

e) In view of the arbitrary or accidental nature of much of the previous history of the monument, its state at any given stage of its history is an imperfect guide to the degree of anastylosis which should be attempted.

The restored northeast corner of the Parthenon

Since there is some conflict between the above principles any solution will necessarily include an element of compromise. But taken together they seem to me to point to the following course of action in respect of the Parthenon Pronaos:

a) East side: anastylosis number two up to and including the architrave of the southern half, but excluding the cast reproduction of the frieze (anastylosis number three seems to involve the use of an undesirable amount of new material).

b) South face: anastylosis number one, up to the architrave.

c) Wall: anastylosis number one.

I consider that it is too early to judge soundly the proper extent of the rebuilding of the cella walls, but the constraints set out above should govern the consideration of this work also.

Finally, I should like to record the following additional observations:

Firstly, no satisfactory conclusion was reached by the conference with regard to the proper surface treatment of exposed new material. The requirement for it to be distinguishable so as not to threaten the authentic integrity of the original work runs counter to the desire for it to be so unobtrusive that it does not disturb the aesthetic coherence of the whole. Provided that new material is adequately marked by incised dating or similar means, and its location properly recorded, the overall visual appearance seems to me in this instance to be the more important consideration.

Secondly, research into methods of reducing the rate of decay of the monument as a result of pollution is the most urgent task in the foreseeable future, a higher priority should be given to it, and a higher proportion of resources devoted to it than to anastylosis.

Wolfram Hoepfner

Institute of Archaeology, Free University of Berlin.

Since their creation, the Classical buildings on the Acropolis have held a special significance. Repairs made in ancient times were of a correspondingly high standard. In modern times, also, the scientists, architects and archaeologists concerned with the excavation, restoration and presentation of the buildings have been aware, for the most part, of their special responsibility. Only now, however, is this responsibility shared by a commission, as it would have been in Classical times in Athens. We can only speculate on the nature of the original building commission's jurisdiction over the architects Mnesikles and Phidias, but we may assume that, like the present commission, it would have provided a forum for experts to discuss the problems fully and arrive at the best possible solutions.

The same approach is being used for the major restoration works in Pergamon, which are concerned with the partial reconstruction of the temple of Trajan. A commission composed exclusively of specialists meets annually to discuss all the important issues and to make decisions on the scope of the work to be carried out in the subsequent year.

At the beginning of the restoration works at the Trajaneum, the commission decided unanimously that the provisions of the Venice Charter for the Restoration of Historic Buildings should be applied in full, with – we are now forced to recognise – unfortunate results. Article 12 of the Charter states: 'Replacements of missing parts must integrate harmoniously with the whole, but at the same time must be distinguishable from the original so that the restoration does not falsify the artistic or historic evidence.' With this in mind, it was decided that all the replacement parts should be executed in artificial stone. This material not only proved to be considerably more expensive than marble, but was of unknown durability. The mistake was not repeated at the Acropolis in Athens. Charalambos Bouras' exemplary restoration of the Stoa in Brauron had shown the wisdom of carrying out all restorations in the same materials as the original, even if this meant that the replacement parts would

become indistinguishable from the old ones after a number of years. This procedure has evident aesthetic advantages: it also avoids the stresses and other internal pressures that arise when a different material is introduced into an existing structure. The structural engineers and chemists working on the Acropolis

Pergamon, Trajaneum with replacement parts in artificial stone

deserve the highest praise for having remained as faithful as possible to the materials and techniques of the ancient buildings.

Article 12 of the Charter of Venice was a reaction to the kind of wholesale restoration that was practised in the nineteenth century. The taste then, in that historicist era, was for a formal integrity, often achievable only through *analogy*. Today a different ground rule prevails: namely, that the restoration or replacement of old structures is possible only with an absolutely clear understanding of the condition of the original. Article 9 of the Charter of Venice states: 'Restoration must stop at the point where conjecture begins . . .'

Manolis Korres' conscientious preparations for the work on the Parthenon revealed, to everyone's surprise, that the building could be restored far more extensively than had been thought possible. Korres was effectively able to cancel out the effects of the explosion of 1687, uncovering a host of minute elements that would have allowed the reconstruction of every detail of the building, up to the roof. The building commission, however, decided not to make use of these scientific findings, wishing to preserve the 'ruined' character that the Parthenon has had for a number of centuries now. In my view, this decision is problematic. Surely Article 7 of the Charter of Venice – 'A monument is inseparable from the history to which it bears witness' – does not mean that we should preserve historic buildings complete with their hotchpotch of inconsequential additions (like the Wrangel Castle in

Berlin). The most important thing, for me, is to try to achieve the original condition of the work as it was conceived by the architect. Here, the building commission has deferred not to Phidias and Iktinos, but to the artillery men who created the ruin.

Article 8 of the Charter of Venice was intended to preserve the integrity of historic buildings. It states: 'Items of sculpture, painting or decoration which form an integral part of a monument may only be removed from it if this is the sole means of ensuring their preservation.' At the time it was written, pollution from cars was not yet a major problem. Today, however, this ruling seems ill conceived. It has also delayed desperately needed measures to protect the sculptures, friezes, mouldings and capitals of the Acropolis from the corroding sulphur and lead in the air. As long as acid rain continues its unbridled destruction of the thousands of works of art that stand in the open air, Article 8 *should* read: 'In the case of air pollution, theft or other threats, valuable integral parts of the building should be removed and preserved in

local museums. They can be replaced on the site with copies.'

Manolis Korres' exemplary documentation of the Acropolis buildings in the course of the recent restoration work has uncovered a wealth of scientific information that is of considerable importance to architectural historians.

Brauron, Shrine of Artemis with replacement parts in natural stone (as restored by C Bouras)

Seldom have restoration and research been so closely linked. Korres has discovered stairs and windows in the east wall of the Parthenon, which point to a close relationship between the carved images forming the metopes and the spacing of the columns. He has found new evidence of how the friezes were assembled and painted. His work has also resolved the debate about the dating of the buildings previously on the site. It is now clear that the forerunner of the Parthenon was begun after the Battle of Marathon. We await with great anticipation his findings concerning the Parthenon's 'grandfather' (to use WB Dinsmoor's phrase).

Judith Binder

American School of Classical Studies, Athens.

In answer to the first three questions, maximum anastylosis (restoration) is to be preferred for the six columns of the Parthenon Pronaos, for the south side of the Pronaos and for the east wall, because it is physically best for the building. A great deal has been heard about symbolic values, cultural heritage, aesthetic viewpoints; it tastes like cold coffee diluted for the fifteenth time and warmed over. As a simple practical-minded American, my interest is in saving what can be saved. From long experience working in American, German and Greek excavations I see that fragmentary material from the smallest bronze pin to the largest architectural complex has a better chance of survival if mended and restored. The more that is put together, the more stays together in better condition. It seems to be a law of physics that architectural fragments are subject to centrifugal forces operating to disperse them further and further away from their original sites. The further they go the more they are drained of meaning.

The Acropolis team did not devote all those years working to recover the stones, to determine their original positions, thereby gaining insights concerning the plan of the Parthenon and making discoveries about the architecture, in order to enrich the pages of books on the history of architecture. They did it for the Parthenon itself. Now that so many stones have been recovered, the best thanks one can give the gods for this undreamt of gift is to reincorporate the stones in the building. Using new material is not, as is often said, a matter of 'falsification' or somehow detracting from the original Parthenon, detracting from its 'authenticity' or from its aura. Nothing is falsified, neither the facts nor the impression on the eye of the beholder.

As for setting up the casts of the Parthenon frieze in place, it makes sense.

The overwhelming majority of visitors to the Acropolis will simply be grateful for the chance of seeing the frieze all together in place and the transparent centrality of the figures will come out in a way not now possible when looking at the scattered originals. Much of the original effect of the frieze will be regained and it is hard to see what loss is involved.

Rowland J Mainstone

Consultant (formerly UK Building Research Establishment; Visiting Professor, Bartlett School of Architecture, University College London; and Hoffman Wood Professor of Architecture, University of Leeds)

I consider that the graphic reconstruction of the Parthenon Pronaos and the further elucidation of its history now presented provide a sound basis for physical reconstruction on the lines proposed, and I am broadly in agreement with the views expressed on pp73-85 and 87-89 of the English version of Vol 2a of the Committee's 'Study for the Restoration of the Parthenon'. I think

that it would be wrong, now that the ground has been so well prepared, not to undertake a considerable measure of reconstruction to give back to the east end of the temple something of its original pre-eminence as well as preserving it for the future, and I see no funda-mental objection to limited

The Parthenon at dusk, as seen from the northwest

'diachronic' anastylosis or to replacing the 'symbol' partly created by Balanos with one that bears a closer resemblance to the original structure. Having also examined what has been done recently on the Acropolis, I am confident that the work is in good hands and that the detailed choices that must be made as it proceeds will be properly weighed, though I feel that it should be undertaken with an eye primarily on the long-term future, and am therefore less easy about the more tentative proposals for public access to the cella.

I warmly support the view that the 'articulated' structural system of closely fitting individual blocks of marble joined only by cramps and dowels is 'part and parcel of the essence and value of architecture' and that any static problems should be resolved without departing from this system, as is indeed desirable structurally also. I am further encouraged by the recogni-tion of the equal importance of line and surface and of the problems created by the substantial losses of outer surface suffered by many of the individual blocks of marble.

Since losses due to thermal fracture of blocks that are still *in situ* bear witness to important episodes in the history of the monument, I feel that attempts to make good these losses are undesirable. Likewise, where only parts of similarly fractured blocks survive as *disjecta membra*, it seems reasonable to complete them (as in the Erechtheion) with a rounded outer face continuous with the surviving fractured face. But where it is necessary to insert a completely new block, I think that it is better to dress this as it would have been before the fire rather than to represent hypothetically the losses that the original block would have suffered – ie that it is better, for instance, to replace lost column drums with new whole drums rather than with drums having simulated fire damage to their west sides.

My chief reservations are about the desirability of re-incorporating in their original places those *disjecta membra* that have lost a large proportion of their original faces or have suffered significant losses on these faces of a kind which they would not have suffered if they had remained *in situ*, and I do not consider that preservation of such elements is necessarily best ensured by their re-incorporation in the wall or column from which they came. To re-incorpo-rate all fragments runs the risk of giving the finished surface an excessively mottled appearance, far removed from any that it ever had previously. Since, also, their re-incorporation would hide from view and render inaccessible to future inspection valuable evidence of the original manner of placing and joining the blocks – evidence which also helped to establish their original locations and thereby served as one important basis for the reconstruction –

would it not be better to place these pieces in a museum or other protected store, and to cut and insert complete replicas of the original undamaged blocks in their places?

Regarding the proposals for the six-columned portico, I would support the larger scheme four, if a partial reconstruction of the northeast anta and adjacent part of the north cella wall were also decided upon, with the rider that where it is necessary to cut new column drums or to cut completion pieces for the west sides of partly preserved drums, no attempt should be made to simulate fire damage.

Without this further reconstruction at the north end, I think that this end would stand in visually disturbing and historically unjustified isolation if scheme four were adopted. Until a decision is reached on the anta and north wall, I therefore favour scheme two.

Regarding the proposals for the restoration of the south side of the Pronaos, I favour scheme two as being consistent with schemes two and four for the Portico, with the same proviso as above in relation to simulation of fire damage.

Regarding the proposals for the restoration of the building's east wall between the Pronaos and the Naos proper, I favour scheme two including the reinstatement of surviving blocks of the second Christian apse, again with the same proviso as above in relation to simulation of fire damage. Though not part of the present proposals as I understand them, I also favour, in principle, the re-erection of part of the later internal colonnade in order to give some impression of the original interior and of its subsequent modification.

I agree about the limited value of elastic analyses (including the latest non-linear analysis presented at the meeting of specialists), about the impracticability (even by more realistic analyses of rocking and shearing displacements) of predicting safety margins against collapse, and about the consequent need to rely primarily on the evidence furnished by the perform-ance of the structure itself. I see the analyses that have been made and shaking-table tests of small models chiefly as aids in interpreting what can be directly observed of this performance. I therefore fully support the approach

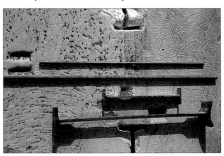

now being taken, with its concentration on restoring to damaged blocks as much as possible of their earlier undamaged strengths.

I also agree with the criteria proposed for the design of necessary rein-forcements and new connective elements. I foresee difficulty only where

Titanium rods and clamps being used by the CCAM

it may be necessary to make good small losses on the top or bottom edges of column drums that nevertheless result in significant reductions in their effective diameters. If a drum that had suffered such a loss were near the foot of a re-erected column, the joint with the completion piece would be sub-jected, in any future rocking about its edge, to high shear and tension. On account of the small size of the loss, it might be difficult to anchor the necessary reinforcement in the completion piece without first cutting into the block to allow the use of a larger piece, and it might be preferable to substitute a complete new drum.

In addition to proposed tests on a shaking table, I suggest that it would be helpful, in relation to the use of lead for bedding the epistyles on the column capitals, to carry out tests on the deformation behaviour of this material at the high rates of straining associated with earthquake movements in order to clarify its ability to absorb energy and reduce shear transfer.

I welcome the attention given to the preservation of the marble from further surface loss and to possible artificial patination treatments. But I leave further comment on these to those who are better qualified.

Regarding further programmes for the cella walls of the Parthenon, the ceiling of the Propylaea, and the temple of Athena Nike, I agree in principle to what is proposed in so far as dismantling is called for to correct previous errors and safeguard these structures for the future.

Leon Krier

Architect, Urbanist.

The Charter of Venice dogmatically asks that all contemporary interventions on historic buildings must stand out against and contrast with the old buildings both in the use of materials and forms. This is in total contradiction with all *traditional* forms of conservation and restoration; it is an expression and result of modernist thinking.

The Charter of Venice, however, claims to be a document of universal value – it also prides itself in being a complement of the Charter of Athens. Now that the influence of the Charter of Athens on our cities is widely recognised as having been disastrous, many consider the principles of the Charter of Venice to be equally outdated. They would prefer to see the missing columns at the Erechtheion to be replaced by a marble rather than a concrete replica. Nobody, of course, can forbid us to want one or the other, but our choice always reveals whether we are traditionalists or modernists at heart.

As for historic buildings, they, I believe, prefer to be restored and reconstructed in the proven ways. After so many tragic experiments is it not about time that the venerable buildings themselves be listened to and have the last say in a matter concerning their life or death?

The 'Theseion' with results of the Charter of Athens

Hermann J Kienast

German Archaeological Institute, Athens.

The Acropolis of Athens has a symbolic value for the whole of the Western world. The fundamental importance of the Classical buildings, combined with the rigour and extent of the restoration, mean that the current works are the most spectacular of their kind. Inevitably, they have attracted worldwide attention – and, simultaneously, a degree of controversy. This, therefore, is an account of the operation by an outsider who has had the privilege of following its progress at close hand, and who knows not only the finished results, but the many layers of problems that had to be resolved to achieve them.

The buildings on the Acropolis have experienced an extensive history of construction and destruction, alteration and renovation. Their present appearance has been shaped in equal measure by Classical and modern times. Building restoration is not a new invention. In fact, the present work on the anastylosis was deemed necessary because of the damage caused by previous attempts at restoration.

The initial phase of this restoration was marked by organisational problems. Who would be responsible for this vitally important project? How could one ensure that the task would be carried out in the most efficient manner possible? Eventually, a fortuitous solution was found. It was decided that the works should be directed by a commission representing all the relevant areas of expertise. All the members of the commission are Greek, making it easier to meet regularly and exchange ideas. Significantly, however, the commission has sought the advice of an international body of experts. It has documented the condition of the monuments with unparalleled care, then it has published its findings, using the papers as the basis for discussion within the profession. Outside experts have even been invited to make a written statement of position – a unique innovation in a project of this kind. Clearly aware of its own responsibility, the commission has challenged the rest of us to acknowledge our responsibility too.

The past restoration work has demonstrated just how sensitive monuments are to inappropriate treatment. Often, short-term cures have led to greater damage in the long term. It is understandable that this experience should have given rise to reservations about the wisdom of intervention *per se*. But a more practical response is to intensify efforts to find a suitable programme of

treatment. This is what the Acropolis commission has done. All previous restorations have been put aside, in order to return the buildings to their authentic substance. In this way, the previous points of damage can be eliminated, allowing work to begin on a completely new basis. The reconstruction work has used marble from the Penteli quarries for the stonework, a simple cement mortar, and titanium for the temporary engineering construction – in other words, it has used only materials which are in keeping with the original, which have stood the test of time. Only further observation over time will show if the current works are suitable. At the very least, it is hoped that the previous damage will have been reversed and no new damage caused. The guiding principle behind this restoration is that all interventions must be reversible, ensuring that elements may be replaced or made good at any time.

All restorations fall somewhere between two extremes: complete reconstruction on the one hand, and radical 'non-intervention' on the other. The approach will vary according to the monument in question. But there are two reasons why the buildings on the Acropolis cannot be allowed to remain in their present condition. First, they are not only historical monuments, but exceptional works of art. Second, failure to intervene in this case will demonstrate not a respect for an historical process, but a lack of will that will lead, eventually, to catastrophe. Since the present damage results to a large extent from previous restorations, remedial action is the only responsible approach. Every restoration is both limited and guided by the prevailing level of scientific knowledge, the technical and economic capabilities and, above all, the spirit of the time. We cannot be bound to the previous restorations of the Acropolis, as they contained substantial errors both in construction and form. New research has completely altered our picture of the buildings, making the errors of the past even more insupportable. For this reason, I am convinced that the present generation not only has the right to intervene, but even the obligation to do so, in order to repair the damage done in the past. One has to have not just a spiritual but a practical approach towards a

monument that is not just a silent witness to the past, but a symbolic marker and memorial. In this regard I consider the present restoration works on the Acropolis to be extremely positive and encouraging. The organisation has been exemplary. Technical problems have been resolved

The Acropolis as seen from the west.

with consummate professionalism. Plans have been opened up to debate.

Once the works are complete, the Acropolis will doubtless look quite different to the way it does today. But the changes will in no way undermine the symbolic value of the buildings. Quite the reverse, they will bear witness to a responsible approach towards the conservation of monuments.

Marcus Binney

Architectural Correspondent for the London Times

Ruskin would have fumed. The Acropolis, being restored. Temples bristling with scaffolding. The Propylaea a mesh of steel poles and wooden planks. Inside the Parthenon a vast crane revolves menacingly on a concrete platform. Outside a gantry hoist glides along special rails.

Yet, contrary to appearances, this is not a wholesale renewal in the spirit of Viollet-le-Duc or Gilbert Scott. It does not involve systematic replacement of eroded stonework or conjectural restoration of missing features. Rather it is the world's most amazing 3-D jigsaw puzzle. The philosophy of the CCAM has been carefully considered given the daunting nature of technical and moral questions related to the restoration of such structures today: it involves returning the maximum ancient masonry possible to the buildings, at the same time adding the least possible new material. The fruits of this work are now visible for all. Within a few years the Greeks have brought the Acropolis alive in a way that a century of classics textbooks never came near to doing.

ΠΑΡΘΕΝΩΝ
ΜΙΑ ΑΝΑΣΤΗΛΩΣΗ
ΤΟΥ ΠΡΟΝΑΟΥ
ΙΣΟΜΕΤΡΙΚΗ
ΠΑΡΑΣΤΑΣΗ

A proposal for a maximum restorative intervention on the Parthenon Pronaos, isometric view from the northwest (drawing by Manolis Korres)

RESTORATION AND VALUE

Demetri Porphyrios

F ar from withering away, the historical is in our days a congested trade. In literature, criticism, art, architecture, interior decoration, tourism, archaeology, or the auction houses, the value of the 'historical' – both cultural and fiscal – is paramount. There is simply too much of it. The myth of the historical is prone to overproduction, rapid turnover and speedy obsolescence. There is no common measure left between the life of a book, a work of art or a building and the life span of the cultural movement that produced it. Given this profound loss of memory on the one hand and the rampant proliferation of the historical on the other, why is it that every now and then the restoration of a national monument gives rise to a most painful debate whereas a hitherto neglected stone is fetishised into a priceless cultural commodity?

Two examples occupying opposite extremes in our understanding of the historical may help my discussion here. What I have in mind is on one hand the Campanile of St Mark's and on the other the bas-relief recently discovered at Canford Manor.

Since the eleventh century the Campanile of St Mark's had taken on a symbolic character that represented Venice herself. The religious, secular and civic values of the republic were all represented in the image of the Campanile and it was such symbolic fortitude that allowed the monument to take hold of experience. When in 1902, therefore, the Campanile fell down, a great debate ensued. Was the disaster to be accepted as the irrevocable consequence of the passing of time consigning the monument to oblivion? Was it incumbent upon the Venetians to restore the Campanile to its former glory? Or was it advisable to organise a competition (as recently the British thought it prudent with the Windsor Castle affair) in search of a contemporary talent to whom the design of the tower in the 'spirit of the age' would be entrusted?

At the time the Campanile collapsed, the London *Daily Telegraph* took the view that the Campanile had 'fallen with all the associations that have clustered around it over the centuries and it may fervently be hoped that no civic zeal for restoration will ever lead the Venetian prefect to try and build it up again . . . (for) the grace its builders gave it is lost for ever in the art they knew.'

The view expressed by the *Daily Telegraph* is surely – with hindsight – that of a nascent modernism. The Campanile was but a relic of the past 'safe upon the canvasses of Canaletto', wrote the newspaper. Its actual building fabric, however, was seen as irretrievable due to an intense suspicion that authentic experience under modern conditions is somehow not available. Once destroyed, historical artifacts lose their rootedness, it was argued, and no restorative scheme can ever give them back a legitimate new lease of life. The history of a ruined monument is unwittingly revealed as a history of disintegration that may afford only aesthetic satisfaction in the form of melancholy nostalgia. It should suffer steady decay left to the action of time.

The opposite view, of course, prevailed. The Campanile of Venice was duly and faithfully restored to its previous familiar shape and form. Not interested in the picturesqueness of decay nor troubled by the alleged inauthenticity of construction,

OPPOSITE: The restored east portico of the Erechtheion, detail of the north column and entablature

The Campanile of St Mark's, Venice, rebuilt after its collapse in 1902

the Venetians chose to restore the Campanile in a faithful manner. Soon there seemed to be no scar in the skyline of the laguna. The paramount symbolic significance of the Campanile overrode the intellectual pretentiousness of a nascent modernism.

A different way of approaching the subject of historical value can be seen in the most recent discovery at Canford Manor in southern England. A stone fragment decorating the snack bar of Canford School – hitherto considered but a mere replica cast of a bygone original – turned out to be an authentic stone panel from the Assyrian palace of King Ashurnasirpal II. Examined and authenticated by the British Museum, it fetched $11.9 million at Christie's London auction house making it the most highly valued bas-relief in the world. Surely its value is not historical for it may be safe to assume that its buyer shares nothing with the civic ideals of the Assyrian kingdom nor with the artistic canons of its sculptor. Its value must rest elsewhere: in the rarity and age-value of the artifact which render the bas-relief priceless by removing it from the nexus of commodification. To possess such an inimitable bas-relief is to strip it of its commodity character conferring on it a fancier's value. Singularity and age-value converge here to produce the idea of the authentic. Age value and rarity are here in direct contrast with the historical value we encountered in the case of the Campanile.

In his essay 'The Modern Cult of Monuments', written only a year after the collapse of the Venice Campanile, the historian Alois Riegl gives an account of the cultural preoccupations surrounding the idea of the monument. Riegl distinguishes between the ideas of *use-value*, *age-value*, and *historical value*.

Use-value refers to the concrete, practical requirements of material life. 'An antique building still in use,' Riegl writes, 'must be maintained in such a condition that it can accommodate people without endangering life or health'. Thus it must be repaired anew irrespective of whether the new stones or timbers may not be authentic. Buildings which are still in use mitigate against their imprisonment as open-air musea. Such buildings may be restored in the artistic and constructional spirit of the existing fabric so that the restored building still in use should have a renewed lease of life. This is good common-sense practice and the Latin word *instaurare* or *reficere* means exactly that: to reinstate and make anew.

Age-value points to an alleged aesthetic and moral requirement that the fabric of a building must 'evidence the slow and inevitable disintegration of nature'. The axiom of age-value, therefore, is fundamentally a modernist sensibility. Its aesthetic claim derives from the eighteenth-century picturesque tradition of the ruin while its moral overtones are inextricably linked with nineteenth-century historicism and the expectation that each and every historical period is indelibly marked by the unique spirit of its age. The collapse of a monument may be mourned but the age-value of its ruinous fabric remains superior to any restoration. Humans, this view maintains, must not tamper with time; yet it is the same ideologues of age-value who embrace the fruits of genetic medicine which, after all, aims ultimately at lengthening human life.

Historical value arises when a particular monument, complex of buildings or townscape transcends over time its use and age values by becoming a symbol that represents 'the development of human activity in a certain field'. Historical value, therefore, is thoroughly a social phenomenon and cannot be assigned by an individual, an expert or a ruler. Historical value depends on a shared form of life and practices of a community within which we pick up the terms of our ethical experience. And inversely, it is our shared recognitions which empower the monument with the capacity to 'refer' to the world. Historical value, therefore, rests on recognition and its characteristic interest lies in conferring legitimacy and honour to the symbolic forms we make and which make us.

After its collapse in 1902, the Campanile of Venice was faithfully restored because in the eyes of the Venetian public the tower had immense historical value. For the London *Daily Telegraph*, however, the Campanile had merely an age value and the heap of rubble it was reduced to was but a sufficient trace of the passing of time. We can see, therefore, how restoration is fraught with difficulties. The difficulties are neither technical nor financial as many would have us believe. Craftsmanship, skilled labour, precision of execution, cost of construction, imaginative talent, etc, are all hurdles; just that: hurdles. When a people have the requisite will all such hurdles can be surmounted

The difficulties instead are ideological. Confronted with a Windsor Castle consumed by fire, the British architectural profession, backed by august art-historical bodies, hastened to proclaim that a rare opportunity had arisen to parade inventiveness in design that would vindicate the 'spirit of our age'. But Windsor Castle is not and has never been about fashion nor about ephemeral contingencies that come and go. As a member of the jury for the restoration of the castle I made it clear that in a culture where everybody is 'talented', one (let alone a nation) needs a peculiar sort of immunity in order to survive.

Historical value is indeed a value whose origins are lost in time, and in that sense, it must always be understood as a synchronic differential structure – but it is a synchronic structure with a memory. In its differential structure, traces of real experience are preserved. That is ultimately, I think, the sense of restoration. 'To restore a building,' writes Viollet-le-Duc, 'is not to preserve it, to repair, or rebuild it; it is to reinstate it in a condition of completeness which could never have existed at any given time.'

Preservation for the sake of preserving borders that repulsive spectacle for a blind rage of collecting the 'dust of (archaeological and) bibliographical minutiae' described by Nietzsche. Repairing or rebuilding is in fact sensible and human but lacks the gravity of a vision. Restoration, however, presupposes real culture, not simply an art historical or archaeological knowledge of culture. Restoration cannot be pursued without such a relation to real culture. When the latter is absent restoration is reduced to the indulgences of the 'heritage industry' where building form becomes reified, loses its transformative ability and cannot serve life.

History as such does not judge. That is done by people, and they can make wrong or foolish judgements. They can slip all too easily in the limbo of cultural relativism and professional neutrality or into the lush self-indulgence of the nostalgia of heritage. In the most recent restoration of the monuments on the Acropolis, thank God, culture sensibly informed judgement.

RESTORING SYMBOLISM

David Watkin

T he question of restoration must, and ought, to be controversial because buildings are concrete reminders of our relationship with our past, and therefore play a key role in our search for a collective cultural identity. This is not a modern phenomenon, for even in the ancient world the restoration of buildings was inevitably a symbolic act. For instance, the Emperor Hadrian, whose claim to the principate was based on an ill-attested deathbed adoption by Trajan, amply demonstrated his affiliation to the imperial dynasty by restoring the buildings of his predecessors. Even when this involved complete rebuilding, such as at the Pantheon, he ensured that the original Augustan inscription of a century and a half earlier, was retained: Hadrian's attempt to emphasise dynastic and cultural continuity at the expense of historical truth would, if repeated today, doubtless be condemned as an unethical falsification of history according to the Charter of Venice (1964). Amongst other precepts this holds that, 'replacement of missing parts ... must be distinguishable from the original so that restoration does not falsify the artistic or historic evidence', and that 'the material used for integration should always be recognisable'.

Such a dogmatic pseudo-moral approach to restoration will more effectively extinguish the last glimmers of life in our historic monuments than any ravages wrought by time and pollution. The Charter of Venice is an unhappy by-product of the erroneous Modernist belief that twentieth-century man no longer needed a living relationship with his past, so that the architecture of the previous two millennia could have no meaning for us except as desiccated museum exhibits, as embodiments of long-dead Zeitgeists that could play no part in the continual dialogue of history.

Since we no longer believe these claims, there is no reason why we should not feel free to restore monuments to a condition as closely resembling their original state as is possible. This has, indeed, been done, in the cases of buildings such as Bruchsal, Pavlosk, or, earlier, Soissons Cathedral, where the greater part of the nave was completely destroyed by German bombardment in 1918. By 1937 it had been faithfully rebuilt in a way which today makes it indistinguishable from the original. Similarly, at the apparently medieval buildings of Magdalen College, Oxford, I was recently shown by the President what he claimed was, after a century of restoration, the single surviving medieval stone.

It seems widely accepted that the recent restoration of the Erechtheion is unsuccessful in that it is neither a comprehensible building, nor a romantic ruin. In either of these forms it could have assisted our understanding of the past and helped cultivate our fictional or real relation to the past. It was, after all, as a result of 'musing amid the ruins of the Capitol, while the barefooted friars were singing vespers in the temple of Jupiter', that Edward Gibbon was inspired to write his *Decline and Fall of the Roman Empire*. Winckelmann, by contrast, conceived his potent image of Greek art as a timeless ideal without ever having visited Greece. However, the Erechtheion seems today to be just a monument to the obstinate historicism of modernist archaeology, failing to provide an idealist vision or associational resonances, so that it could inspire neither a Winckelmann on the one hand, nor a Gibbon on the other.

If there is, as I suggest, no rational reason why the monuments on the Acropolis should not be fully restored as completely and coherently as our knowledge of ancient Greek architecture allows, why does such a project seem so unlikely? I think in our heart of hearts we all shy away from restoring the Parthenon to its pristine state, complete with gorgeous polychromy and with a barbaric chryselephantine cult statue, as envisaged by Quatremére de Quincy, because the result would undoubtedly destroy it as a secular icon of absolute perfection. For we seek in Periclean Athens the origin of those things which make us civilized: philosophy, democracy, art, and literature. We conveniently forget about Greek slavery, pederasty, bloody animal sacrifice, and the dark mysteries of Greek religion. Winckelmann, who refused invitations to visit Athens, could not bring himself to confront the reality of ancient Greece, and neither can we.

In the Enlightenment, architects resurrected the Vitruvian myth of the superiority of Greek architecture to Roman, and saw in the trabeated skeleton of the Greek temple the ultimate embodiment of their ideals of structural rationalism, moral purity, and geometric perfection. The discovery of such seemingly irrational enrichments as entasis, polychromy, horizontal curvature, and even engaged orders, should have shattered this myth, but did not. If we want thus to continue deluding ourselves and see a Greek temple in a state which represents this Enlightenment ideal, we should visit the unfinished temple at Segesta in Sicily, a Greek monument far more eloquent than anything on the Acropolis today.

Schinkel, one of the greatest of all Classical architects, was bold enough to propose building a modern palace on the Acropolis in the grounds of which the Parthenon would become the ultimate in garden ornaments. Though Schinkel's iconoclasm is unlikely to return, the notion of a Periclean apogee to our civilisation, which still prevails today, has surely outlived its usefulness. Until we are able to face the irrationality of the ancient Greeks, we will not understand the darker side of twentieth-century civilisation. Yet whether the monuments on the Acropolis were to be fully restored or not, their historic role as the rarest surviving icons of western civilisation would make them too precious for the public to be allowed to have much contact with them. Thus they are doubtless doomed to remain as desiccated archaeological objects, unattractively preserved in whatever state of partially suspended decay the Athenian smog allows. Instead, perhaps the Getty Museum might be persuaded to build in Malibu a full-scale replica of the Parthenon it its pristine form so that we might for the first time fully experience Greek architecture.

The Erechtheion from the southeast

211

ANASTYLOSIS AND HISTORICAL INTEGRITY

Oswyn Murray

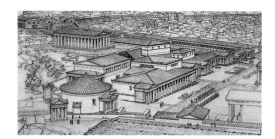

One of the great pleasures of the last ten years has been the excitement of reliving the Periclean Age on the Acropolis. I remember vividly my amazement early one spring morning when I arrived there to hear the sound of saws and stonemasons' hammers, and to discover that the Acropolis was once again a building site: I was hearing the sounds and watching many of the skills that went towards the original construction of the Erechtheion. Similarly now that the Parthenon is largely dismantled, and the cranes and scaffolding are in place, we await with excitement that aural and visual experience which accompanied the original work on the Parthenon almost 2,500 years ago. It is indeed a unique privilege to visit the Acropolis in this period, simply because, in the process of rebuilding according to the ancient techniques, it has come alive again, and we can return to the past.

But that is not of course the point of the operation, or the reason why it is thought controversial. Let me begin from the symbolic meaning of the Acropolis.

The fifth century complex of the age of Pericles was an ideological construct, demonstrating the power and glory of Athens as a result of her rule over other Greeks; it was funded by her imperial revenues and the booty from the successful defence of Greece against Persia. If we are to believe the normal view, the Acropolis had stood in ruins as a symbol of Persian impiety for a generation, before the Athenian imperial democracy decided to declare its own independence from this assertion of piety towards the past. The decision to build was controversial; so much is clear from Thucidides' comparison of the Athenian display in building with Spartan restraint (1.10), and from the debate recorded in Plutarch's *Life of Perikles* 12, where the speaker accuses Athens of 'decking herself out like a prostitute with thousand talent temples'. Pericles himself would doubtless have defended the programme by the doctrine proclaimed in the Funeral Oration, that it was the privilege of Athens to stand out as the education of all Greece.

From the start the Parthenon was symbolic, and built anew on the ruins of an earlier (and arguably more beautiful) succession of archaic temples. It remained symbolic of Athenian culture (though not democracy) throughout antiquity: its changes in use reflect the changes in Athenian history. The Greek Macedonian 'liberator' Demetrios Poliorketes used it as a drinking room; the Roman age filled it with symbols of their own power and respect for Athenian culture, until Athena finally had to share her residence with a statue of the greatest Philhellene, the emperor Hadrian himself. In the age of the traveller Pausanias (second century AD) the Parthenon arose from a clutter of statues, victory monuments and dedications, designed to recall the glorious past of Athens. In late antiquity it was restored as a symbol of paganism by Julian the Apostate, and as a Christian basilica by Justinian. Under the Turks it was at various times mosque, harem and (with tragic consequences, thanks to the Venetians) powder magazine. Historically the Parthenon is a creation of the Greek experience in all its manifestations, and every ruined element, every scar from use, reuse and abuse has its meaning.

It was the Romantic Age which made the Parthenon a symbol of antique

Reconstruction of the Athenia Agora (drawing by Manolis Korres)

perfection, and which raised it from a picturesque ruin to an icon of architectural design. With that move the Acropolis gained two new functions, as a symbol of the new idealised Philhellenic national revival, and as an archetype for an aesthetic classicism. Inevitably the picturesque elements of the *Turkokratia* were ruthlessly removed, and the monument was restored, not as the Christian church which the Byzantine age had known, but as a symbol of pure classicism. Archaeologists worked in the name of scholarship to strip the entire Acropolis and expose it to the rock, seeking two contradictory goals, to discover the origins of everything there, and to restore on scientific principles the single Classical moment of the fifth century. In the course of a century of restoration by successive generations from 1834 to 1933, much of the later history of the Acropolis was lost.

We are the inheritors of a neoclassical idealised icon; we cannot go back in history, except to the Classical age and except through their eyes. Moreover, we have become used to their view of the past, which is now our symbol. There is a physical need for repair and for reversing the damage of modern pollution: what goals should we pursue other than freezing this late nineteenth century vision for another century to enjoy? Quite apart from a better understanding of the use of restoration materials, our generation has acquired infinitely more knowledge of the techniques of construction of ancient buildings, through the study of their reconstruction. No-one who works on the Acropolis can afford to ignore the pioneering reconstruction by the Austrians at Ephessos, the Americans at Nemea and the Greeks at Brauron: we now know how the ancient Greeks constructed their temples, and how to replicate their techniques. Since we can do this, we are able to go further in restoration than our predecessors; the caution with which this is done underlines our unease in presuming to disturb the ghosts, as much of the archaeologists Kavvadias and Balanos as of the original architect Iktinos: we insist on using different coloured stone, and on the principle of reversibility. Every move involves a compromise with the past; but our justification must be that in the case of the Acropolis this compromise is with a nineteenth century past which we have grown used to, not with the earlier Parthenon or with our own modern standards of restoration.

Those who object to the present programme for restoration seem therefore to me to be objecting to the disturbance of their personal memories, not of the symbol itself. The temple of Athena has been continually rebuilt since before the Parthenon to the present day, and if our interventions are more scientifically controlled, they are still attempts to create an icon, albeit an archaeologically founded one. Contrarily those who wish the programme to go further, and produce a theme park reconstruction like that of the Stoa of Attalos, turn their backs entirely on the principle of historical integrity, in favour of the creation of a pure symbolic icon.

In European culture, Greece is both a symbol and a reality with a historical past. The problems of the Acropolis are the problems of that balancing act which lies at the heart of the Classical tradition; as we build we do more than merely restore: we present a vision for our age of the meaning of the Hellenic tradition. We are right to work with vision, as well as with caution and restraint.

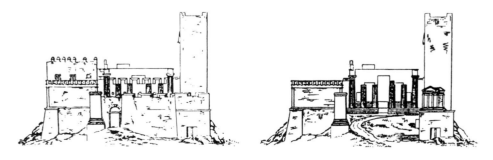

View of the Propylaea, before and after the demolition of the later additions to it, as depicted by Ed Schaubert, 1836 (L Ross, E Schaubert, C Hansen, Der Tempel der Nike Apteros, Berlin 1839)

A BUILDING SITE ONCE AGAIN

PHOENIX'S RISE OR THE SWAN'S LAST SONG?

Lothar Haselberger

The materials used were stone, bronze, ivory, gold, ebony, and cypress wood, while the arts or trades which wrought and fashioned them were carpenters, moulders, founders, stonecutters, dyers, goldsmiths, ivory-workers, painters, embroiderers, engravers, and besides these the carriers and suppliers of the materials . . . As then the buildings arose, no less impressive in size than exquisite in form, the artists strove to out vie the material and design with the beauty of their workmanship. And yet the most wonderful thing was the speed with which they were completed . . . In fact, the entire project was carried through in the high summer of one man's administration . . . created in so short a span, and yet for all time. (Plutarch, *Life of Pericles*, 12f, second century AD)

O nce again, the Athenian Acropolis is a building site. A romantic ruinscape, elevated high above a tumultuous city, has drastically changed its appearance and has turned – returned, rather – into a state-of-the-art working place, thus forcefully recalling what this Rock was like throughout the primetime of Classical Athens: a building site of highest technological and artistic achievement, involving 'every age and condition in Athens', from the first man of the state to the oxen prodder.

Recent work on the Acropolis' crowning monument alone, the Parthenon, has already amounted to a full decade – the time span once needed to create the entire edifice (447-38 BC). Starting in 1979 with the restoration of the Erechtheion, which was finished in 1986; continuing with the Parthenon, the dismantling of which was begun in 1984; recently extending to the Propylaea; and scheduled finally to include the Temple of Athena Nike as well: the ongoing work will need at least one further decade to be concluded. That work is dedicated to the consolidation, conservation, and investigation of the four major Classical buildings on the Acropolis. It is unprecedented in scale and intensity. Despite a long series of earlier modern restorations – beginning with the paradigmatic stone-for-stone rebuilding of the Temple of Nike in 1835-36, and concluded, for a while, with a preceding ten-year restoration of the Parthenon in 1923-33 – the current intervention is the most thorough architectural treatment these monuments have ever undergone since the time they were erected. On the whole, the present rebuilding may well match the span it took to build them, intermittently, between 447 BC (when, with the Parthenon, the Periclean building programme on the Acropolis was started) and 406 BC (when the Erechtheion was finished, shortly before the collapse of Athenian military power). These monuments were already seen by their ancient contemporaries as the lasting testimonies of what Athens, 'the school for all Hellas' (Pericles according to Thucydides, *Peloponnesian War* I, 10), could achieve in art and architecture. And ever since they have been recognised as the visual sum and summit of Athenian – and Grecian glory. For two and a half centuries now, these monuments have attracted uninterrupted passionate attention across the world from

OPPOSITE: The east portico of the Propylaea wrapped in scaffolding

scholars and lay audiences alike, starting with the pioneering studies of James Stuart and Nicholas Revett in the mid-eighteenth century. Meanwhile, the four Classical buildings on the Acropolis constitute the most thoroughly explored historic buildings worldwide.

In many respects, we know these monuments incomparably better, down to the fractions-of-inches refinements of their design, than most of the ancient Athenians did. And thanks to the congenial work done by the ancient masterbuilders' modern successors – who are able to locate the original positions of the tiniest bits of scattered fragments – these monuments will soon be rising again to a state of completeness that seems to reverse time and decay in a wondrous way. We are experiencing the high tide of what ingenious research and conscientious restoration can obtain: will Phoenix be rising from the ashes?

At the same time, scientists and restorators find themselves in a desperate race against an exponentially progressive loss of substance compared to which one and a half millennia of disregard and destruction appear as an almost negligible quantity. Imminent is the loss of original substance on a grand scale under the blight of a rampant city's aggressive heating and traffic exhaust. For the first time ever, the bare material existence of the original surfaces is at stake – the survival of the very medium, stone, that for ages has been modelled into the product of human ingenuity and artistic excellence.

The new kind of 'patina' does not add another historical layer to the epidermis of the monuments underneath which the integrity of the historic document remains untouched, as in the case of Michelangelo's frescoes in the Sistine Chapel now restored in their original blaze: on the contrary, this patina corrodes, eats away, turns into volatile dust the skin and essence of these creations.

While this deplorable fact holds true for all monuments of stone and metal exposed to a polluted atmosphere, the intensity of the phenomenon as well as the quality of the target seem to reach an unparalleled peak in the buildings of the Acropolis.

The alarming corrosion of art and history has been seen and stated for quite some time now. It is tangible in the pieces of comparison and their nearly intact skin in the British Museum where the 'Elgin Marbles' have been well-preserved and well-presented since 1817. And for decades, the Eleusinian plain right next to Athens has presented devastating evidence of what political *laissez-faire* together with aggressive private entrepreneurship lead to – so far without effective results for the Acropolis.

That beautiful bird will hardly even rise to sing its last song. Before that, it will have been deprived of its 'feathers' by the rescue of the sculpture, together with samples of architecture, and their transfer to an isolated, climate-controlled space (whose new construction has, incidentally, been halted) – the rest being left exposed to further decay, as a plucked 'corpus' respectfully stabilised and equipped with new artificial 'feathers' in the shape of weatherproof copies.

Notwithstanding all this ingenious rescue work, the original substance will shrink ever more rapidly. What used to be a unique ensemble of art and architecture under the open sky, a *Gesamtkunstwerk* without parallel, is intentionally torn apart, for lack of any better solution, and unintentionally left to fall apart. Chemical 'weather-proofing' cannot halt this; such coating is doomed to fail and create even faster decay.

The problem is not a technical one. Even the most drastic technical solution proposed so far, sheltering the entire Acropolis under a giant plastic dome, could not prevent the complex, however ruinous, from losing its integrity and urban context, its historic wholeness. To my mind, such a dome would nevertheless be the perfectly appropriate technical response to the present environment; it forces us to visualise dramatically the all-too-limited rescue efforts, despite the earnestness and skill of the teams at work on the Acropolis. Not the least of the unacceptable consequences is that they leave the people of Athens outside the protective environment, teary-eyed and with lungs as damaged as the monuments' marble epidermis.

The issue is political. An holistic approach is imperative, one that comprises the entire polis in its full social as well as topographical extent and exerts strictest legislative control of, and bans, the smog and acid rain producing sources. Cost is a side issue compared to the political will and energy needed to succeed.

Post-war London was able, effectively, to eliminate its notorious smog. Pittsburgh in Pennsylvania, having suffered second to none from sky-darkening pollution, is under blue skies again. Will the Athenians, together with their administration, be able to act? A heroic, unselfish and unanimous effort is called for, as great as the ancient Athenians' feats at Marathon, Thermopylae, and Salamis. Then, the enemy came from the outside, and, though eventually defeated, succeeded in destroying the Acropolis – which in turn led to its Classical flowering. This time, however – much harder to accept and control – it is from within that the destructive forces come. And the imminent second destruction of the Acropolis will be the final one.

Maybe, in their mercilessly inhumane environment of today, these monuments have fallen behind the times: after all, they were created in an age whose gods were idealised humans. Whether the Acropolis' message is reflected powerfully enough to the outside world, where for the moment human lives themselves do not appear to count enough to turn things around, remains obscure. At present, the smog is too dense.

The Caryatids silhouetted against the Athenian sky

ARCHITECTURE AND POLITICS IN THE CLASSICAL CITY-STATE

Helen Tatla

(. . .) all artificial things are generated either from something which bears the same name as themselves [eg a house from a house, inasmuch as it is generated by mind; for the art is the form *(eidos)*], or from something which contains some part; (. . .) And it is the same with natural formations as it is with the products of art. For the seed produces just as do those things which function by art. It contains the form *(eidos)* potentially, and that from which the seed comes has in some sense the same name as the product.[1]

The Interpretation of Classical Architecture

Idea or eidos, whether in Plato's or Aristotle's sense, taken as the source and the essence of Classical architecture, constitute metaphysical boundaries, absolute presuppositions in any discussion of the problem of origin; for, as Aristotle puts it, they indicate 'the ultimate subject, which cannot be further predicated of something else'.[2] The absolute autonomy of the notion of *idea* or *eidos* consists in its universal and immutable character. As Aristotle suggests, it is approachable by us only through its corporeal expressions.

Political Freedom and Equality as Expressed by the Form of the Classical Temple

The notion of justice *(themis)* conceived as the basis of social order by Homer and Hesiod, remained subject to the will of the Olympian gods until the early sixth century. The new justice of the *polis* as conceived by Solon, however, although maintaining its claim to divine protection, was rational as opposed to metaphysical in principle, being based on a cause and effect relation between free individuals. In Solonian justice, the determinant agency of social order was sought in the ensuring of individual freedom, and through this of common freedom, in intelligible terms.

The concept of individual freedom underlied the form of the temple through the broader cultural quest for self-sufficiency both of the notion of *whole* and of the parts within it. In this spirit, formal self-sufficiency, or independence, in temples was achieved through the mastering of the interaction between cause and effect in their members. The causal relation between the members of a temple was expressed as a constant evolution of form aiming at the achievement of maximum results with minimum effort. Thus, in the course of time, the Doric capital became less tapered and more conical, the columns more slender, and the intercolumnations larger. Representing the political realm, the conceptual order of the temple predescribed the causal relation between its parts in such a way as to ensure the individual character of each, by connecting it directly to an ordered, intelligible whole. This evolution was ultimately controlled by the *idea* or *eidos*, as is clear in the case of columns which throughout antiquity remained much thicker than was structurally necessary. The independence of the parts was in fact achieved by resisting mere expression of their material function. Fluting, for example, visually released columns from their material existence, while tapering stressed their individuality by manifesting an active response to their supportive function.

In the late sixth century, with Cleisthenes' reforms, through which political justice was emancipated from the concept of religious morality, a merging of individual liberty and equality before law was accomplished. The causal relation that underlied the process towards individual liberty in Solonian justice gave its place to a dialectic relation between free individuals interacting on equal terms within the political system.

As far as the Classical temple is concerned, equality was built upon a form of visual and formal dialectics. The fact that temples of different size from this period do not follow a uniform scale, but differ from each other in the relation of their parts for instance, illustrates the idea of equality based on a dialectic relationship of constituent elements. Regularisation and formal individuality developed in parallel for a certain period, but diversity continued to be understood as part and parcel of the greater concept of equality.

However, it seems that the evolution of the temple onwards, towards the actual perceptual representation of the ideal of justice, gradually turned into an opposite kind of evolution away from the *idea*. The fifth century BC can be characterised as a transitional period. Towards the end of the fifth century, the excesses of individualism destroyed the concept of *polis* as a harmonic interaction between economically and intellectually free individuals acting within the framework of universal justice. The Parthenon can be considered as representative of the climax of the transition, as it embodies the unity of political and religious attitudes, and, at the same time, hints at the increasing estimation of the aesthetic aspect of the temple as an expression of power and wealth as opposed to moral purity.

As the separation between morality and politics continued on its course, lifeless typification and lack of formal precision marked the deterioration of the idea of the temple in the Classical sense. The notions of morality and politics as expressed by Classical architecture in its later phases of decline rather than in its flowering have their equivalents in the Modern situation.

The Modern Aftermath

One could argue that the Classical and the Modernist eras represent the two critical, opposite nodes in the shift of human thinking from metaphysical into secular within the Western world. In Modernist thought, equality and freedom in the political field, far from having any moral foundation, operate in economic terms. In art, the current autonomy of the aesthetic reflects its separation as much from morality as from reason, and in this sense from both the metaphysical and the empirical worlds.

If autonomy in the Classical era was manifested through the potentiality of a work of architecture for an infinite number of distinct corporeal expressions prescribed by the *eidos*, in Modernist architecture it refers to a unique work considered as a disjointed aesthetic entity independent of the essence.

Notes

1   See Aristotle, Metaphysics 1034a23-b2, translation by H Tredennick, The Loeb Classical Library, Harvard University Press, 1933.

2   Ibid, 10172b20

THE VOICE OF TEIRESIAS

THE PERICLEAN MONUMENTS AND THE INDUSTRIAL METROPOLIS

Richard Economakis

The restoration of the Acropolis monuments has brought them once again to the forefront of Western cultural consciousness. This time, however, they have returned not as the radiant beacons of certainty that they were in older times of intellectual and spiritual crisis, but as tokens of a lost innocence – effigies charged with our secret aspirations, like charms against the darkness that lies ahead. We invoke these magnificent, ageing creations of human genius as Odysseus did the spirit of the wise Teiresias of myth: where Odysseus offered sacrificial blood to allow the blind seer to retrieve his voice, we have promised to restitute the ancient structures. Like Odysseus we seek prophetic guidance – and though we may not yet have completed our task, we are moved already to appreciate what a previous generation cannot possibly have recognised.

Here more than anywhere our bifrons relationship to the past is revealed; for we stand awestruck in the shadow of the Parthenon and the Erechtheion while all around us resound the calls of a brave new technological world that would have humanity accept the Periclean monuments, like all other creations of pre-industrial times, as products of a transcended cultural reality that may no longer directly inform our 'evolving' sensitivities. Yet the student of the Acropolis monuments cannot possibly share this view; for it is evident that, inspite of its technological prowess, our present age falls far short of the combined universality, exactness, and clarity of vision that still emanates out of the ruins of fifth century BC Athens. The gnostic cannot but appreciate the Acropolis monuments for what their creators themselves made no secret they intended them as: namely, comprehensive essays in what for us is eternally relevant.

In the unparalleled suppleness and formal resolution of the monuments' architectural and sculptural elements we recognise the as yet uncorrupted fruit of our first fully conscious attempt to wrest order out of the material world, universal truths out of the tenuousness of corporeal existence. Here the guiding principle is nothing less than perfect harmony – *apolyte harmonia* – the precise joining of parts into a balanced whole. The result is beauty, as Phidias, Iktinos, Callicrates, and Mnesikles were aware, and it is as worthwhile and precious today as it was two and a half thousand years ago.

The Neo-Platonist philosopher Plotinos of Alexandria (AD 204-70) perhaps best summarises the Classical appreciation of beauty in his 'Enneads', thus:

> Only a compound can be beautiful, never anything devoid of parts; and only a whole; the several parts will have beauty, not in themselves, but only as working together to give a comely total. Yet beauty in an aggregate demands beauty in details: it cannot be constructed out of ugliness; its law must run throughout.[1]

In varying degrees this sensitivity has marked the history of Western art and architecture. Yet to many of us today such words seem distant, or, at best, quaint. It is claimed that the very nature of our appreciation of the natural and built environments is undergoing a 'revolutionary' change. But who can ascend the

OPPOSITE: The Erechtheion from the east with the modern city spreading across the Attic plain. The nineteenth-century town hugs the foot of the Rock, at the edge of the ancient Agora

Acropolis without a sense of exasperation and outrage at the cancerous expansion of revolutionary unsightliness over the Attic plain, a region once renowned for its natural beauty and remembered to the western world through the magical idyll of Shakespeare's *Midsummer Night's Dream*? In the Athens of the nineties the difference between absolute beauty – both of nature and human creations – and mediocrity can be appreciably measured; between a responsible focusing of intellect – the Periclean monuments – and narcissistic, *laissez-faire* industrial-age individualism; between the crystal purity of the Attic sky – which occasionally reappears briefly after rainstorms and high winds – and the deathly atmosphere of the industrial metropolis.

Like most modern cities, the greater part of contemporary Athens was not built by architects but by a combination of unchecked speculation and unprincipled construction. Yet that point in time when the attitudes and values that had so caringly rebuilt the town after its investment as the capital of a new Greek state – values that did not reject the idea of *language* in architecture, derived of the logic of load-bearing construction; of *civic space*; or of *urban scale* regulated by the notion of pedestrian, mixed-use neighborhoods and formal hierarchies – that change of mind that precipitated the indiscriminate march of concrete and steel was brought about by the shortsighted adventurism of the authors of the Modern movement, who preached intolerance toward all normative architectural and urbanistic methodologies. Tradition, continuity, commonality, pleasurability, propriety, and common constructional sense were placed under a common heading – *Expired* – and passed as mere historical terms. The new banners proclaim 'temporality', 'flux', 'idiosyncracy', and more recently – and cynically – 'deconstruction' as the highest standards of culture. It is only now, with the abolition of all rational criteria, when so many natural and human creations of beauty have been defiled by the encroachment of desensitised, pointedly unsympathetic new constructs and the average person is helplessly reliant on the wasteful products of our consumerist economies, that one recognises the magnitude of the dangers confronting our world.

Sit on an edge of the Areios Pagos or the Philopappos hill in Athens some evening – any evening – and try to imagine the sounds of the ancient city over the feverish din of automobiles and machines, or visualise the beauty of a place that once was at peace with itself across miles of carelessly built, randomly shaped 'functionalist' rooftops with rusting television antennae or the glare of neon lights and endlessly darting and twisting headlights. This was still possible only thirty years ago.

The atmospheric pollution that is dissolving the surfaces of the ancient marble monuments in Athens is not so much a cause as an effect of the greater illness that eats into our minds today. For we continue to build and expand zoned, monocentric cities that rely on the automobile, shuttling a growing sea of humanity from one single-use area to another in a seemingly unending, macabre dance that leads to alienation and impassivity. At the same time we are discouraged to reclaim the proven systems of urban habitation for fear of being branded reactionaries or naive sentimentalists. The rich formal hierarchies built into the evolved regional languages of architecture are dismissed as mere stylistic, outdated conventions; yet the fortunate urban dwellers among us are considered by all to be those who reside in historic districts which are protected by our modern planning departments in a patronising gesture of historicist appreciation.

Modernism will continue its attempts to rationalise and intellectualise its anti-urban and fundamentally anti-humanist attitudes. Yet the truly responsible architect today cannot continue to hope for redemption in the causes of destruction, no matter how reformed these may claim to be. The new generations must fortify the ground

The north porch of the Erechtheion overlooking the modern urban sprawl

222

that has been gained by the first post-war efforts to reclaim a civic realm. The recent revival of Classical and humanist values – evidenced in the expanding body of projects, treatises, and built work from around the world[2] – comes at a critical point in time. If the built environment is to be rescued we must learn to look upon the Acropolis monuments not as the mere archaeological artefacts (worthy, perhaps, of our care but nevertheless irrelevant) that they are made out to be by contemporary culture, but as potent bearers of meaning on a cultural, civic, and architectural level. Whether one chooses conservation, restoration, or reconstruction, what matters is not so much the extent of restitution of the specific object but our willingness to let it inform our own sensitivities in everyday life. When we turn our gaze to the Acropolis we must picture it in its true context, namely that of sacred temenos overlooking a city which knew its limits and limitations; which consisted of well-matched private and civic realms; in which civic and public buildings received the greatest architectural attention; where citizens participated directly in the formulation of common policy; and where freedom was not regarded merely as a right of the individual, but as the fruit of responsible social conduct. The Acropolis monuments could not have been conceived or produced by any other social system. As such we cannot restrict our appreciation for them to purely aesthetic or architectural considerations.

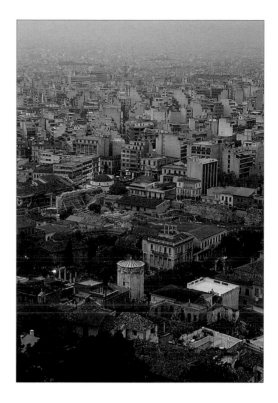

Teiresias' words can just be made out: there is nothing wrong in seeking to restore the scale, size, and formal hierarchies of the traditional city; nothing wrong in utilising the techniques of load-bearing construction or the specific languages that were developed out of this system, so long as one does so correctly and appropriately.

In their perfection, the Periclean buildings represent not the culmination of a cultural evolution but true beginnings. It is to these origins that we turn time and time again for our new inspiration, which to be relevant must always seek to relive its greatest moment, when creation was inseparable from the communal spirit. It is this spirit that informs the work and efforts of the Committee for the Conservation of the Acropolis Monuments.

Notes

1 Plotinos, *Enneads*, Penguin Classics, Translated by S MacKenna, London 1991.
2 See *Building Classical*, R Economakis (ed), Academy Group Ltd and Ernst + Sohn, London 1993.

The Tower of the Winds in its modern context

The raising of the flag ceremony, performed on the Acropolis by the Euzone guards every Sunday at sunrise